Foundation Expression Blend 2
Building Applications in WPF and Silverlight

Victor Gaudioso

friendsof

DESIGNER TO DESIGNER™

an Apress® company

Foundation Expression Blend 2: Building Applications in WPF and Silverlight

Credits

I would like to dedicate this book to my loving wife, Shay, who always believed in me and pushed me to reach for the stars.

I would also like to dedicate this book to my three beautiful kids, Brianna, Tristan, and Luke.

Finally, I would like to dedicate this book to my wonderful, close-knit family—my parents, Ralph and Elfie, and my two awesome uncles, Joseph Gaudioso and Charles Elliot.

CONTENTS AT A GLANCE

CONTENTS

ABOUT THE AUTHOR

 **Victor Gaudioso** is a senior software application engineer at Identity Mine, a top-tier software company specializing in designing and developing cutting-edge software applications in WPF and Silverlight, creating customized WPF/Blend and Silverlight training programs, and creating tools for designers and developers. Because Victor's company is a Gold Vendor for Microsoft, they have worked with Fortune 500 companies such as Microsoft Games for Windows, Harrah's, Mattel, NBC/Universal, Disney, Best Buy, GameStop, Vivendi Universal Games, and New Line Cinema, among others. Victor also teaches a WPF/Silverlight course at R. Blank's Rich Media Institute in Venice, California. Victor travels around the world to give seminars and/or private instruction on WPF/Silverlight to companies such as Adobe and RMI in Toronto and Vancouver. Victor, a former Flash/ActionScript engineer, still stays active in the Flash community by writing articles and tutorials on www.actionscript. org, where he is also a moderator.

ABOUT THE TECHNICAL REVIEWER

 **Jason Cook** is a software engineer and user interface designer based in Hollywood, California. He has a highly decorated background in developing Rich Media Applications, winning more than a dozen coveted industry awards over the last ten years. Jason has built a number of groundbreaking applications for industry-leading entertainment and consumer products clients such as ABC, NBC/Universal, Disney, Mattel, MTV, VH1, Honda, New Line Cinema, Sony Computer Entertainment America, Sony Pictures, and Touchstone Pictures. Jason has led seminars, conducted professional training programs, and offered personalized consulting for Fortune 500 software companies.

ABOUT THE COVER IMAGE DESIGNER

Corné van Dooren designed the front cover image for this book. After taking a brief from friends of ED to create a new design for the *Foundation* series, he worked at combining technological and organic forms, with the results now appearing on this and other books' covers.

Corné spent his childhood drawing on everything at hand and then began exploring the infinite world of multimedia—and his journey of discovery hasn't stopped since. His mantra has always been "The only limit to multimedia is the imagination," a saying that keeps him moving forward constantly.

Corné works for many international clients, writes features for multimedia magazines, reviews and tests software, authors multimedia studies, and works on many other friends of ED books. You can see more of his work at and contact him through his web site, www.cornevandooren.com.

If you like Corné's work, be sure to check out his chapter in *New Masters of Photoshop: Volume 2* (friends of ED, 2004).

ACKNOWLEDGMENTS

I would like to acknowledge the people who helped to make this publication possible. First and foremost, I would like to acknowledge my good friend and mentor Andrew Whiddett, who took me under his wing and has taught and continues to teach me ever inventive ways to develop applications. I would also like to acknowledge my friend John Grden, who forced me to embrace the principles of object-oriented programming, and my wonderful aunt, Zan Gaudioso, who helped me with a ton of authoring questions. Further, I would like to acknowledge the team at Apress/friends of Ed: my go-getter project manager whom I have come to think of as more of a friend than colleague, Kylie Johnston; my editor, Ben Renow-Clarke, whom I overworked with my horrible punctuation; my copy editor, Ami Knox, with her incredible attention to detail; and my production editor, Laura Esterman, who put it all together into what you see now. I would also like to acknowledge my friends over at Electric Rain. And finally, I acknowledge my very talented technical editor and personal friend, Jason Cook, who helped me to keep my facts correct, my tutorials functional, and my explanations clear. Thank you all from the bottom of my heart, I couldn't have done it without any single one of you.

INTRODUCTION

Welcome to *Foundation Expression Blend 2: Building Applications in WPF and Silverlight*! I am very excited about this book, as I love Windows Presentation Foundation (WPF) and Silverlight, and I have a passion for teaching them both. Throughout the course of the book, I am going to take you step by step from being a novice in Blend/WPF/Silverlight to being a skilled practitioner, able to create your own dynamic Rich Media Applications with animations, stunning effects, and even 3D objects. As well as these innovative tools from Microsoft, you will also use some third-party applications that will really make your creations visually stunning.

Because this technology is so new, only a handful of people in the world know how to develop in it, and those who can are compensated very well and are highly sought after. It's a rapidly expanding market, and more and more companies are looking for Silverlight and WPF developers—if you have those skills, then you'll be a developer in demand! To give you an example from the real world, the company I work for, Identity Mine (www.identitymine.com), is always on the lookout for talented WPF and Silverlight developers, and if someone were to approach us with a portfolio of skills similar to those you'll learn in this book, we'd pretty much hire that person on the spot! And that doesn't just go for us; Silverlight and WPF are hot topics, and there are many more companies out there looking designers and developers who can use them well. In fact, if you've worked through this book and think you've got what it takes, feel free to e-mail your résumé with code samples to me at wpfauthor@gmail.com.

So, before you roll up your sleeves and get started, let me start off by introducing you to WPF/Blend and giving you some important information about the rest of this book.

Who this book is for

Throughout my career, I have purchased many technology books and then come to realize that I was not part of the target audience for the book. In order to help potential readers avoid this situation with my book, I decided to outline exactly who this book is for. This book is for you if you know the basics of object-oriented programming (OOP) and have some programming experience in languages (such as JavaScript, ActionScript, C++, Visual Basic, Java, and C,) but have not used WPF. If you understand even just a little about OOP, you can benefit from this book and start to develop in WPF; however, if you do not have any experience in any of these languages, I suggest you buy a beginners guide on C# to go through first. *Beginning C# 2008: From Novice to Professional* by Christian Gross (Apress, 2007) is a good book and will give you far more information than you will need to make good use of this title.

What this book will teach you

Following is a complete list of what exactly this book will teach you so that you know what you will be able to accomplish in WPF/Blend once you have completed the book. You will

- Understand the typical WPF/Blend workflow for creating WPF applications.
- Understand the Blend IDE—what tools are available and how to use them.
- Understand XAML and C# basics.
- Know the basic WPF framework element controls.
- Understand the WPF MediaElement and how to use it to create video and audio for your application.
- Learn how to create reusable Styles and control templates.
- Understand and know how to create events and EventHandlers.
- Learn about and create ObservableCollections of data.
- Create 3D objects and know how to bring them into WPF and use them.
- Learn about WPF visual brushes and how to use them.
- Understand the difference between timelines and Storyboards and know how to use timelines to create compelling Storyboard animations.
- Put all of the new knowledge you learn together to make two very fun and dynamic 3D WPF applications, as well as two Silverlight applications that you will be able to reuse as you continue to develop in Silverlight.

What WPF/Blend is and what C# and XAML are

WPF has a large number of framework elements or controls such as Buttons, Grids, and MediaElements, among others. These are all written in the Extensible Application Markup Language (XAML), an XML-based markup language. XAML also allows you to create Storyboard animations. These UI controls can be controlled partially in the XAML by Storyboards, but for the most part they are controlled with C#. This type of structure is very similar to HTML and JavaScript, as HTML displays the content, while JavaScript adds functionality to the interactive parts of the HTML such as mouseover effects. Conversely, controls can be created in C#, but, again, most controls are created in XAML. XAML can also display assets such as images, audio, and video.

C# is a very robust object-oriented programming language developed by Microsoft and is part of the .NET Framework. Basically, I like to think of XAML as the pretty exterior of a cool car and C# as the powerful engine under the hood. So the typical way that WPF creates and displays content goes like this:

1. XAML describes how the controls, images, video, and other assets are shown.
2. C# gives these assets their functionality.

3. The compiler then puts the XAML UI and functionality together into an executable (EXE) file for a Windows application or a XAML browser application (XBAP) executable for online applications.

4. The browser or Windows then displays the application.

The real power of WPF is the robustness of C# and the capability of using XAML to create the interface as well as to make use of 3D objects.

What tools you will need

It is worth mentioning here that C# is created and edited in Visual Studio 2005 or C# Express, and XAML can be edited in both Blend and Visual Studio 2005 or C# Express. Visual Studio 2005 is a developer tool for creating applications with the .NET Framework and has been around for some years. Some of the tools offered by Visual Studio 2005 are the control toolbox for adding controls to an application as well as tools to assist in writing code such as IntelliSense (discussed in Chapter 2). Blend, however, is a new instrument that allows you to create and display WPF assets such as controls and images in code or visually. The Selection and Brush Transform tools, as well as the various shape tools, are just a few of the features that Blend offers the developer. I will go into these and other tools in Chapter 3, and you will master these development tools in later chapters.

What Silverlight is and how it differs from WPF

Silverlight, formerly known as Windows Presentation Foundation Everywhere (WPF/E), is a cross-platform version of WPF. Basically, it is a scaled down version of WPF that can run on a Mac or PC. WPF can only run on Windows Vista or Windows XP with .NET 3.0 or later installed (Windows XP ships with .NET 2). There are other differences, but most important, for me anyway, is WPF can make use of 3D objects, while Silverlight cannot without third-party plug-ins. This is because it is difficult to port 3D hardware acceleration across different platforms. The other major difference is that Silverlight 1.1 can use C#, JavaScript, and Python, among others, for its code-behind language, and Silverlight 1.0 can use only JavaScript for its code-behind language (the code that gives functionality to XAML assets), while WPF can use only C# or Visual Basic. The final difference is that Silverlight integrates right into an HTML page by using the Silverlight browser plug-in, while WPF needs to be inserted into an IFrame to mix with HTML content. Silverlight is still being developed, so the differences I have just explained may not exist in future Silverlight releases.

Online resources

Throughout this book, I will point you to online WPF examples I have created as well as code snippets and video tutorials. In the appendix of this book, I will also point you to additional resources that can help you grow as a WPF/Blend developer. These resources include web blogs, online tutorials, code examples, and much more.

Layout conventions

To keep this book as clear and easy to follow as possible, the following text conventions are used throughout:

Important words or concepts are normally highlighted on the first appearance in **bold type**.

Code is presented in `fixed-width` font.

New or changed code is presented in **`bold fixed-width font`**.

Menu commands are written in the form Menu ➤ Submenu ➤ Submenu.

Where I want to draw your attention to something, I've highlighted it like this:

> *Ahem, don't say I didn't warn you.*

Chapter 1

SETTING UP THE WPF DEVELOPMENT ENVIRONMENT

What this chapter covers:

- Downloading Visual Studio 2008 Beta 2
- Installing Visual Studio 2008 Beta 2
- Downloading Microsoft Silverlight Tools Alpha Refresh for Visual Studio 2008 Beta 2
- Installing Microsoft Silverlight Tools Alpha Refresh for Visual Studio 2008 Beta 2
- Downloading Blend 2 September Preview[1]
- Installing Blend 2
- Creating a WPF test application in Visual Studio 2008
- Creating very simple content in your WPF test application
- Compiling/running your WPF test application
- Opening your WPF test application in Blend 2

---

1. At the time this book was written, the version of Blend 2 was the September Preview. At the time this book was released, the version is the December Preview. There may be a new version by the time you are reading this. The information provided here is still relevant with the only difference being the Preview version.

Before we delve into the download and installation of the WPF/Silverlight development environment, I feel it would be good to make certain you and your machine are able to handle the tasks that will be asked of you in this chapter. This chapter assumes the following:

- You have a computer that is running either Windows XP with Service Pack 2 installed or any version of Windows Vista.
- Your system has at least 1GB of RAM.
- Your hard drive has at least 5GB of free space available.
- Your PC has a relatively fast CPU.
- Your system has a relatively good video card.
- You have Internet access (high speed is preferred).
- You know how to navigate the Internet.
- You know how to download, save, and install programs.
- You have a DVD burner with DVD burning software.

If I have not scared you off, you can start downloading and installing the WPF/Silverlight development environment.

> The installation instructions provided in this chapter are for the pre-release versions of these products. Therefore, the installation instructions may change slightly with the final release of these products.

Until recently, installing the WPF/Silverlight development environment was very difficult to do. You had to install the Microsoft .NET Framework 3.0 (if you were not running Windows Vista), Microsoft Visual Studio 2005 or Visual C# 2005 Express, the MSDN Library for Visual Studio, Expression Blend, and finally, the Microsoft Visual Studio 2005 Extensions for Windows Workflow Foundation. The download and install process took a very long time, and oftentimes the install would fail. Fortunately, Microsoft has streamlined the install process for WPF and Silverlight in that now you only need to download and install Visual Studio 2008, Blend 2, and the Microsoft Silverlight Tools Alpha Refresh for Visual Studio 2008 Beta 2 (this last one is just for Silverlight development). In this chapter, I am going to tell you how to find these downloads and then show you how to install them step by step. You are then going to open Visual Studio 2008 and create a new WPF project to ensure you have installed everything correctly, and finally, you are going to open that same WPF project in Blend 2, again, to make certain you have installed the WPF development environment correctly.

> If you want to use Windows XP for WPF development, you need to have Service Pack 2 installed, or you cannot develop in WPF (earlier versions of XP are not supported).

Downloading and installing Visual Studio 2008 Professional

> *This download will require you to download an image file that will, when run, require you to burn a DVD. If you do not have a DVD burner, download this file onto a computer that does have a DVD burner.*

Unfortunately, URLs can and do change over time. For that reason, I am not going to provide you with specific URLs to downloads. I am, however, going to point you to the Microsoft Download Center where you can search for the programs you will need.

1. Type the following URL into your web browser:

www.microsoft.com/downloads/

2. Once you navigate there, you enter visual studio 2008 professional in the search input box at the top of the page as I have done in Figure 1-1 and click the Go button.

Figure 1-1. Finding Visual Studio 2008 from the Microsoft Download Center page

With any amount of luck, you will see the results that match what I have in Figure 1-2.

2 results found; results **1-2** shown.		
Title	Release Date	Popularity ▲
Visual Studio 2008 Beta 2 Professional Edition Microsoft Visual Studio 2008 is the next-generation development tool for Windows Vista, the 2007 Office System, and the Web.	7/23/2007	#388

Figure 1-2. Your search should return the Visual Studio 2008 Beta 2 Professional Edition link.

3. Click the Visual Studio 2008 Beta 2 Professional Edition link and then click the Download button. You will be prompted to Open or Save the file to your local hard drive as shown in Figure 1-3.

4. Choose to Save the file on your local hard drive and make note of where you saved it. It will then start to download. The file is about 3GB, so this may be a good time to make and enjoy a cup (or possibly a pot) of coffee. This may seem like a very long download to you, but the previous installation method for Visual Studio 2008 required you to download eight files, seven of which were almost a gigabyte each!

5. Once the file has finished downloading, navigate to wherever you chose to save it on your local hard drive and double-click it. It will then open your default DVD burning software (mine is Nero), and attempt to burn a DVD. This should take under 10 minutes on most modern computers.

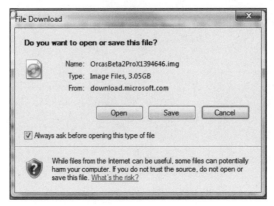

Figure 1-3. Save the IMG file to your local hard drive, and make a note of where you saved it.

6. Once the DVD is complete, the fun begins! Open the DVD drive that contains the new Visual Studio 2008 Beta 2 installer DVD and close it again, and it should automatically run. Some PCs may not have autorun enabled. If this is the case, use Window Explorer to navigate to your DVD drive and double-click the setup.exe file. You will then see a screen like the one in Figure 1-4.

> *Some DVD burning software may not recognize an IMG file. If this is the case, you may have to install another DVD burning software such as the trial version of MagicISO to convert the IMG file to a more common ISO file.*

Figure 1-4. Once you run the Visual Studio 2008 Beta 2 installer DVD, you will see this screen.

7. Click the Install Visual Studio 2008 link. The installer will then perform a check to make certain that Visual Studio 2008 can be installed on your machine and which components your particular machine will require to develop WPF applications (see Figure 1-5).

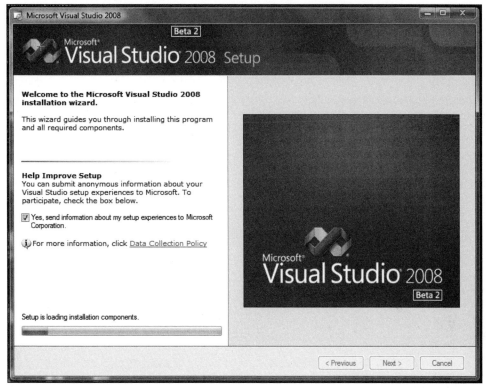

Figure 1-5. The Visual Studio 2008 Beta 2 installer will determine which components it needs to install on your machine.

8. You will then be asked to read and accept the license terms. To do that, select the appropriate radio button as I have done in Figure 1-6, and click Next.

> *Notice too that the product key has been entered for you and grayed out. This is because Visual Studio 2008 is still in Beta form and thus free, for now. Once the final product is released, you will need to purchase it and enter a valid product key to continue the installation process.*

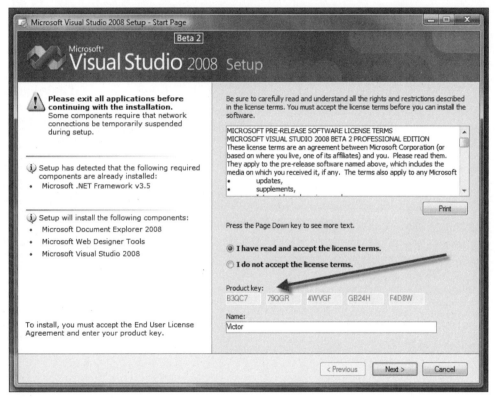

Figure 1-6. Accepting the license terms

9. The installer will then ask what features you want to install for Visual Studio 2008. Choose Default like I have done in Figure 1-7, and then click Install.

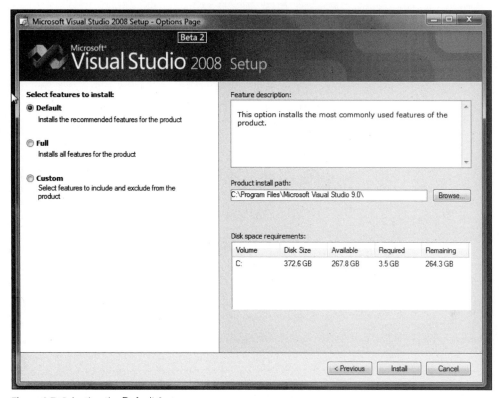

Figure 1-7. Selecting the Default features

At this point, the installer will then start to install a host of components that will allow you to create WPF applications (see Figure 1-8).

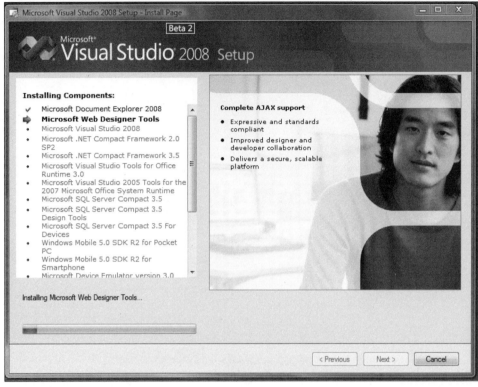

Figure 1-8. The install process begins.

The best advice I can offer you to make the installation process easier is to be patient. Personally, I have witnessed the installation of Visual Studio 2008 be as short as one hour and as long as two hours. Two components that take particularly long to install are the .NET Framework 3.5 and Microsoft Visual Studio 2008. The good news is that this version of the installer will install components that previously had to be downloaded and installed separately. For example, previously you had to download and install the .NET Framework 3.0 and the Visual Studio Tools for WPF separately.

10. Once the installer has completed, click Finish and then you can move on and download and install the Silverlight Tools for Visual Studio.

Downloading and installing Microsoft Silverlight Tools Alpha Refresh for Visual Studio 2008 Beta 2

The program you'll download in this section allows you to create Silverlight 1.1 applications in Visual Studio 2008. This book primarily covers WPF development, but because Silverlight 1.1 is a subset of WPF tools, much of the content is relevant to Silverlight 1.1 as well. Also, later in this book, I present some Silverlight 1.1 tutorials.

1. You can find the download under the "DOWNLOAD THE RUNTIME AND TOOLS" section located here: http://silverlight.net/GetStarted/.

2. Select the link that reads Microsoft Silverlight Tools Alpha Refresh for Visual Studio 2008 Beta 2 (July 2007).

3. You will then be redirected to a download page. Click the Download button on that page.

4. When prompted, save the file to your hard drive and make a mental note of the name of the file and where it was saved.

5. When the program has finished downloading, navigate to where you saved it on your hard drive and double-click it.

6. Run through the installation process. It is very simple and fast (no longer than 5 minutes).

Downloading and installing Blend 2

If you already own a copy of Blend 2, you can skip this section. If you do not have Blend 2, this section will describe where to find and install the free trial version.

1. To find the Blend 2 trial, head back to the Microsoft Download Center (located here: www.microsoft.com/downloads/) and in the search field enter blend 2 september like I have done in Figure 1-9.

Figure 1-9. Navigating to the Microsoft Download Center and entering blend 2 september in the search box

Again, with any degree of luck, your search will yield the same results that mine did, as the only result returned to me was exactly the one I was looking for (see Figure 1-10).

Figure 1-10. My search yielded one result, and it was just the result I was looking for.

2. Click the Expression 2 September Preview link, and you will be taken to the download page for Microsoft Expression Blend 2 as I was in Figure 1-11.

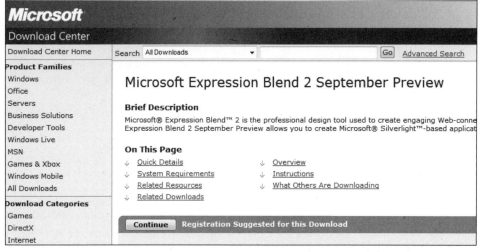

Figure 1-11. Your search result should take you to the download page for Microsoft Expression Blend 2.

3. Click the Continue button, and you will be taken to a page asking whether you want to register to receive the download. Registration is optional, and can be skipped if you prefer. Once that's done, you will be redirected to the page that will actually let you download the program (see Figure 1-12).

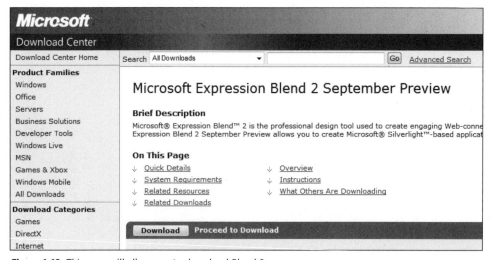

Figure 1-12. This page will allow you to download Blend 2.

4. You are then asked whether you want to Run or Save the file. In my experience, I have found that it is best to save it locally and then run it once it has completed downloading. That being the case, save the file to your local hard drive (making note of the file's name and location). Once the file has completed downloading, navigate to where you saved it on your hard drive and double-click it.

5. Click Run (see Figure 1-13).

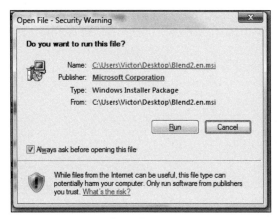

Figure 1-13. When the Open File dialog box appears, click Run.

6. Click Next (see Figure 1-14).

Figure 1-14. Click Next on the Blend 2 installation screen.

7. Accept the end-user license agreement and click Next (see Figure 1-15).

Figure 1-15. Accept the end-user license agreement

8. You will then be prompted to choose the setup type that best suits your needs. Select Typical (see Figure 1-16) and then click Install. You will then see the Blend installer progress bar (see Figure 1-17).

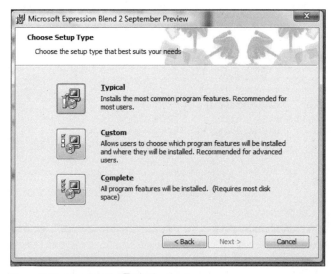

Figure 1-16. Selecting the Typical setup type

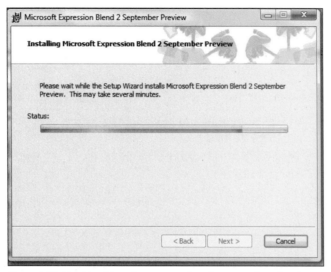

Figure 1-17. The Blend installer progress bar shows you how far along the install is.

9. After only a few minutes, the Blend 2 installer will inform you that it has completed the installation and will ask you to finish the process; choose Finish (see Figure 1-18).

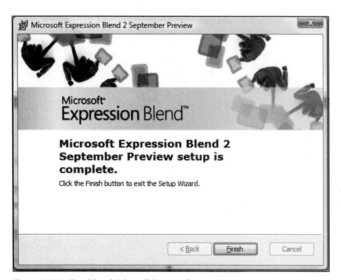

Figure 1-18. The Blend 2 install is complete.

Okay, now the moment of truth; you are going to open Visual Studio 2008 and create a new test WPF application. Getting excited yet? I am!

Creating your first WPF project

When I create WPF projects, I like to create them in Visual Studio 2008, even if I create the project and then immediately switch over to Blend to work on it. This is because Visual Studio and Blend 2 create WPF projects a little bit differently from each other.

- Blend doesn't offer the option for creating a WPF online application.

- As soon as Blend 2 creates projects, it starts to name the UIElements that the developer then, if so inclined, has to change.

- When Blend 2 creates a WPF project, it automatically closes off the main UIElement like this:

  ```
  <Grid x:Name="LayoutRoot"/>
  ```

  If you wanted to add something to the preceding root element in the XAML, you would have to open up the element like this:

  ```
  <Grid x:Name="LayoutRoot">

  </Grid>
  ```

  But Visual Studio 2008 does it for you like this:

  ```
  <Grid>

  </Grid>
  ```

- By default, a WPF project created in Visual Studio has more reference assemblies (I will explain reference assemblies later in the book in Chapter 10).

- Visual Studio is a little more tidy when it creates a WPF project: VS puts all of the project's properties inside of a Properties directory, while Blend 2 just creates a file called AssemblyInfo.cs in the root of the project. And, Visual Studio's AssemblyInfo.cs file (located in the Properties directory) is much more advanced.

Granted, these are subtle differences, but altogether they make it a good idea to create your WPF applications in Visual Studio.

That being said, let's move on and create a new WPF solution:

1. In your Start menu, navigate to where you see Microsoft Visual Studio 2008 and select it like I have done in Figure 1-19.

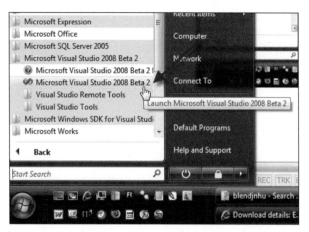

Figure 1-19. Navigating to Microsoft Visual Studio 2008 Beta 2 and selecting it

If you would rather not use the Start *menu, you can start Visual Studio 2998 by double-clicking this file:* C:\Program Files\Microsoft Visual Studio 9.0\Common7\IDE\devenv.exe.

2. At this point Visual Studio may ask you what developer settings you would like. Set this for C#.

3. Once Visual Studio 2008 Beta 2 opens, select File ➤ New ➤ Project like I have done in Figure 1-20.

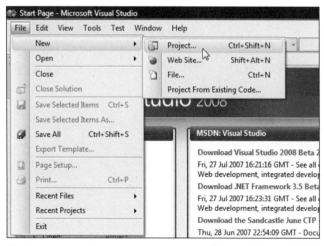

Figure 1-20. Opening a new project

The New Project dialog box will appear. Under Visual C#, you will see the project templates available to you, two of which will be WPF Application (for stand-alone Vista WPF applications) and WPF Browser Applications (for online browser WPF applications).

   4. Choose WPF Application, name your project WPFTestApplication, select C:\Projects (you will have to create this Projects directory by clicking Browse and creating a new folder in the New Project dialog box) for the location, and then click OK (see Figure 1-21).

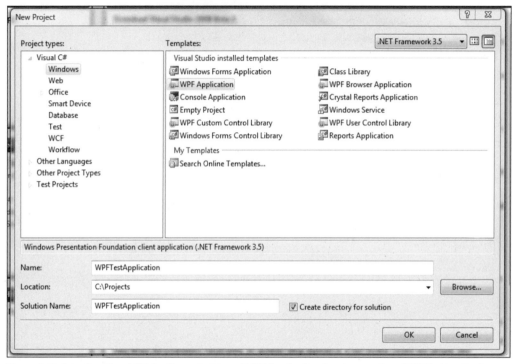

Figure 1-21. Selecting Visual C# for the project type, WPF Application for the template, WPFTestApplication for the name, and C:\Projects for the location

> You are currently creating a WPF stand-alone Vista application, but under C# the option for creating a Silverlight application should also be available.
>
> I have you create a new directory called Projects and save your project there because by default Visual Studio 2008 and Blend 2 save their projects in different locations. This can make it difficult to open projects created in Visual Studio in Blend and vice versa. This Projects directory can help solve that problem.

Visual Studio 2008 will then create a new WPF solution for you. A WPF solution is essentially a directory with one or more WPF projects that have associated files in them made up of XAML and C#. So Visual Studio has created a solution for you named WPFTestApplication and inside of that a project with the same name.

Visual Studio has a design tab that attempts to show you your project visually. Personally, I like to use Blend for my visuals and Visual Studio strictly for code. That being the case, I like to turn off the Visual Studio Designer. To do this, continue with the following steps:

5. Right-click any XAML file in Visual Studio's Solution Explorer (located in the top right of Visual Studio) and click Open With as shown in Figure 1-22.

Don't let terms like "Solution Explorer" and "the Visual Studio Designer" scare you, as I'll go over all of these terms in depth in upcoming chapters.

Figure 1-22. Turning off the Visual Studio Designer

6. A dialog box will then appear. Select XML Editor, click the Set as Default button, as shown in Figure 1-23, and click OK.

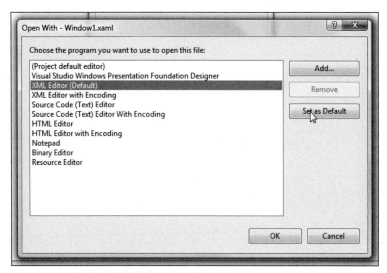

Figure 1-23. Selecting XML Editor as the default

7. Visual Studio will then ask you if you want to close your XAML file; click Yes. Visual Studio will then close the Designer and open your XAML file in XML view as shown in Figure 1-24.

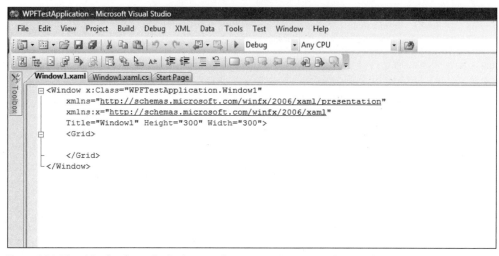

Figure 1-24. Visual Studio closes the Designer and opens your XAML page in XML view.

8. Now, just to be certain you can compile and run your project, give it some very basic content. In between the Grid tags, create a simple TextBlock as shown here:

```
<Window x:Class="WPFTestApplication.Window1"
    xmlns="http://schemas.microsoft.com/winfx/2006/xaml/presentation"
    xmlns:x="http://schemas.microsoft.com/winfx/2006/xaml"
    Title="Window1" Height="300" Width="300">
    <Grid>
      <TextBlock Text="FOO"/>
    </Grid>
</Window>
```

9. Now press F5 to run the application, and you should see something very similar to what I have in Figure 1-25.

Figure 1-25. Press F5 to run your test application, and you should see this.

> *I am using the terms "compile" and "run" interchangeably, but technically, they are not. "Compile" means to create an executable application from your project, while "run" means to create an executable application from your code and run it immediately afterward. Oftentimes throughout the book, I will use them interchangeably; however, if I want you to compile the application but not run it, I will be sure and explicitly tell you to do that. So for now, just know that I use both terms to basically mean "start the application."*

It is worth noting here that when you compiled your application, Visual Studio automatically saved your project. So now you can leave Visual Studio open, and fire up Blend and open your project.

10. To open Blend 2, look under your programs for Microsoft Expression; in that folder, click Microsoft Expression Blend 2 September Release, as shown in Figure 1-26.

Blend will open and will show you a welcome dialog box. Personally, I don't like dialog boxes when programs start, so I uncheck the Run at startup box and click Close (see Figure 1-27). If you ever want this screen back, you can click Help ➤ Welcome Screen. You can also check Run at Startup to make it reappear every time Blend is started.

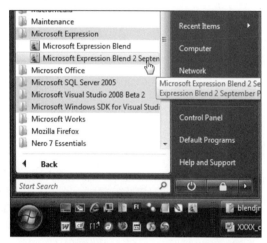

Figure 1-26. Navigating to Microsoft Expression Blend 2 September Preview

Figure 1-27. Blend's startup dialog box

11. Now select File ➤ Open Project/Solution and then navigate to where you saved your WPFTestApplication (I saved mine under C:\Projects). Then double-click the .sln (solution) file (see Figure 1-28).

Figure 1-28. Navigating to where you saved your WPFTestApplication and double-clicking the .sln file

You will then see that Blend opens your project and shows it to you in Split view, that is, you see the project visually as well as its XAML code . . . this is a brand new feature to Blend 2 (see Figure 1-29).

Figure 1-29. Blend shows your project in the brand new Split view.

Now that you have verified that you have installed the WPF development environment correctly by creating a new WPF project in Visual Studio 2008 Beta 2 and opening that same project in Blend, you can move ahead and make your first real WPF application.

Summary

In this chapter, you have downloaded and installed Visual Studio 2008 Beta and Blend 2 as well as Microsoft Silverlight Tools Alpha Refresh for Visual Studio 2008 Beta 2. You also verified that you installed the WPF development environment correctly by creating a new WPF project in Visual Studio and opening that project in Blend 2. In the next chapter, you are going to get down and dirty with WPF and create an application that has some very cool functionality. It will be fast paced, and I won't explain everything in detail because the next chapter is meant to generate excitement by showing you how fast and easy it is to create a very cool WPF application. Then in subsequent chapters I will discuss everything in greater detail.

Chapter 2

THE WPF/BLEND WORKFLOW AND YOUR FIRST WPF APPLICATION

What this chapter covers:

- The WPF/Silverlight improved workflow
- Creating your first WPF application

Microsoft has addressed problems with the designer/developer workflow with WPF and Silverlight. In this chapter, I will discuss that workflow and talk about how Microsoft thinks it has come up with a solution. I will also discuss a typical way of working in WPF and Silverlight using Blend 2 and Visual Studio 2008. Finally, I am going to show you how to create your very first WPF application, "Hello World!" with a twist, literally.

A new way of working

One of the major selling points for WPF and Silverlight is that Microsoft has recognized some of the difficulties that sometimes crop up when designers and developers try to work together, and provided a better set of tools and workflow to allow them to interact more easily. Blend 2 is intended to be used by designers to visually manipulate the application user interface (UI)—they can control layout, create visual Storyboard animations, add in assets such as graphics and video, etc. Developers, on the other hand, can use Visual Studio to interact with the application through code, in an environment they are familiar with—connecting it up to data sources, providing button interaction, creating `MediaElement` controls, etc. This makes the workflow between designers and developers much more simple, harmonious, and time efficient, and thus cost effective.

Before I started working in WPF and Silverlight, I was an ActionScript engineer for a large advertising firm in Los Angeles where we made large web sites for entertainment companies such as Disney, Universal, Mattel, and Warner Bros. Here I will describe a typical workflow between the developers, the designers, and myself, pointing out the limitations of that workflow along the way and then describing to you how WPF and Silverlight address those problems.

- First, the designers design the entire site, top to bottom, as a series of Photoshop mockups.
- Once the mockups are agreed upon and signed off, the Photoshop PSD files are handed off to me and my team to "make work." This is a typical workflow not only for Flash development, but also for other technologies as well (HTML, Java, etc.).
- I use the Photoshop file as a guide and re-create an object, let's say something simple like a button. I re-create it in Flash, or sometimes if I'm lucky I can copy it from Adobe Illustrator as a vector graphic.
- Then we plug the functionality into the newly created Flash objects, for example, the event handlers that handle the functionality for buttons.

This sounds pretty effective, so what then are the limitations? Let's say for some reason the client changes his mind and wants the button to look radically different. Being that I am not much of a designer, the job then falls upon the designers to make the change. They go back and make the required change to their Photoshop or Illustrator file. When they have completed the change, they then inform me that the files have been updated. I open up their Illustrator or Photoshop file and then either re-create the Photoshop file or copy the new vector graphic from Illustrator into Flash. This may not seem problematic, and in fact, it is not. It is, however, time consuming.

Microsoft's solution is to have the developers and the designers working on the same set of files in the same project so that if the style of a `Button` has changed, the designers can go into the same files that I, the developer, am working on and make the change. Further, WPF/Silverlight allows you to use something called `Styles` to specify the way user interface elements (`UIElements`) appear in your application. And these `Styles` are 100% reusable so that if I or the designer change the `Style` file (commonly defined in a WPF Resource Dictionary, which we will get to in Chapter 7) of, say, the navigation `Buttons`, that change is then reflected in any WPF/Silverlight `UIElements` that make use of that `Style`, which could be hundreds of `Buttons` in a large application. As you can ascertain, this saves a good amount of time. Now if you take into account that this type of scenario takes place many times during a project, the amount of time that is saved is dramatically increased. And as we all know, time is money, and money is what allows us to be able to pursue our hobby of developing Rich Media Applications.

So, how does WPF create a harmonious workflow? To explain this, I think it would be a good idea to provide you with a real-world example. Recently, I was part of a team that was developing a complex kiosk application. There was one developer on the project and two designers. The developer worked solely on the functionality of the application, in the C# code-behind files, while at the same time the two designers were creating the UI layer in the XAML files. Typically, as I explained before, the designers would finish the UI layer, usually in a separate program such as Photoshop, and then hand it off to the developer to "wire up." But now with WPF, the designers and developers could work on the application at the same time, thus saving vast amounts of time. This proved to be a much more effective and thus harmonious workflow.

I have included a few screenshots in the last part of this section to show the similarities as well as the differences between Visual Studio 2008 and Blend 2. Figure 2-1 shows how XAML code looks in Visual Studio, and Figure 2-2 shows the same XAML code in Blend in the XAML view. Figure 2-3 shows the same project in Blend's Design view. Finally, Figure 2-4 shows the same project in Blend 2's new Split view, which displays the Design view and the XAML view on the same screen.

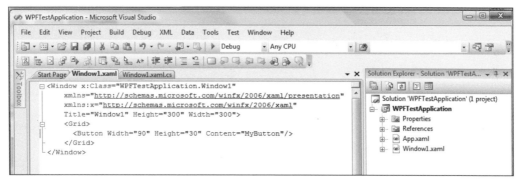

Figure 2-1. Sample XAML code in Visual Studio

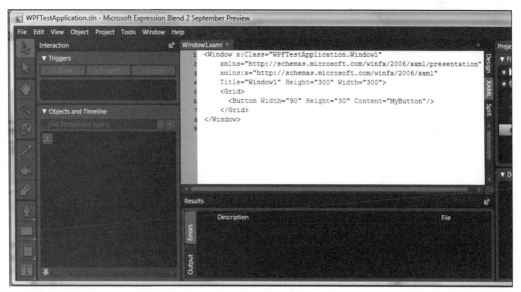

Figure 2-2. Sample XAML code in Blend

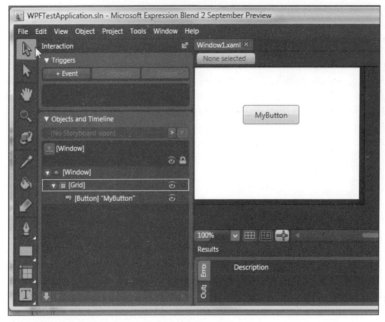

Figure 2-3. The same project in Blend's Design view

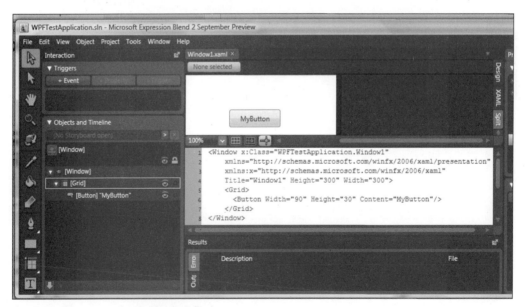

Figure 2-4. The same project in Blend's Split view

Your first WPF application: "Hello World!"

Without further ado, let's start you building your first WPF application. If you have ever read any programming books before, I am certain you know what your first application is going to be . . . yes, you guessed it, "*HELLO WORLD!*" Because "Hello World!" is the first application of almost every technical publication, everyone, including myself, usually hates it, as it tends to be very boring. So, I decided to make this particular "Hello World!" application one that harnesses the real power of WPF. This "Hello World!" application is going to have gradient colors, Buttons, and Storyboard animations that are run from EventTriggers. I can pretty much guarantee you that this will be the most exciting "Hello World!" application you have ever created. So get ready and let's create "Hello Word!" but with a twist . . . literally!

1. Open Visual Studio 2008 and click Create: Project or click File ➤ New ➤ Project.

   The New Project dialog box appears. Here, you want to make sure you have a few things selected (see Figure 2-5):

   - **Project type**: Under Visual C# select Windows.
   - **Template**: Select WPF Application.
   - **Name**: Type HelloWorld.
   - **Location**: It is very important to know where your project is being saved. Visual Studio 2008 will attempt to place your project in a default location on your hard drive. This is fine, but be sure you know where this location is; you will be opening this project in Blend 2, and in order to do that, you need to know where it is on your local hard drive.

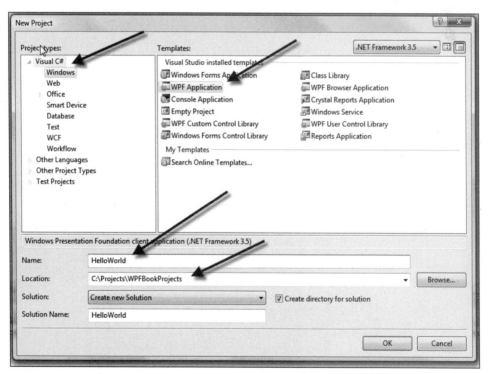

Figure 2-5. This is how your New Project dialog box should look in Visual Studio 2008.

This creates and opens up a new project named HelloWorld, as you may have expected. In later chapters, I am going to explain what everything is, but for now I am just going to give you a taste of working with WPF and Blend. So if I use terms you don't quite understand, fear not, as I will go over everything in depth in later chapters.

Visual Studio 2008 shows the new project in its Design view. I talked about how to close Visual Studio's Design view in Chapter 1, but because Visual Studio 2008 loses this setting for every new project you create, I will explain how to close the Design view again:

2. In Visual Studio Solution Explorer, top right of the Visual Studio integrated development environment (IDE), right-click Window1.xaml and select Open With (see Figure 2-6).

3. Now select XML Editor.

4. Click Set as Default.

5. Click OK (see Figure 2-7).

6. Visual Studio 2008 will now ask you if you want to close Window1.xaml. Click Yes.

Figure 2-6. Selecting the Open With context menu option

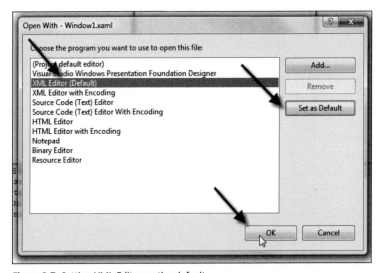

Figure 2-7. Setting XML Editor as the default

Visual Studio 2008 now shows you the XAML for Window1.xaml.

Getting to know Solution Explorer

Before I continue, let me tell you about Solution Explorer and what it is for. You can see where Solution Explorer is located in Figure 2-8. Solution Explorer is exactly that—a tool that lets you explore all of the different parts of your solution or project. Here you can see all of the directories as well as all files included in your application, XAML documents, CS files (C# code-behind pages—files that, along with their companion XAML files, describe a WPF application or control), images, audio and video files, XML files, etc. It allows you to easily look and see what files you have and where they are located.

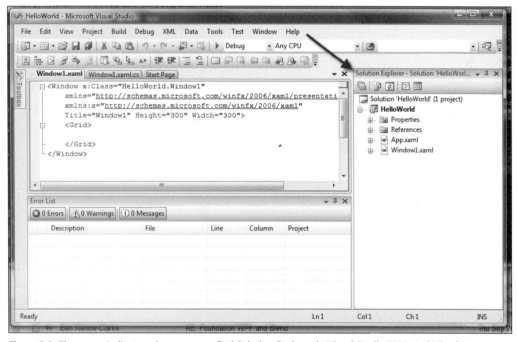

Figure 2-8. The arrow indicates where you can find Solution Explorer in Visual Studio 2008. A similar feature, called the Project panel, appears in the same place in Blend 2.

1. Now take a look at the code—what you should currently see in the XAML window is this:

```
<Window x:Class="HelloWorld.Window1"
    xmlns="http://schemas.microsoft.com/winfx/2006/xaml/presentation"
    xmlns:x="http://schemas.microsoft.com/winfx/2006/xaml"
    Title="Window1" Height="300" Width="300">
    <Grid>

    </Grid>
</Window>
```

You are now going to add some code to your application:

2. Place your cursor in between the open <Grid> and the closing </Grid> tags.

3. Enter the following bold line so that your code now looks like this:

```
<Grid>
        <TextBlock/>
</Grid>
```

> *Did you notice that when you started to type, Visual Studio attempted to figure out what you wanted and offered you a list of options? This is an autocomplete function called IntelliSense and is a very handy tool.*

Great! Now you have a TextBlock, the only problem remaining is that it is an empty TextBlock. You want to fix that by adding in a Text attribute to tell your TextBlock what text to contain:

4. Change the TextBlock line so it matches the following bold one:

```
<Grid>
  <TextBlock Text="Hello World!"/>
</Grid>
```

5. Now run your application and see what you get! Press F5 to compile and run the application. Provided you did not make any mistakes, you should see a window with the words "Hello World!" in the upper-left corner as shown in Figure 2-9.

Figure 2-9. Running the "Hello World!" application

Time for Blend 2!

Amazing, huh? What do you mean it looks boring? OK, OK, I know, it is not much to look at, but now that you've got the simple programming part out of the way, you can open the project in Blend 2 and make your "Hello World!" application look a little cooler.

1. Open Blend 2 and then select File ➤ Open ➤ Project/Solution.

2. Blend will then prompt you to provide the location of the solution file (.sln). Navigate to where you created your project and double-click the .sln file.

Once you open that file, you will notice immediately that Blend has a cool Design view as well as a XAML view. So I am sure you can see your "Hello World!" TextBlock. But shown in Figure 2-10. But it is almost as plain as it looked in the window when you ran it before. *That* is about to change.

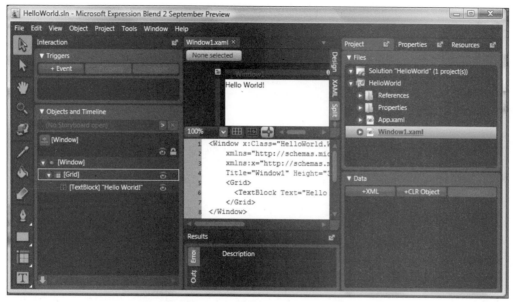

Figure 2-10. This is what your "Hello World!" application looks like in Blend's new Split view.

Changing the size of the application

First thing you are going to want to do is to give yourself a little breathing room by setting the Width and Height properties of Window1.xaml. Window1.xaml is the first page that the user will see when running your "Hello World!" application. Visual Studio 2008 created Window1.xaml by default because you chose to create a WPF application. If you had chosen to create a WPF browser application or a Silverlight application, the default would have been Page1.xaml. In order to manipulate [Window]'s properties such as Width and Height, you need to select it. To do that, follow these steps:

1. Go over to the Objects and Timeline panel located on the left side of the Blend IDE and double-click the [Window] UIElement until it is highlighted, as shown in Figure 2-11 (it will appear outlined in yellow on your screen).

Figure 2-11. Selecting elements in the project by clicking them in the Objects and Timeline panel on the left side of the Blend 2 IDE

2. Next, go over to your Properties panel (located on the right side of the Blend IDE), select the Properties tab, and change the Width and Height values to 800 and 600, respectively, as shown in Figure 2-12.

Figure 2-12. Changing the Width and Height settings of the [Window] UIElement in the Properties tab

Styling the Background

Ahh, nice, a little breathing room. Now with [Window] still selected in the Objects and Timeline panel, you'll give your Background a little style.

1. In the Properties tab, find the Brushes section, and if it is not already expanded, click the arrow to turn down the content for the Brushes bucket as shown in Figure 2-13. Once you turn down the arrow for the Brushes bucket, you will see the Background property for [Window].

2. Select the Background property (step 1 in Figure 2-14) and follow these steps:

    a. Click the Gradient brush (step 2 in Figure 2-14).

    b. Click the default black color stop (step 3 in Figure 2-14).

    c. Click the color bar and drag it to a color you like (step 4 in Figure 2-14).

    d. In the large square color editor, click a color (step 5 in Figure 2-14).

Figure 2-13. These are the arrows to click to expand each section.

Figure 2-14. Making changes to the "Hello World!" application's background

Notice your Background changed to reflect your choices. Fun, huh?

3. Notice also that your gradient is going from left to right; you want it to go from top to bottom, so grab the Brush Transform tool, shown by the arrow in Figure 2-15.

Once you select the Brush Transform tool, you will see that your Background now has an arrow. You can use this arrow to change the gradient properties, one of which is rotation.

4. Place your mouse over the handle of the arrow until it turns into a semicircular arrow, and then click and drag to rotate it so that it goes from top to bottom.

> Holding down Shift while you rotate limits rotation to set degrees so that it is easy to get the gradient arrow and the resulting gradient perfectly up and down.

Figure 2-15. The Brush Transform tool allows you to adjust gradients.

Starting to look better, isn't it? To see more of the design, you can click the Design tab, shown by the arrow in Figure 2-16, so that you can no longer see the XAML for your project (this can also be done by clicking View ➤ Design).

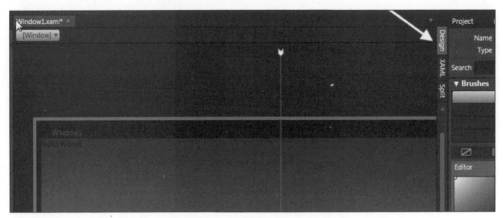

Figure 2-16. This shows what the project looks like in Blend 2's Design view.

Styling the TextBlock

Now that you have your Background looking somewhat cool, you can move ahead and make your [TextBlock] UIElement look good.

1. Click the Selection tool (or press the V key to select it), as shown by the arrow in Figure 2-17.

2. Double-click your [TextBlock] so that it is highlighted in the Objects and Timeline panel like I have done in Figure 2-18, and in the Layout section (sometimes referred to as a **bucket container**) of the Properties panel change its Width setting from Auto to 400 and its Height setting to 100 as shown in Figure 2-19.

Figure 2-17. The Selection tool is used to select UIElements in the Workspace.

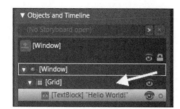

Figure 2-18. Selecting the [TextBlock] in the Objects and Timeline panel

Figure 2-19. Changing the Width and Height of your [TextBlock] to 400 and 100, respectively

Notice that this centered the [TextBlock] to the stage; if you don't want it centered, select it in the Objects and Timeline panel and then use your Selection tool to drag it to wherever you want.

Now that you have it where you want it, you'll change the text to look a little more aesthetically pleasing.

3. With the [TextBlock] still selected (it should have a blue line around it in the Workspace when it is selected), go to the Properties panel and under the Brushes section click Foreground. (The Foreground is the color property for the actual text.)

4. Grab the color selector and slide it to a color you want; you will see that the text changes colors on the fly in Blend's Design view. I chose a neon greenish color that has a Hex value of #FF16FA45, as you can see in Figure 2-20.

> *You can visually set the color of the* Foreground *property like you did earlier for the* Background *property, or you can manually type in a value yourself.*

Figure 2-20. Choosing a color for your
selected [TextBlock]

The hex values for Blend are much like the hex values in other visual programs such as Photoshop and Illustrator, the only difference is that Blend requires FF before the 6-character hex code.

The reason that the hex color value requires an FF is because WPF uses 32-bit 8-hex character codes as opposed to the more familiar 24-bit 6-hex color code. 32-bit hex colors are represented in WPF as AARRGGBB (two characters alpha, two characters red, two characters green, and two characters blue).

Once you've changed the color of your text, your changes should be reflected onscreen, as demonstrated in Figure 2-21.

Figure 2-21. Your [TextBlock] will change colors dynamically in
the Design view as you change the color in the Brushes section
of the Properties panel.

Next, you'll make your text a little more colorful and change the foreground from a solid color to a gradient color.

1. To do this, make sure that the [TextBlock] is still selected and then click the Foreground property (step 1 in Figure 2-22).

2. Click the Gradient button (step 2 in Figure 2-22).

3. Select the first color tab (step 3 in Figure 2-22).

4. Drag your color selector until your first color is a shade of red (step 4 in Figure 2-22).

5. Click in the center of your gradient to add another color tab stop (step 5 in Figure 2-22).

6. Slide the color selector around until the middle color tab is white (step 4 in Figure 2-22).

7. Select the color tab stop furthest to the right (step 6 in Figure 2-22).

8. Drag your color selector until it is a shade of green (step 4 in Figure 2-22).

Figure 2-22. The final gradient setting for the foreground

Figure 2-23 shows that the [TextBlock] is starting to look pretty cool. Note: I have made the size of my [TextBlock]'s text bigger to show the gradient more clearly. In the next step, I will show you how to do this.

Figure 2-23. The [TextBlock] with a three-color tab stop gradient

1. Now change the size and font of the [TextBlock]. To do that, drop down to the Text bucket in the Properties panel and change the font size to 72, as shown in Figure 2-24.

Because you set your [TextBlock] to have a Width of 400 and a Height of 100, your text should all show without being cut off. But if it was, as shown in the example in Figure 2-25, it can be fixed by grabbing the size handles on the right and dragging them out until all text shows clearly.

Figure 2-24. Changing the text font size to 72 in the Text bucket of the Properties panel

Figure 2-25. If the text is being cut off, grab the size handle and drag it to the right until all text is visible.

2. Press F5 to run the application and take a look. Not a bad little "Hello World!" application for a short amount of work, huh?

Making the "Hello World!" application more exciting

I think at this point your "Hello World!" application already blows the competition away, but let's go forward and really make this thing do something cool. And if, at this point, you are starting to get a little confused because we are moving fast, don't worry, as everything you are doing here will be covered in depth in later chapters. Keep in mind this exercise was intended to get your hands dirty with WPF. So, next you'll move forward and really make your "Hello World!" application sing . . . or should I say spin?

Creating a WPF button

OK, now for the additional functionality. I thought it would be cool to create a simple button that when clicked fires an event that runs a Storyboard animation that will make the "Hello World!" TextBlock spin around 360 degrees—hence "Hello World!" with a spin! Are you up for it? I know you are, so let's start making this application better than any other "Hello World!" application ever created.

> *The button will be styled with a default skin that comes as standard in Blend; I will cover custom styling later on in Chapter 7.*

First you need to create your Button. To do that, follow these steps:

1. Locate the Button tool in the Blend 2 toolbar. If another control is selected, hold the mouse button down until all controls show up, and then click the Button tool as shown in Figure 2-26.

Figure 2-26. Selecting Button in the toolbar

> *You may have already noticed that many of the ways the user interacts with Blend's tools are much like those for popular development and drawing tools in such applications as Photoshop, Dreamweaver, Flash, and Illustrator. Personally, I think this was a great move by Microsoft, as many of us in the technology field have been using these tools for years, and it makes learning this new tool much more pain free and fast.*

2. With the Button tool selected, draw a Button control in the Workspace (this is the same area as what's known as the stage in Flash) by clicking and dragging the mouse. You can make the Button any size you want. Figure 2-27 shows my Button control relative to the TextBlock in the Workspace.

Figure 2-27. Drawing a Button control in the Workspace

> *An alternative way to put a Button control in the Workspace is to double-click the Button tool on the toolbar, and Blend 2 will place a Button control into the Workspace for you with default dimensions. I rarely use the default dimensions, as I personally like to draw my controls by hand.*

That went easy enough, right? Now let's be a little creative and give the Button some text other than the default of "Button."

3. First make sure the Button is selected in the Objects and Timeline panel, and then in the Properties panel find the Content property under the Common Properties section as shown in Figure 2-28.

Figure 2-28. To change the Button text, change the Content property in the Properties panel.

> *The* Properties *panel has a search field that allows you to enter the name of the property, such as* Content, *that will then filter the properties for you based upon your search criteria. This is very convenient when you don't know what bucket a particular property is in.*

4. Change the Content property (where it currently says Button in Figure 2-28) to read something like Spin the Text.

5. Press Enter, and you will see the Button now reflects your change (see Figure 2-29).

Figure 2-29. Your Button control will update once you change the Content property in the Properties panel.

Now you have your Button set up, but currently it doesn't do anything. You need to tell the Button what you want it to do—in order to control a Button it, must have a unique name, so give it one:

6. Go to the Properties panel and change the Name property to spinBtn, as shown in Figure 2-30.

Figure 2-30. To control a Button with code, you need to give it a unique name.

> *I had you name your* Button *using a common naming convention whereby the first letter is lowercase and subsequent words in the name start with a capital letter. Oftentimes, .NET programmers will in general follow this convention, but sometimes start the name off with a capital letter such as "SpinBtn." You may see me using this latter naming convention in subsequent chapters, as I do in Figure 2-30, as I occasionally use both.*

Now that you've given the Button a name (an **instance name**, in official terminology), you can start to give it functionality in a number of different ways. You could, for example, animate it visually in Blend using the Animation Workspace or do it using XAML in the Blend XAML view, or you could even do it in either C# or in XAML using Visual Studio. Eventually, I will show you how to supply functionality in all these different ways, but for now I am keeping it simple and very visual, so you will do it in the Design view of Blend.

Creating EventTriggers for the spinBtn

At this point, you want to give the Button a Trigger. A Trigger is basically something that occurs when a user does something. The Trigger you are going to make use of is known as an EventTrigger. In this case, the clicking of your Button is going to fire an EventTrigger. When the Trigger is fired, you are going to run an animation called a Storyboard (I cover Storyboards in more detail in Chapter 10).

> *A Storyboard is basically an animation sequence that you create and can then reuse whenever you want—a Storyboard will change the value of an object's properties over time. As an analogy, say we have a friend named Bri, and Bri can do a cool little dance. Say we took Bri's dance and turned it into a Storyboard. We would have access to Bri's dance Storyboard at any time—basically, Bri's dance Storyboard is a Resource that we possess to be reused. So, in our analogy, we could take Bri's dance Storyboard and apply it to her friend Tristan, who could then perform Bri's dance. It is worth noting that Storyboards are much like traditional timeline animations that are seen in animation programs such as Flash or After Effects.*

You are not going to make a dance Storyboard but rather a spin Storyboard. That Storyboard will be a Resource available throughout the application, but will never be used unless you tell the application to make use of it. So, when the user presses the spinBtn button, you are going to "trigger" your spin Storyboard, and voilà! Your text will spin. Storyboards are created using the timeline feature, a feature that you will find very familiar if you've ever used Flash before. Blend 2 has made some radical changes to the Objects and Timeline panel that have made it much easier to create very cool Storyboard animations. Some of the changes to the Objects and Timeline panel in Blend 2 are

- The ability to copy Storyboards
- The ability to click one button in Blend and reverse a Storyboard

This last feature makes creating animations for ButtonEnter (when the mouse moves over a Button) and ButtonLeave (when the mouse moves off a Button) a breeze. But we'll get into that in later chapters.

I think at this time it would be a rather smart idea to show you Triggers, timelines, and Storyboards in action. So let's go ahead and start using them.

Make certain your Button is selected in the Objects and Timeline panel and then press F7 to switch Blend 2 from the Design Workspace to the Animation Workspace (the Animation Workspace can also be shown by clicking Window ➤ Animation Workspace). At the bottom of the page, you will see the Interaction panel (see Figure 2-31).

Notice that the Objects and Timeline panel has moved to the bottom of the page. You can also see there is a Triggers panel. This panel may be collapsed; if it is, click anywhere on the collapsed Triggers panel as shown by the arrow in Figure 2-32.

Figure 2-31. Blend 2's Animation Workspace shows an Interaction panel at the bottom of the page.

Figure 2-32. Click anywhere in the collapsed Triggers panel to expand it.

Figure 2-33 shows an expanded Triggers panel.

Figure 2-33. This shows expanded Triggers and Objects and Timeline panels in Blend 2's Animation Mode.

Let's run through some steps one by one to create the Triggers and Storyboards:

First, however, make sure your spinBtn is still selected; sometimes when you are clicking around, selected objects can become unselected. If it is not selected, you can select it by clicking it in the Workspace or by selecting it in the Objects and Timeline panel (this panel appears at the bottom of Blend while Blend is in the Animation Workspace), as shown in Figure 2-34. When your button is selected, it will have a blue line around it with size and rotate handles, and it will be highlighted in your Objects and Timeline panel.

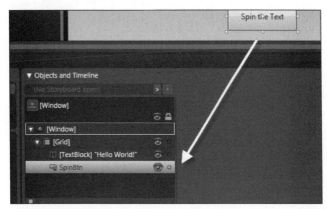

Figure 2-34. The button is selected.

1. With spinBtn selected, click the + Event button as shown in Figure 2-35 to create a new event.

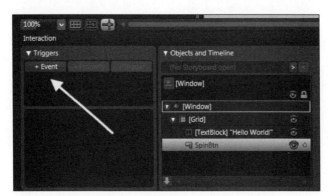

Figure 2-35. With spinBtn selected, click the + Event button in the Triggers panel to create a new event.

The default event that Blend creates when you click + Event is a [Window].Loaded event (see Figure 2-36). You don't want a [Window].Loaded event—because this will fire the event every time the [Window] is loaded . . . you want to fire the event when your spinBtn is clicked.

Figure 2-36. Clicking the + Event button in Blend 2 creates a [Window].Loaded event by default.

In order to change your Trigger to fire on a click Event, do the following:

2. Click the When drop-down menu (see Figure 2-37).

3. Select the spinBtn button (see Figure 2-38).

Figure 2-37. Clicking the When drop-down menu

Figure 2-38. Selecting spinBtn from the When drop-down menu

> If spinBtn is not selected in the Objects and Timeline panel, you will not see it as an option in the When drop-down menu.

4. Click the is raised drop-down menu (see Figure 2-39).

5. Select Click (see Figure 2-40).

Figure 2-39. Selecting the is raised drop-down menu just to the right of the When drop-down menu

Figure 2-40. Selecting Click from the is raised drop-down menu

This is a visual way create a narrative of what is going to occur. You can read it like a sentence that says "When spinBtn Click is raised" (where "raised" means when the event occurs). Make sense? But now what? What do you want to happen "When spinBtn Click is raised?" Good question, and here is how you add that piece:

6. Click the + button as shown in Figure 2-41 to add a new action that will fire when spinBtn is clicked.

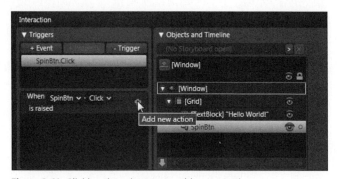

Figure 2-41. Clicking the + button to add a new action

7. Blend 2 will then pop up a dialog box that informs you that no timeline exists for you to begin and that it is going to create an empty one for you. This is what you want to happen, so click OK.

Blend 2 now creates a timeline in your Objects and Timeline panel as shown in Figure 2-42.

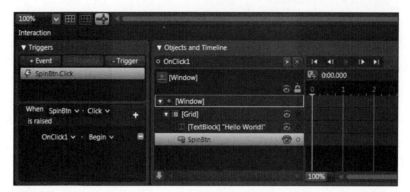

Figure 2-42. Blend 2 creates an empty timeline for you in the Objects and Timeline panel.

Blend 2 also places a red frame around your Workspace indicating that anything you do now is being recorded (see Figure 2-43).

At this point everything you do on the Workspace is being recorded into a Storyboard with the default name of OnClick1. You can change the name of this Storyboard by right-clicking OnClick1 and selecting Rename from the context menu as shown in Figure 2-44.

Figure 2-43. Blend 2 places a red line around your Workspace indicating that anything you do is being recorded.

Figure 2-44. Selecting Rename to rename your Storyboard

> *When I say that "everything in the Workspace is being recorded," I mean that Blend is taking note of every action you are performing and placing it into the Storyboard. This is much like recording actions in Photoshop or the using the AutoKey function in After Effects.*

8. Rename OnClick1 Storyboard to SpinTextSB.

Now at 0 seconds (this is the default position of the playhead), you need to record your original position.

Why do you need to do this, you ask? Because if you drag your playhead out to, say, 2 seconds and then spin the text on your Workspace and then run the application, this is what will happen:

The TextBlock will spin to the new angle that you determine in the Storyboard.

What's the problem? What if you click the spinBtn again? What would happen? See where I am going with this? Nothing would happen. Why? Because your Storyboard would tell the TextBlock to spin to the angle you declared in the Storyboard, but since the TextBlock is already at that angle, nothing would happen. To remedy this, you tell your TextBlock to start out at a 0 angle at 0 seconds and then 2 seconds later to be at another angle. Thus when you click the spinBtn a second time, the text will spin again, over and over and over. So, let's now record the angle of your text at 0 seconds.

9. With your TextBlock selected in the Objects and Timeline panel, click the Record Keyframe button, as shown in Figure 2-45.

Figure 2-45. The Record Keyframe button

Now you can look at your timeline and see that a dot representing the angle of your TextBlock has been recorded at 0 seconds (see Figure 2-46).

Figure 2-46. A dot represents the angle of your TextBlock in the Objects and Timeline panel at 0 seconds.

10. Move your playhead out to 2 seconds as I have done in Figure 2-47.

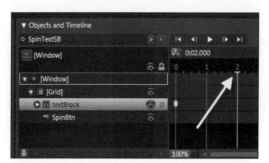

Figure 2-47. Moving the playhead out to 2 seconds in the Objects and Timeline panel

The playhead represents where you are in the timeline. So if the playhead is at 2 seconds in the timeline, as shown in Figure 2-47, any action recorded there will occur at 2 seconds into the Storyboard animation.

11. Set the TextBlock's Angle property to 180 in the Transform bucket of the Properties panel like I have done in Figure 2-48.

Figure 2-48. Changing the TextBlock's Angle property to 180

Notice two things:

Your TextBlock is now upside down (see Figure 2-49).

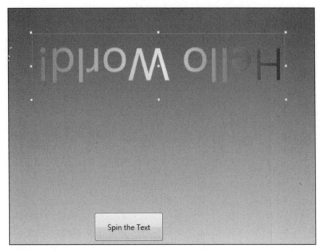

Figure 2-49. Your TextBlock is now upside down, representing the change to the Angle property you made.

There is a dot on your Objects and Timeline panel at 2 seconds representing the Angle property of your TextBlock (see Figure 2-50).

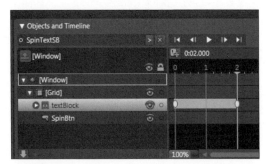

Figure 2-50. Your Objects and Timeline panel now has a small dot at 2 seconds, representing your TextBlock's changed Angle property.

12. Now, move the playhead out to 4 seconds and change the TextBlock's Angle property to 360.

Again, your TextBlock changes—it is now right side up again. And a small dot appears at 4 seconds in the Objects and Timeline panel that represents your new TextBlock's Angle property.

So, now your timeline should look like what I have in Figure 2-51.

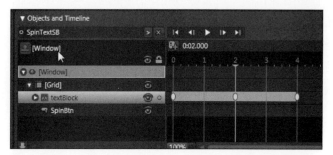

Figure 2-51. Your Objects and Timeline panel now has three small dots, representing your TextBlock's changed Angle property over time.

You can click and hold the playhead and scrub back and forth through the Storyboard animation. You can also click the Play button on top of the timeline to run the Storyboard. These tools are great for getting your Storyboard just the way you want it.

13. Now close your Storyboard by clicking the X button as shown in Figure 2-52.

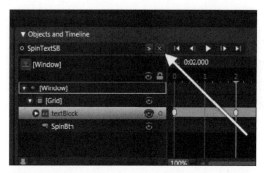

Figure 2-52. Clicking the X button to close your Storyboard

Notice the red line goes away as well as your Objects and Timeline panel? Now, the moment of truth:

14. Press F5 to run the application, and voilà! You click the spinBtn and your TextBlock does in fact spin 360 degrees over a 4-second time span. Click it again, and voilà again! It does it once more.

Well, congratulations! You have just created your very first real WPF application. And dare I say it, probably the best darn "Hello World!" application to date! Now that I have you all excited about WPF, let's continue through the rest of the book and really make some very cool WPF apps, with me over your shoulder guiding you all the way!

You will find the executable for your "Hello World!" application in the bin\Debug *directory of your project so that if you like, you can keep it on your desktop or even give it to your friends so they can run it. My executable* .exe *file is located at* C:\Projects\WPFBookProjects\HelloWorld\HelloWorld\bin\Debug.

A compressed file containing a finished version of the application you just created can be found at http://windowspresentationfoundation.com/bookDownloads/helloWorld.zip.

Summary

You just created your first WPF application. Congratulations! Now honestly, have you ever seen a "Hello World!" application do anything like this before? I don't think so. This exercise was intended for you to get hands-on experience with creating a WPF application in Visual Studio 2008 and Blend 2. You will be doing a lot of work in Visual Studio 2008 as well as Blend 2 in the upcoming chapters, but before you create any more applications, I will cover some Blend, C#, and XAML basics in the following chapters. Along the way, you will perform little exercises, and when you have learned all the basics, you will move on to learn several exciting creative techniques, including those for two 3D applications that will absolutely blow your mind and wow your friends! So let's get moving!

Chapter 3

THE BLEND 2 INTEGRATED DEVELOPMENT ENVIRONMENT

What this chapter covers:

- The Blend 2 toolbar
- The Objects and Timeline panel
- The Project panel
- The Properties panel
- The Resources panel
- 3D objects that can be created in Blend 2

Now that you have your development environment set up and you have had a taste of how fun and easy it is to create a cool looking and interactive WPF application, we can take a step back and get to the basics and discuss some of the major features of the Blend 2 integrated development environment (IDE). As we proceed, I will explain each major feature and then task you with little exercises that will help you to familiarize yourself with these tools and features. Some of these tools and features I will discuss briefly here and in more depth in later chapters. Now we are going to jump right in and start to explore some of Blend 2's major features.

The Blend 2 toolbar

If you are familiar with any of the popular design/development products such as Adobe's Photoshop, Flash, and Illustrator, the Blend 2 toolbar will be nothing new to you, as Microsoft has apparently attempted to make its toolbar functionally match that of the Adobe suite of development/design products. This, in my humble opinion, was a very smart move on the part of Microsoft, as it makes transition from an Adobe product to this new product quite easy. If, however, you are not familiar with the toolbar concept, this section will serve as a good introduction. The toolbar is a set of tools that allows you to create and edit user interface (UI) content that the users of your WPF/Silverlight applications can interact with. The Blend 2 toolbar is located on the left side of the Blend 2 IDE as shown in Figure 3-1.

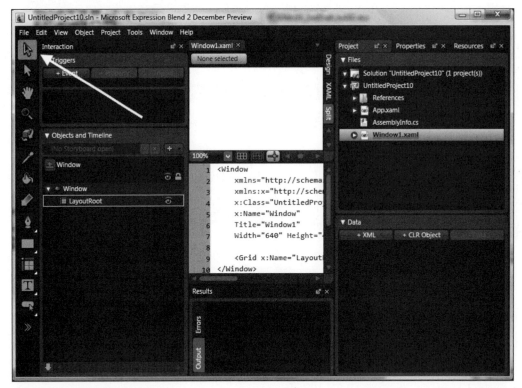

Figure 3-1. The Blend IDE

Figure 3-2 shows an isolated view of the toolbar. I will cover some of the tools you see in more depth than others in this chapter, as I will discuss some of the others in greater depth in later chapters.

Figure 3-2. The Blend 2 toolbar

The Selection tool

The Selection tool, as shown in Figure 3-3, is the tool that is used when you want to select UIElements (user interface elements that the user of your WPF/Silverlight applications will interact with) in the Workspace (known as the stage in Flash). This tool allows you to select UIElements to change their properties, such as modifying their size or shape or changing their Opacity or color (you will see how to do all of this later). This is probably the most used tool in all of Blend, so it would make sense for you to become very familiar with its location on the toolbar.

Figure 3-3.
The Selection tool

> Most of the tools on the toolbar can be selected by using keyboard shortcuts. For example, to select the Selection tool, you can press the V key. You can see the keyboard shortcut in the tooltip when you hover the mouse cursor over a tool's icon in the toolbar.

The Direct Selection tool

The Direct Selection tool, as shown in Figure 3-4, is a tool that allows you to see and edit the different nodes that make up a custom shape known as a Path (drawn using the Pen or Pencil tool). If you are not familiar with vector drawing tools such as Illustrator, I probably just lost you. Because I don't want to lose you, I will jump ahead a little and show you how to use the Pen tool to create Paths.

Figure 3-4.
The Direct Selection tool

55

The Pen/Pencil tools

The Pen/Pencil tools (as shown in Figure 3-5) allow you to create custom shapes or Paths in WPF/Silverlight. By default, you will see the Pen tool in the Blend 2 toolbar. To get to the Pencil tool, you can click and hold or right-click the Pen tool until you see the option appear for the Pencil tool. The Pen tool basically allows you to create a series of points that can be manipulated with the Direct Selection tool. In order to demonstrate this, I will show you how to use the Pen tool to create a Path.

1. Select the Pen tool from the Blend 2 toolbar.

2. Click to make a series of points.

3. Click the first point to complete the shape.

The Pen tool icon has helper features that help you to understand the action that is about to be performed by the tool. For example, when you have created a series of points (see Figure 3-6) and mouse over the first point, the Pen tool cursor shows a circle icon, indicating that if you click, you will complete the Path. Also, once you have created a Path and mouse over a line on the Path, a plus icon appears next to the Pen tool cursor indicating that you are about to add a new point. Finally, if you mouse over a point in the Path, you will see a minus icon appear next to the Pen tool cursor; this indicates that if you click, you will remove the point.

You have just created a custom Path. Now you can select the Direct Selection tool and modify those points (see Figure 3-7).

4. To move a point, place your cursor directly over it, click, and drag it. If you want to add a Bezier curve to a point, hold down the Alt key and then click and drag a point like I have done in Figure 3-7.

The Pencil tool allows you to create a shape by clicking and drawing in the Workspace like you would on a piece of paper (see Figure 3-8).

The Pen and Pencil tools in conjunction with the Direct Selection tool are very handy for creating shapes that are not symmetrical as opposed to simple Ellipses and Rectangles.

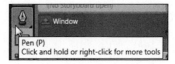

Figure 3-5. The Pen tool

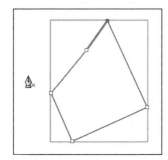

Figure 3-6. Use the Pen tool to create points. Click the first point to complete the shape.

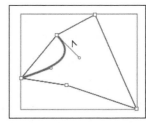

Figure 3-7. You can use the Direct Selection tool to modify your shape.

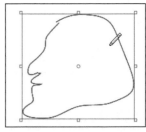

Figure 3-8. Using the Pencil tool, you can create shapes by drawing like you would on a piece of paper.

The Pan tool

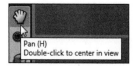

Figure 3-9. The Pan tool

You should now have a better idea of Paths and what the Direct Selection tool does, so let's jump back up the toolbar and carry on from where you left off. The Pan tool, as shown in Figure 3-9, allows you to navigate around the Workspace. This is very handy for large applications. You will notice that when you select this tool, your cursor turns into a hand icon. If you click and drag your mouse, you will notice that you can move your Workspace. Directly selecting this tool, however, is very impractical, because you can get the same result by holding down the spacebar and clicking and dragging your mouse. For this reason, I don't think I have ever directly selected the Pan tool from the toolbar, but there is something else that I find this tool very useful for: double-clicking it snaps into view the item that is currently selected on the Workspace or the Objects and Timeline panel. Sometimes I find myself so far off of the Workspace that I don't know where it has gone; in these times, I can just double-click the Pan tool and voilà! I have the UIElement that I am working on right in the center of my view—very handy.

The Zoom tool

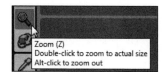

Figure 3-10. The Zoom tool

The Zoom tool, as shown in Figure 3-10, allows you to click the Workspace to zoom in. You can also click and draw out the area you want to zoom in on. Further, if you hold down the Alt key and click, you will zoom out. Finally, if you double-click the Zoom tool, you will be shown your Workspace at 100% with no zoom at all. I find this tool very handy for doing design details such as complex glass Buttons with many gradients.

The Camera Orbit tool

Figure 3-11. The Camera Orbit tool

If you are only familiar with 2D design/development tools such as Photoshop or Illustrator, you probably won't recognize the Camera Orbit tool, shown in Figure 3-11. This tool is surely familiar to any designer with 3D experience, from hardcore 3ds Max animators to those who only tinker with the 3D plug-in for Adobe Illustrator. This tool is for manipulating the camera view of WPF 3D objects known as Viewport3Ds.

> *The Camera Orbit tool is available in WPF but not Silverlight, as Silverlight does not support 3D without the use of third-party plug-ins.*

Figure 3-12. Here I am using the Camera Orbit tool to rotate the position of my camera in my Viewport3D.

You can see that in Figure 3-12 I am using the Camera Orbit tool to rotate a Viewport3D that I created from an Image control (you will see how to do this later in Chapter 10).

The Eyedropper tool

The Eyedropper tool, shown in Figure 3-13, is a very handy tool for selecting colors. The Eyedropper tool will select any color that is directly underneath it, whether it be a color of a vector shape or an image. Using the Eyedropper tool from the toolbar is rarely done because the same tool can be found on the Brushes palette, which is much handier to use. I will discuss this more in later chapters, but for now just be aware that it exists.

Figure 3-13. The Eyedropper tool

The Paint Bucket tool

The Paint Bucket tool, shown in Figure 3-14, is just like the Paint Bucket tool in Flash and Photoshop. You can select this tool and click an object to effectively "paint" your selected color onto that object like I have done in Figure 3-15.

Figure 3-14. The Paint Bucket tool

Figure 3-15. Here I am using the Paint Bucket tool to "paint" a Rectangle a different color.

The Brush Transform tool

The Brush Transform tool, shown in Figure 3-16, is perhaps one of my personal favorites because it is so powerful. This tool allows you to manipulate an object's gradient. To demonstrate this tool, follow these steps to create a Rectangle with a gradient and then use the Brush Transform tool to manipulate its gradient.

Figure 3-16. The Brush Transform tool

1. Select the Rectangle tool as shown in Figure 3-17.

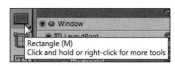

Figure 3-17. Selecting the Rectangle tool from the toolbar

2. Draw a Rectangle in the Workspace as shown in Figure 3-18.

Figure 3-18. Drawing a Rectangle in the Workspace

3. Activate the Selection tool (by pressing the V key) and click the Rectangle to select it.

4. In the Brushes section of the Properties panel, click the Fill property as shown in Figure 3-19.

Figure 3-19. Clicking the Fill property in the Brushes section of the Properties panel

5. With the Fill property selected, click the Gradient brush button as shown in Figure 3-20.

Figure 3-20. Clicking the Gradient Brush button

Notice now your Rectangle has a black-to-white gradient that runs from left to right as shown in Figure 3-21.

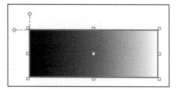

Figure 3-21. Your Rectangle now has a gradient that runs from left to right.

But say you want this gradient to run from top to bottom instead of left to right. Well, as you might have guessed, you would use the Brush Transform tool to make it so. You'll do that now:

6. Click the Brush Transform tool (shown previously in Figure 3-16).

Notice now your Rectangle has an arrow over it running the same direction as your gradient (starting left and pointing right), as you see in Figure 3-22. You can now use this arrow to manipulate your gradient, so do that now.

Figure 3-22. The gradient arrow

7. Place your cursor over the arrow until it turns into a hand . . . when it does, click and drag your mouse to change the size of the gradient.

8. Next, move your cursor around the tip of the arrow until your cursor turns into a curved two-headed arrow; you can now click and hold the mouse to rotate your gradient from top to bottom like I have done in Figure 3-23.

> *When rotating your gradient using the* Brush Transform *tool, you can hold down the Shift key to constrain the angles so that it is easier to get a perfect up-to-down gradient.*

Figure 3-23. When your cursor turns into a double-headed arrow, you can then rotate your gradient from top to bottom.

Because the Rectangle is longer than it is tall, your gradient will be too big when you rotate it. You can size your gradient so that it starts exactly at the top of your Rectangle and ends perfectly at the bottom like I have done in Figure 3-24.

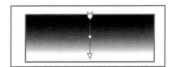

Figure 3-24. Rotating and resizing your gradient

We will get into gradients in much more depth in later chapters, but this provides the gist of the Brush Transform tool. With that, you can move forward.

The shape tools: Rectangle, Ellipse, and Line

There are three shape tools. The one that shows by default is the Rectangle tool (see Figure 3-25). If you hold down your mouse over the Rectangle tool or right-click it, you will see the options for the Ellipse and Line tools, which you can then select. Since you have already seen how the Rectangle tool works, let's move on to the other shape tools:

1. Click and hold on the Rectangle tool, and when you see the option for the Ellipse tool, select it.

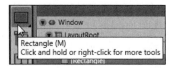

Figure 3-25. The Rectangle shape tool

2. With the Ellipse tool selected, draw an Ellipse in the Workspace like I have done in Figure 3-26.

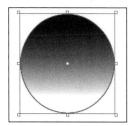

> *If you hold down the Shift key while drawing a shape (specifically a Rectangle or Ellipse), your shape will be perfectly symmetrical. Also, if you hold down the Alt key, the shape will be drawn from the center rather than the corner.*

Figure 3-26. Here I have drawn an Ellipse in the Workspace using the Ellipse shape tool.

Notice how Blend drew out the Ellipse with the same gradient that you used on the Rectangle earlier? This is a pretty cool feature and can save some time when making objects that are meant to look exactly alike.

Now try out the Line tool:

1. Hold down the Ellipse tool on the toolbar until the Line tool becomes visible, and select it.

2. Now draw a line in the Workspace like I have done in Figure 3-27.

> *If you hold down the Shift key while drawing a line, your line's angle will be constrained so that it is easier to make a line that is perfectly vertical or horizontal.*

Figure 3-27. Using the Line shape tool to draw a line in the Workspace

The shape tools, as you will see in later chapters, allow you to make very cool objects such as custom Buttons.

Layout controls

Next we see the layout controls, as shown in Figure 3-28. The default layout control shown when Blend first starts is the Grid. That is because the Grid is by far the most popular layout control. As a matter of fact, when you create a new WPF project, the default layout control that is placed in your Workspace is a Grid named LayoutRoot. Basically, layout controls are the controls that handle the layout of your WPF application; that is, they are the containers that house your UIElements. You could think of them almost like HTML tables because without them, you would not be able to view tabular content in a structured way. You will see an example of this in Chapter 5.

There are a many different layout controls, and they are all used at different times to accomplish different goals because they each display their content differently. I will go into these controls in depth later on in the book, but for now just be aware that there are nine layout controls: the Grid, the Canvas, the StackPanel, the WrapPanel, the DockPanel, the ScrollViewer, the Border, the UniformGrid, and finally the Viewbox (see Figure 3-28). Again, don't worry about what these are and what they do now because I am going to really break them down for you and work through exercises on how to use them properly in Chapter 5.

Figure 3-28. If you click and hold the Grid tool on the toolbar, all nine layout controls will appear.

Text controls and text input controls

The next tool on the toolbar is the TextBox tool. If you hold this tool down, other controls will appear (see Figure 3-29). These are controls that allow you to add text to your applications as well as text input controls such as a TextBox (a text input field) and a PasswordBox. I will discuss these controls in depth later in the book.

Figure 3-29. If you click and hold the TextBox tool, the other text and text input controls will appear.

Input controls

The next tool on the toolbar you will see is the Button control. If you hold down this tool, you will see the other input controls available to you (see Figure 3-30).

These controls are essential because they allow your application to interact with the user. Probably the most common of these input controls is the Button control. If you have done any web development, most of these controls will already be familiar to you. We will use most of these controls later on in the book.

The Asset Library Last Used tool

The next tool on the Blend 2 toolbar is the Asset Library Last Used tool. This is a handy little feature that will turn into the last control you have used from the Asset Library. Say, for example, I select the

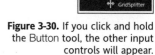

Figure 3-30. If you click and hold the Button tool, the other input controls will appear.

CheckBox tool from the Asset Library to create a check box. The Asset Library Last Used tool will turn into a CheckBox control. What is an Asset Library you ask? Find out in the next section.

The Asset Library

The next button you will find on the toolbar is a very handy one called the Asset Library. This is a collection of *every* control available to you in WPF/Silverlight (see Figure 3-31).

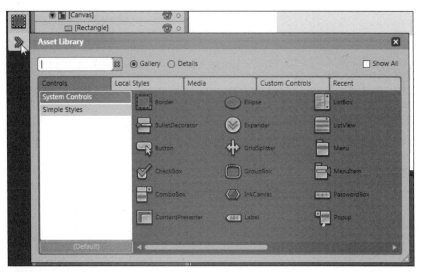

Figure 3-31. The last tool on the Blend 2 toolbar is the Asset Library.

This tool is great for a few reasons. First, it has a search feature that will filter out the controls you see. For example, if you type B in the search field, all controls that have the letter B in them will appear. If you continue to type the word Button, all controls with the word Button in them will appear. Currently, there are four controls with the word Button in them . . . I know that not because I am a genius but because I just tried the search I just mentioned while writing this chapter. Which brings up a good point: oftentimes we WPF/Silverlight developers forget the name of controls. When we do, the Asset Library is a great place to come to browse through them.

The other reason why I think this is a great tool is because if you make custom UserControls (we will do this in a later chapter), they show up here under the Custom Controls tab. This makes it so easy to implement the Custom UserControls that you have made, you won't believe it. But for now, you are just going to have to take my word for it until you get to the custom UserControl tutorial found in Chapter 7.

There are so many controls in the Asset Library that it would be impractical and out of the scope of this book to discuss them all. In fact, I could imagine an entire book on all of these controls. Anyway, because I am not going to discuss all of these controls, I thought it would be nice to talk about three that I really am fond of: InkCanvas, Tab, and Frame.

The InkCanvas control

In order to use the InkCanvas control, follow these steps:

1. Click the Asset Library, search for "ink," and select the InkCanvas control.

2. Draw an InkCanvas in your Workspace.

3. Press F5 to run the application, and you'll find that you can draw directly onto your InkCanvas like I have done in Figure 3-32.

Figure 3-32. The InkCanvas control allows you to make a drawing application with no programming whatsoever.

Is this cool or what? You didn't have to do any programming at all; Blend does all of the work for you.

The TabControl

The TabControl is a really awesome control that allows you to add content to a tab-based window in a matter of minutes. Take a look at Figure 3-33—I was able to make that example in less than two minutes. And it is skinnable, too. In case you don't know, **skinning** is a term used to describe the redesigning of a control to fit the look and feel of the rest of the project.

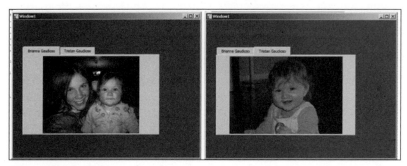

Figure 3-33. In a matter of minutes, I was able to use the TabControl to create a tabbed Window application.

The Frame control

The Frame control is another one I go absolutely nuts for. The Frame control allows you to embed a frame in your WPF application. The source of that frame can even be a URL. Check out Figure 3-34. That is an actual functioning instance of Google. Amazing, huh?

Figure 3-34. The Frame control acts as a web browser in WPF applications.

The Objects and Timeline panel

Now that you are familiar with the toolbar, let's move on to the Objects and Timeline panel of the Interaction panel located on the left side of the Blend IDE, just to the left of the toolbar, as shown in Figure 3-35.

If you place an object in your Workspace, say a TabControl, it will show up here as an object because it now becomes part of your Visual Tree. The Visual Tree is just a list of any objects in your Workspace. As you can see in Figure 3-36, the Visual Tree consists of a window. Inside that window you can see the LayoutRoot Grid (this is created automatically when the project is created). Inside of that you can see my TabControl, and if you look inside of that, you can see it has two TabItems that each have a Header and an Image. That is my Visual Tree, and if I want to select an item, say the TabItem1 image, I can just click it here in my Objects and Timeline panel. Oftentimes I prefer to select items here because it can be difficult to select an item in the Workspace when there are a lot of things going on. For example, say I want to select a Button I have in the Workspace, but it is being covered by a StackPanel. It would be very tricky to select the Button without moving items around. In this case, it would be much easier to simply select the Button from the Objects and Timeline panel.

Figure 3-35. The Objects and Timeline panel is located just to the left of the toolbar in the Blend 2 IDE.

Figure 3-36. An easy way to select items is through the Objects and Timeline panel.

Another thing you should know about this panel is that there are little eyeball icons for each object in the Visual Tree, as shown in Figure 3-36. If I were to click the eyeball icon of the TabControl layer, my TabControl would become invisible in the Workspace, and the eyeball icon would be replaced by a small blank circle icon. To reveal the item again, just click the blank circle icon, and it will reappear. Also, if there are any items in that object (as in the case of my TabControl), they and their eyeball icons would be invisible as well. This is because they are

65

children of the TabControl. Keep in mind it hasn't been deleted, it's just hidden. And, it is only hidden in the IDE, so if you were to run the application, you would see the TabControl again. If you actually wanted to make it invisible to the user, you would have to set it to be invisible in the Properties panel—but we will get to that a little later.

If you look at Figure 3-36, you will see that each object has a little circle icon next to its eyeball icon. That circle icon will change to become a little padlock icon when you click it, effectively locking the object and all of its children. This is helpful because when you get an object designed and positioned perfectly, you can lock it so that nothing accidentally changes that object while you are working on other objects.

I have now covered the basics of the objects part of the Objects and Timeline panel, but I have yet to address the timeline aspect of it. I will do so in Chapter 12, which covers the Storyboard and animation, as that's where you'll actually put the timeline feature to use.

The Project panel

The Project panel (see Figure 3-37) shows you all of the assets that make up your application.

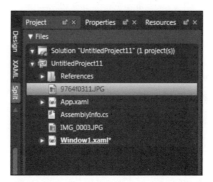

Figure 3-37. The Project panel shows all of the resources of the current application.

The assets that make up the project are as follows:

- The first thing you see is the name of your project solution; mine is named UntitledProject11.

- Next you see a directory called References. This folder holds references to other DLLs that make the application work. You will not need to worry about that directory in this book. But, just so you know, you can add references to other WPF projects and have all of the resources available in that project available to your new project.

- Next you see 9764f0311.JPG (and later IMG_0003.JPG). These are the images that I used to populate the TabControl that I made in Figure 3-33.

- Next you see app.xaml. This is a file that is automatically generated by Blend, and it holds information about resources, dictionaries, and the like.

- Then you have AssemblyInfo.cs. This file is automatically maintained by Visual Studio and Blend. There is no need to edit it manually.

- Now you finally come to Window1.xaml. This is the file that you have been working with when I asked you to create a shape, Rectangle, etc. We will talk about XAML and C# in depth in the next chapter, but it is worth mentioning here that XAML is the UI layer. Everything the user sees will be contained in this file. Notice there is an arrow next to this file. If you were to turn that arrow down, you would see Window1.xaml.cs. This is called a **code-behind** page. Most every XAML page has a code-behind page. This code-behind page is written in C#. Code-behind files can be written in C# or Visual Basic for WPF and Silverlight 1.1 projects. Silverlight 1.0 code-behind pages are written in JavaScript. Code-behind pages are edited not in Blend 2, but in Visual Studio 2008. But again, we will talk in depth about this in the next chapter.

The Project panel is important because it allows you to easily navigate to any file you want by double-clicking it. If you double-click a XAML file, it will open in Blend, but if you double-click a CS (C#) file, it will open a new instance of Visual Studio 2008, and you can edit it there. Another reason why the Project panel is important is that it allows you to right-click the solution and add a new folder. This is important when trying to keep your image, video, and audio assets organized. Also, you can add items to a project solution in the Project panel. Via a context menu command, you can navigate to your assets (images, video, audio, XML, etc.). Blend then makes a copy of whatever item you select and places it in the project in the folder you specify. To put an asset into a new folder you created, follow these steps:

1. Right-click that new folder.
2. Click Add Existing Item.
3. Navigate to an item, say an image on your hard drive, and double-click it.

A new feature that was added to Blend 2 allows you to actually drag and drop images from your hard drive right into the Project panel.

The Properties panel

This Properties panel, shown in Figure 3-38, is where you set the properties for controls in your Workspace. You can get from the Project panel to the Properties panel by clicking the tab that reads "Properties."

Figure 3-38. The Properties panel

The Properties panel is so important, and you will use it so often, I feel that it would be a good time to start some serious hands-on work with Blend 2 in order to demonstrate this panel.

Brushes

We've already taken a brief look at the Brushes panel, but let's take a closer look at it now and set up a very simple project that you'll use to view the effects of some of the other panels.

1. Create a new project in Blend and call it PropertiesPanel.

2. Select the Rectangle tool and draw a Rectangle on the Workspace. Make it any size you wish as you will change it later.

3. Make certain that the Rectangle is selected.

4. Find the Brushes section of the Properties panel. If it is not already turned down, do so now so that you have something that looks like what I have in Figure 3-39.

Figure 3-39. The Brushes section of the Properties panel

First let's take a look at the Fill property. Notice right now this property is set to a solid color (see Figure 3-40).

Figure 3-40. The Fill property of your Rectangle is set to a solid color of white.

5. Change the color from white to another color. You can do this a few different ways:

a. You can just click in the color palette, and the color will change to whatever color you clicked (step 1 in Figure 3-41).

b. You can adjust the RGB values individually (step 2 in Figure 3-41).

c. You can change the color by setting the hexadecimal value (step 3 in Figure 3-41).

d. You can change the color value by using the Eyedropper (step 4 in Figure 3-41). The Eyedropper will pick up any color that is underneath it. This goes for your Workspace or the Blend application as well.

e. You can change the color by making use of a color resource (step 5 in Figure 3-41). You will create a color resource and apply it to another object a little later in this tutorial.

You can also choose a gradient for your object by selecting the Gradient brush option, as shown in Figure 3-42. Let's take a look at gradients in a little more detail.

Figure 3-41. These are the different ways you can change the solid fill of an object.

Figure 3-42. With your Rectangle selected, you can also fill it with a gradient by choosing a gradient fill.

Once you choose a gradient fill, you will notice that your object by default now has a white-to-black gradient across it. This can be changed much like it is changed in popular design programs such as Adobe Flash and Photoshop. To change one of the gradient colors, follow these steps:

1. Select the color handle for the gradient color you want to change, as shown by the arrow in Figure 3-43, and then change the color by any method you learned about in the preceding exercise.

2. Drag the color slider (step 1 in Figure 3-43) to pick a hue, and then select a suitable color from the color palette (step 2 in Figure 3-43).

To add more color handles, and therefore add more colors to the gradient, simply click in the gradient bar, and a new handle will appear below where you clicked. To remove a handle, click it and drag it away from the gradient bar.

If you notice, your gradient runs from left to right. What if you wanted it to run from top to bottom? In this instance, you could select the Brush Transform tool from the toolbar and manipulate the gradient arrow like you did earlier in this chapter. Play with the gradient colors and the Brush Transform tool until you get your gradient looking cool.

This is a good time to talk about **color resources**. Say you have a gradient or even a color that appears in many different places in your application. As you may know, designers are very particular about maintaining their designs, and any deviation from the developer can cause problems. Because of this, developers in the past had to be meticulous and re-create the gradient or color for every object. But now you can create a color or gradient once and then create a color resource so it can be applied to any object. But it goes much further than just color resources. Any property can be saved as a resource such as a fill, the source of a MediaElement, the angle of an object, anything. Other objects can then use these resources. If the resource changes, all of the objects using that resource will automatically be updated throughout the project.

Back to our gradient example; say your new gradient is exactly to the designer specifications.

1. Click the +Brush button, shown in Figure 3-44, to create a color resource.

Figure 3-43. Changing one of the colors that make up your gradient

Figure 3-44. The +Brush button allows you to turn your gradient into a color resource that you can use again throughout your application.

Now a dialog box pops up and asks you a few questions about your new color resource (see Figure 3-45):

2. The Name (Key) field is where you specify what name you would like for your new resource. The default name of Brush1 is fine for this demonstration so you can leave it as is.

3. In the Define in area, Blend is asking you if you would like this new resource to be available to 1) the entire application, 2) the current document only, or 3) a ResourceDictionary (we'll cover this in a minute). For your single-page application, select This document to make the resource available only to the current document.

4. Once you have set both the parameters in the dialog box, click OK.

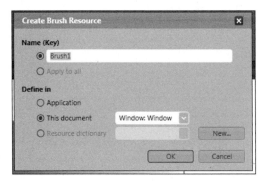

Figure 3-45. The Create Brush Resource dialog box

Because I told you that any property can be set as a resource, I feel it would be good to show you how to do that as well. Here are the steps to create a resource for the source of a MediaElement:

1. In the Asset Library, select MediaElement.

2. Draw a MediaElement in the Workspace.

3. In the Properties panel in the Media bucket, click the Source button.

4. When the Add Existing Item dialog box appears, navigate to an image or video on your local hard drive

5. Double-click the file.

6. Now click the Advanced property options button shown in Figure 3-46.

7. Click Convert to resource.

8. In the Create Resource dialog box, give the resource a name and click OK.

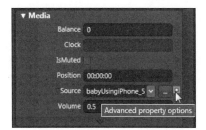

Figure 3-46. The Advanced property options button

You have now created a resource out of your MediaElement Source property.

This is a good time to talk about ResourceDictionaries. You can define a custom ResourceDictionary that holds reusable templates such as gradients. It is a good way to keep your custom resources organized. So, go ahead and create one by following these steps:

1. Create a new Rectangle on the Workspace.

2. Give it a gradient fill of your choice. I left mine the default of Brush1.

3. Click the +Brush button in the Brushes bucket of the Properties panel.

4. Give the new Brush Resource a name of your choice.

5. Where you see the grayed out Resource Dictionary radio button at the bottom, click the New button.

6. Blend will now ask you what name you want to give your new ResourceDictionary. You can just use the default and click OK.

7. Then click OK in the Create Brush Resource dialog box. Notice now that Blend has switched over to the last option of Brush Resources, as shown in Figure 3-47. You can see a list of resources. By default, your new brush is selected. Blend has also created a new XAML file called ResourceDictionary1.xaml. That file holds the information for your new gradient.

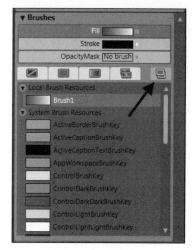

Figure 3-47. Blend has now switched your color over to the Color Resources option and has selected your new brush gradient.

> Remember earlier in the chapter that I said that most XAML files have C# code-behind files? A ResourceDictionary is an example of a XAML file that does not have a C# code-behind file.

So now let's go ahead and see how you can apply your new brush resource.

1. Select the Ellipse tool.

2. Create an Ellipse in the Workspace.

3. Make sure your new Ellipse is selected.

4. In the Brushes section of the Properties panel, click the Brush Resources button.

5. Select your new brush; mine is named Brush1.

Notice your Ellipse now has the same exact gradient fill as your Rectangle (see Figure 3-48).

> It is possible that Blend remembered the last gradient you created and made your Ellipse that color by default. If that occurred, select your Ellipse and in the Brushes section give it a solid default color of black, and then follow steps 3 through 5 earlier.

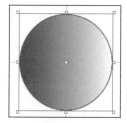

Figure 3-48. The Brush1 resource gradient applied to the Ellipse

You also have the option of editing the alpha of either one of your colors in a gradient or your entire color in a solid fill. You can see the slider for this right under the RGB sliders in the Brushes section of the Properties panel. I find that not to be very useful. If I want an object to fade out, I want the entire object to fade out, not just the fill of the object. This brings us to the OpacityMask property, as shown in Figure 3-49.

Figure 3-49. An OpacityMask allows you to edit the alpha of an entire object.

If you wanted the entire object to be see-through, there is an Opacity setting for the object that you can set. You will see that later. But say you want the object to fade out, like a reflection, for instance. The object does not have a setting for that, but fortunately the Brushes section does and it is called OpacityMask. To demonstrate this, go ahead and create a reflection for your Rectangle:

1. Select the Rectangle, and copy it by pressing Ctrl+C.
2. Paste in a new Rectangle by pressing Ctrl+V.
3. Move your new Rectangle directly beneath the original one.
4. Move your cursor over the top-right handle of the new Rectangle, and rotate it 360 degrees so that it appears to be a mirror image of the original Rectangle as shown in Figure 3-50.

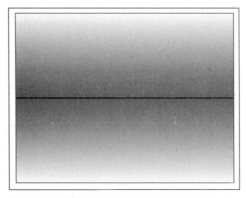

Figure 3-50. Creating a duplicate copy of your Rectangle, moving it below your original, and rotating it 360 degrees

5. Now select your new Rectangle.

6. Click OpacityMask, as shown in Figure 3-51.

Figure 3-51. With your bottom Rectangle selected, click OpacityMask.

7. Select Gradient brush, as shown in Figure 3-52.

Figure 3-52. Selecting Gradient brush for the fill of your OpacityMask

Now here it is important to understand that the colors you select are irrelevant in an OpacityMask. What *is* important is the alpha of the colors.

8. Set the alpha of one of the colors to 0% as I have done in Figure 3-53.

Figure 3-53. Setting the alpha of one of the gradient colors to 0%

Notice that now half of your Rectangle is invisible. But wait, that does not look like a reflection, as the gradient for the OpacityMask is going the wrong way (see Figure 3-54).

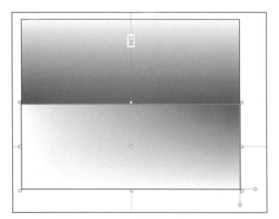

Figure 3-54. Your OpacityMask is working, but the gradient is going the wrong way (left to right instead of top to bottom) and does not look like a reflection.

9. Select the Brush Transform tool, rotate the gradient, and size it until it runs from top to bottom and looks something like what I have in Figure 3-55.

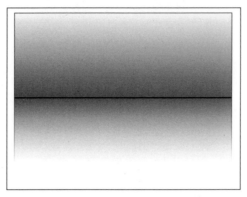

Figure 3-55. With the `OpacityMask` gradient adjusted properly using the Brush Transform tool, you get the reflection effect you are looking for.

Now *that* looks like a reflection!

Let's go through the other options located in the Brushes bucket of the Properties panel very quickly:

- The BorderBrush allows you to set the border color of an object.
- The Foreground option allows you to set the color of text in the foreground. This is most commonly used for text controls.
- The last thing I need to mention is that you can choose to give any one of these no color at all by clicking the No Brush option shown by the arrow in Figure 3-56.

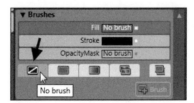

Figure 3-56. The Background, BorderBrush, Foreground, and OpacityMask settings can have the No Brush option applied.

I think we have adequately addressed the Brushes section of the Properties panel. Next we will briefly go over a few other sections in the Properties panel.

Appearance

The Appearance bucket of the Properties panel, shown in Figure 3-57, controls how the object will appear. Click the little arrow at the bottom of the Appearance bucket to see all of the properties that can be set. You can set an object's `Opacity` and `Visibility`, and give it bitmap effects. Let's look at that now.

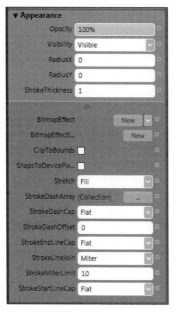

Figure 3-57. The Appearance section
of the Properties panel

Go ahead and give the Ellipse you made earlier a bitmap effect.

1. Select the Ellipse in the Workspace.

2. Click the BitmapEffect drop-down arrow, not the New button. Click Drop Shadow.

Notice now your Ellipse has a drop shadow, as shown in Figure 3-58.

Figure 3-58. The Ellipse with a
drop shadow bitmap effect

Also, notice that in your Appearance section a BitmapEffect (DropShadow) properties section has appeared, as shown in Figure 3-59. This allows you to control the properties of your newly created drop shadow.

Figure 3-59. This is the properties section for your new drop shadow bitmap effect. The arrow points to the collapsible arrow button.

Layout

Moving along, you come next to the Layout bucket of the Properties panel, as shown in Figure 3-60. This section allows you to set how the object is laid out in the Workspace. You can

- Set an object's Height and Width to a specific number or let Blend do it for you by setting one or both to Auto.

- Set the Row and Column of an object that resides in a Grid.

- Set the RowSpan and ColumnSpan if the object is in a Grid and wants to span across rows and columns much like HTML tables.

- Set the Horizontal Alignment and Vertical Alignment of an object.

- Set the Margin of an object that will describe in numbers how far an object is from the Top, Bottom, Left, and Right of its parent object (Grid, StackPanel, etc.).

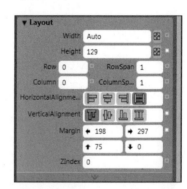

Figure 3-60. The Layout section of the Properties panel

- Set the ZIndex of an object, that is, whether it is on top of or under other objects. (A higher ZIndex will place the object higher in the stack, that is, an object with a ZIndex of 1 will appear on top of an object with a ZIndex of 0.)

- See advanced properties by clicking the collapse arrow at the bottom of the bucket.

- Set advanced properties such as whether an object has horizontal or vertical scrollbars.

There are other advanced layout properties, but this is sufficient for you to know for the time being.

Common Properties

The Common Properties section of the Properties panel, as shown in Figure 3-61, is a section that contains properties common to all UIElements or controls. Here you can set properties such as

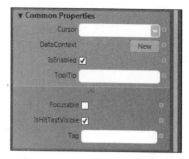

- What cursor an object will display when the mouse is over it (by specifying a value in the Cursor field)

- Whether the object can detect hits (by enabling the IsHitTestVisible option)

- Whether the object will display a ToolTip and what it will read (by specifying text in the ToolTip field)

Figure 3-61. The Common Properties section of the Properties panel

One thing I want to cover in more depth is the Cursor property. In WPF/Silverlight, no control by default has the hand cursor when you mouse over it, not even the Button controls. Personally, I think that the hand cursor creates a very good call to action for users; they see the hand cursor, and they know they can click the object and something will happen. So, for any clickable object in my applications, I always set the Cursor property to Hand. There are different options that are quite useful when creating interfaces, so I suggest you investigate them.

Text

The Text bucket of the Properties panel, as shown in Figure 3-62, will only appear when controls that have text are selected. This bucket has properties for the font, paragraph, line indent, and lists. These are all pretty self-explanatory, and I urge you to play around with these settings.

Figure 3-62. The Text section of the Properties panel

Transform

The Transform section of the Properties panel, shown in Figure 3-63, allows you to transform objects. Basically, you can make your transformations such as rotate, skew, etc., here or directly on the object like you did when you rotated your Rectangle. Personally, I would rather make my transformations directly on the object in the Workspace. However, this is useful for making exact transformations or for making sure that a series of objects are transformed in the same way. There are two types of transformations that you should be aware of: RenderTransform and LayoutTransform. RenderTransform will transform an object after it has already been drawn out or rendered in the application. A LayoutTransform will occur prior to the object being drawn or rendered. What is the difference

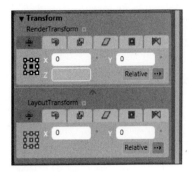

Figure 3-63. The Transform section of the Properties panel

you ask? Say we had three Rectangles laid out in the Workspace. The first one is at the top, and second one starts at the bottom of the first one, and the third one starts at the bottom of the second one. If we were to apply a LayoutTransform to the middle one that rotated it 90 degrees so that it was laying on its side and run the application, the top Rectangle would move up to accommodate the rotated second one, and the third one would move down to accommodate the second one. That is because the second one was transformed before anything was drawn or rendered. However, if we performed a RenderTransform and rotated the second Rectangle 90 degrees and then ran the application, the second Rectangle would be over the top of both the first and third Rectangles because they were all laid out before we transformed the second Rectangle.

Miscellaneous

The Miscellaneous section of the Properties panel (see Figure 3-64) contains any properties that don't fit into the previously described buckets. Here you can set values such as Clickmode (available for controls that can handle click events such as a Button or RadioButton), which specifies how you want to handle click events. Release, Press, and Hover are just some options.

Figure 3-64. The Miscellaneous section of the Properties panel

Search

The final section we will go over for the Properties panel is the Search section, as shown in Figure 3-65. This is a very handy and time-saving feature that I use regularly. Because the Properties panel is very large and has many properties for any given control, it is difficult sometimes to remember where exactly a property is located. Say for example I want to change the Cursor property, but I cannot remember where it is located in the Properties panel. I can just start to type the word cursor into the search field, and Blend will locate it for me as is shown in Figure 3-65. To clear the Search panel so you can see all of the properties again, just click the X button at right.

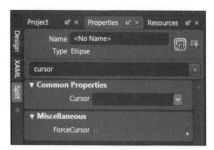

Figure 3-65. The Search section of the Properties panel

The Resources panel

The Resources panel, shown in Figure 3-66, contains a list of all resources of your application. Remember the ResourceDictionary1.xaml file you created? It shows up in this list, and inside of it shows the Brush1 resource color gradient you created. You can use this to actually apply the resources, which you'll do now by following these steps:

1. Select your Rectangle tool and create a Rectangle in the Workspace.

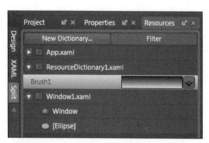

Figure 3-66. The Resources panel, which contains all resources available to your project including the ResourceDictionary you created earlier

2. In the Resources panel, turn down the ResourceDictionary1 arrow so that your custom gradient named Brush1 is shown as it is in Figure 3-66.

3. Click and drag Brush1 to your new Rectangle in the Workspace and let go.

4. Blend will now ask you what property you want to apply Brush1 to; click Fill.

You will see that now your new Rectangle has the Brush1 gradient applied to it.

Blend development views and Workspaces

Previously, Blend had two different development views. With the release of Blend 2, there are now three. At some point, you as a developer will have to work in all three, so you need to be familiar with them. I will discuss them briefly here and in depth in later chapters. So let's get started.

The Design view

Blend's real power is the Design view. You can get to the Design view by clicking the Design button, shown in Figure 3-67. Visual Studio 2008 also has a Design view, but it is not nearly as powerful as Blend's, which can visually represent complex applications.

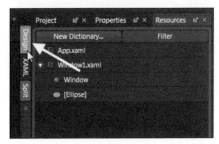

Figure 3-67. The Design view can be accessed by clicking the Design button.

The Design view allows you to basically do what you have been doing in these exercises, and that is to draw controls in the Workspace visually instead of with code. What you may or may not know is that Blend 2 *is* actually creating the code for you in the XAML. You could (and at one time had to) write the XAML code manually, but that becomes cumbersome and takes quite a bit of time.

Another advantage of the Design view is that you can easily tweak UI controls and see the effects immediately. Remember a while back when you were making your Rectangle reflection, and it looked all wrong until you adjusted the stroke with the Brush Transform tool? You were able to do that visually and keep tweaking it until it looked the way you wanted it to look. Imagine now if you wanted to tweak that gradient in the code. To better illustrate this point, let me show you the code that Blend created for you due to your adjustments:

```
<Rectangle.OpacityMask>
  <LinearGradientBrush EndPoint="0.487,0.236" StartPoint="0.487,1.387">
    <GradientStop Color="#FF000000" Offset="0"/>
    <GradientStop Color="#00FFFFFF" Offset="1"/>
  </LinearGradientBrush>
</Rectangle.OpacityMask>
```

See what I mean? This would have been much more difficult if you had to come to this exact code by trial and error. This provides a good segue into your next development view, the XAML view.

The XAML view

Whereas the Design view is more for designers, the XAML view is primarily for developers. The XAML view can be turned on by clicking the XAML button as shown in Figure 3-68, next to the Design button. This view reveals the code that is generated by the Design view. UI controls can be added solely in the XAML view, but this is not a very good idea for a couple of reasons. First, Blend does not have IntelliSense, which is a feature found in Visual Studio that helps predict what code you need to write and fills in the blanks for you. Another huge advantage, in my humble opinion, for using Visual Studio to write XAML is the fact that it has collapsible code. That is, I can collapse a huge chunk of code so that it is not visible save for a couple of lines. This is invaluable in WPF because some 3D objects (called `Viewport3Ds`) can be literally thousands of lines of code. There are other advantages as well, but these are my favorite two.

Figure 3-68. The XAML view can be accessed by clicking the XAML button.

So basically, the XAML view in Blend 2 is helpful at times, but I prefer to use Visual Studio to edit my XAML.

The Split view

The Split view is a brand new feature to Blend 2, and it allows the developer to view half of the screen in Design view and half of the screen in XAML view. If you have ever played around with Dreamweaver, this concept is nothing new to you. I think it is a real blast to draw out a control, say a `Rectangle`, on the Workspace, and then instantly see the XAML be created.

> *You can choose to split the screen horizontally by clicking* View ➤ Split View Horizontally.

Workspaces

You already know about views such as the Design view and the XAML view. Now you need to understand what Workspaces are. The Blend 2 IDE provides you with two distinct Workspaces: the Design Workspace and the Animation Workspace. In each of the two Workspaces, the Blend 2 IDE will change to allow the developer to focus on different aspects of development, namely design and animation.

The Design Workspace

You are already familiar with the Design Workspace, as that is what you have been working in. As a matter of fact, you even worked a little with the Animation workspace in Chapter 2. The Design Workspace focuses on the Visual Tree, properties, and resources. Also, features that allow you to create `Storyboards`, namely the Objects and Timeline panel's timeline editor, are not visible. This allows the developer more room to see the application visually and thus makes it easier to design. By default, Blend 2 opens in the Design Workspace. If you are in the Animation Workspace, you can press F6 to get back to the Design Workspace.

> *You can view the timeline editor in the Design Workspace, but it is docked to the right of the* Objects and Timeline *panel and is very narrow, and thus not very easy to work with.*

The Animation Workspace

The Animation Workspace is a place where you can create Storyboard animations in the Objects and Timeline panel and create EventTriggers in the Interaction panel. Both of these panels are docked along the bottom of the IDE, and thus allowing it more vertical space. This lends itself very well to creating Storyboards as you can see more of the timeline.

Go ahead and create an animation that will run when your application is loaded:

1. Delete everything off the Workspace except for your cool Rectangle and its reflection.

2. Select the Rectangle, hold down the Shift key, and click the reflection.

3. Select Object ➤ Group Into ➤ StackPanel, as shown in Figure 3-69.

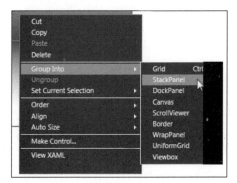

Figure 3-69. Creating a StackPanel

4. Give your new StackPanel a name of ReflectionSP, as shown in Figure 3-70.

Figure 3-70. Giving your new StackPanel a name of ReflectionSP

5. Center your new StackPanel in the Workspace and move it just below the Workspace so when the application starts, it will not be visible, as shown in Figure 3-71.

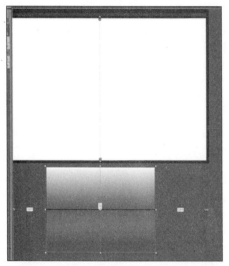

Figure 3-71. The Rectangle and reflection Rectangle are now in a StackPanel named ReflectionSP, which is below the Workspace so that when the application starts, it will not be visible.

6. Press F7 to view the Animation Workspace.

7. With the StackPanel selected, click the New Storyboard button as shown in Figure 3-72.

8. When the Create Storyboard Resource dialog box appears, leave the default name and click OK.

9. A new timeline will appear, as shown in Figure 3-73.

Figure 3-72. Clicking the New Storyboard button

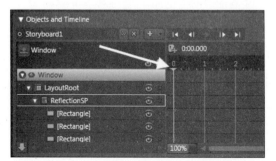

Figure 3-73. A new timeline appears that will allow you to create a new Storyboard resource.

10. Move the playhead out to 1 second, like I have done in Figure 3-74.

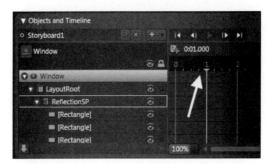

Figure 3-74. Moving the playhead out to 1 second

11. Move the StackPanel to the center of the Workspace.

12. Click the Close Storyboard button as shown in Figure 3-75.

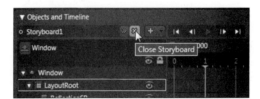

Figure 3-75. Closing the Storyboard by clicking the
Close Storyboard button

13. Press F6 to go back to the Design Workspace.

14. Press F5 to run the application, and you will see that the Rectangle StackPanel will animate
into the application.

Easy, right? You will get into more complex animations later in the book, but for now I think you
should be comfortable with both Design and Animation Workspaces.

Creating 3D objects in Blend

The current version of Blend only allows you to create one type of 3D object, and that object has to
be an Image control. Other programs such as ZAM 3D can be used to export 3D objects into XAML,
but we will go over ZAM 3D in Chapter 10. For now, let's create a 3D object using an image.

> *If you would like to jump ahead and learn about Electric Rain's ZAM 3D, you can read
> about it here:* http://www.erain.com/Products/ZAM3D/DefaultPDC.asp.

1. In Blend, create a new project and call it 3DImage.

2. Right-click the Project panel on your project and click Add Existing Item.

3. Choose an image on the hard drive of your choice and double-click it.

4. Double-click the image in the Project panel, and it will be added to the Workspace inside of an Image control, or simply drag it to the Workspace.

5. Select the Image and click Tools ➤ Make Image 3D.

6. Now with the Image selected, give it a name of 3DImage in the Properties panel.

7. In the search field, type clipto, and the ClipToBounds option will appear. Uncheck it. ClipToBounds means that no matter what you do to this Image, it will not be constrained by the bounding box of the original Image.

8. Press F7 to open the Animation Workspace.

9. Click the New Storyboard button as shown in Figure 3-76.

Figure 3-76. Clicking the New Storyboard button

10. In the Create Storyboard Resource dialog box, give your new Storyboard a name of AppLoad and click OK.

11. Move your playhead out to 1 second, and make sure your Image is selected.

12. Grab the Camera Orbit tool, as shown in Figure 3-77.

Figure 3-77. Selecting the
Camera Orbit tool

13. Move your Camera Orbit tool around while holding down the Alt key, and move the mouse to zoom in and out. Once you understand how this tool works, set the Image back to close to its original size.

14. Move your playhead out to 2 seconds and move and zoom it around a little more.

15. Repeat this for the playhead at 3, 4, 5, and 6 seconds. Try to reposition the last frame, frame 6, so that the Image looks somewhat like it did when you started. If you have trouble with this, I will tell you an alternative method of manipulating the Image without using the Camera Orbit tool:

a. Grab your Selection tool and double-click the Image. You should now see a pivot point rotator. You can use these arms to better control your rotation, as shown in Figure 3-78.

b. Turn off your timeline recording by clicking the red dot on the top left of your Workspace that says "Timeline recording is on" so that it reads "Timeline recording is off."

c. Close the Storyboard by clicking the X button in the Objects and Timeline panel next to the Storyboard named AppLoad.

Figure 3-78. Rotating the image with the pivot point rotator

16. Click F6 to go back to the Design Workspace.

17. Click F5 to run the application.

Pretty cool, huh? If that went a bit fast or you got lost, you may want to go back and review some stages, as everything I told you to do has screenshots associated with it in the previous pages. I would guess that you did perfect, though.

> *You can download the source application at* http://www.windowspresentationfoundation. com/bookDownloads/3DImage.zip.

Summary

In this chapter, you learned all about the Blend 2 IDE and how to make use of the toolbar and all the tools that Blend makes available to you. You also learned about the different layout controls that allow you to house controls in the Workspace. Finally, you learned about the different Workspaces, Design and Animation. In the next chapter, I will cover XAML and C# in greater detail.

Chapter 4

C# AND XAML

What this chapter covers:

- C# and the .NET Framework
- What is XAML

In this chapter, I am going to give an overview of the programming languages C# and XAML (Extensible Markup Language). I will not go into very much detail because I will do that later in the book in a practical "hands-on" manner. Here, I will give you a little bit of background history of the origins of each language and then explain to you in more detail how each interacts in order to create WPF applications. So with that, let's get started and discuss the very robust language known as C# (pronounced C sharp).

C# and the .NET Framework

C# is a very robust **object-oriented programming** (OOP) language that was based on C++ syntax developed by Microsoft. C# is designed to use the tools in the .NET Framework efficiently. The **.NET Framework** is a series of technologies and products also developed by Microsoft that has continued to evolve with releases of .NET 1.0, 1.1, and 2.0, and most recently with 3.0 and 3.5. The .NET Framework is shipped as part of the Microsoft Windows operating system. It was created to be a very easy-to-use programming solution to many common programming needs including, but not limited to, web application development (.aspx and the older .asp pages), database connectivity, network communications, user interface components, and numeric algorithms. The .NET Framework allows for programmers to use methods of its class library in conjunction with their own code to create robust applications, in this case, WPF applications.

The .NET CLR

The .NET **common language runtime** (CLR) ships as part of the .NET Framework. It is an important part of the .NET Framework and worth giving a quick mention. The CLR is a "virtual machine" similar to Adobe's Flash Player that interprets code and translates it into a language the computer can understand. The main purpose of this layer of abstraction between the programmer and the computer is to simplify management of memory, exceptions, threads, garbage collection, and security. The second purpose of the CLR is to allow the developer to write code in any CLR-supported language and know that it will execute the same way once compiled. This allows for WPF and Silverlight applications to be developed in C# as well as Visual Basic, JScript, JavaScript, Python, Ruby, and other languages (although C# and Visual Basic are by far the most common).

In case you don't know, **exception handling** is a programming mechanism whose job it is to handle exceptional occurrences, also known as errors, in a programming routine of an application. In the .NET environment of Visual Studio 2008, every time an exception is thrown (i.e., there is an error in your code), the development environment will record debugging information known as **stack** and **heap values**. This debugging information is then given to you so that you can tell exactly what the exception thrown was. The debugging values can seem at times to be very cryptic and not at all intuitive as to what the error was.

You may also not know what memory management is so I will take a few moments and explain that now. **Memory management** is simply the act of managing computer memory by allocating chunks of a computer's memory to programs that are running. For our purposes, this is an adequate description of the .NET CLR.

> I find it useful to take the exception errors and do a web search on them, because chances are very good that any problem you run into has been encountered by another programmer in the past. Also, the MSDN forums are a great place to post questions about exceptions.

Why C#?

C# is a very popular OOP development language in both online and offline development communities.

What makes OOP so special, you ask? OOP uses **objects** to create applications. An example of an object would be the Button in the "Hello World!" application that you created in Chapter 2. Objects are important because they have the following characteristics:

Encapsulation Any complex software system may have hundreds or even thousands of individual "moving parts"—each one with its particular responsibilities. Encapsulation is a principle that states that each part is responsible for itself and its duties and knows as little as possible about the other parts. This leads to more stable, easier to understand code because making a change to one part is less likely to affect the rest of the system.

Classes In OOP, objects get their instructions, or how they will function, from classes. Classes include two very important things: **properties** and **methods**. If objects are like nouns, the "things" in an application, properties are the adjectives that describe objects, like their color or position. Properties can be built-in or custom-made. Using a Silverlight version of the "Hello World!" application as an example, Page1.xaml has a code-behind page called Page1.xaml.cs. This page has in it a class called Page1. Page1 has built-in properties such as a Background property. You can create your own custom properties in a class. The following code is the entire code for Page1.xaml.cs. I have modified it so that it creates a Boolean (true or false variable) called thisBookRocks, sets it to true, and then prints out the result in the Output window as shown in Figure 4-1.

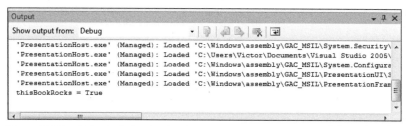

Figure 4-1. The Output window in Visual Studio shows the value of the thisBookRocks Boolean variable.

Methods are an object's verbs—the things an object can do. Classes come with a built-in method called a **constructor**. A constructor is a method that is named the same as the class and will run every time the object is instantiated (that is, every time the object is placed in the Workspace, either physically or by code). You can see the constructor in the following code as well; it is called Page1. If you are new to classes, properties, methods, and constructors, fear not, I will be showing you how to work with them in great detail later on in the book.

```
using System;
using System.Collections.Generic;
using System.Text;
using System.Windows;
using System.Windows.Controls;
using System.Windows.Data;
using System.Windows.Documents;
using System.Windows.Input;
using System.Windows.Media;
using System.Windows.Media.Imaging;
using System.Windows.Navigation;
using System.Windows.Shapes;
using System.Diagnostics;

namespace HelloWorldSample
{
    public partial class Page1 : System.Windows.Controls.Page
```

```
    {
        Boolean thisBookRocks = true;
        public Page1()
        {
            InitializeComponent();
            Debug.Print("thisBookRocks = "+thisBookRocks.ToString());
        }


    }
}
```

Inheritance Inheritance actually belongs to classes, but I want to give it its own section because it is a very important part of OOP. A class can be a child of another class and have children classes of its own. Basically, a class "inherits" all of the traits of its parent. I will use the classic example that I have seen in every OOP book: imagine you have a class called Fruit. Fruit is the parent class or superclass (a parent class with no parent of its own). Fruit has some child classes, say Apple, Orange, and Peach. All three of the subclasses Apple, Orange, and Peach inherit from their parent class of Fruit. So they all know they are a fruit and have all of the traits of the Fruit class, those being they are edible containers for the seed of a plant. So what is the advantage of inheritance? Imagine if you didn't have inheritance. In the preceding example, you would have to tell Apple, Orange, and Peach via code that they are all edible containers for the seed of a plant. That would mean you would have to write the code three times, once for each class. That is a big waste of time, and most importantly, prone to errors, because if you type a block of code once, you have one chance of getting it wrong; type it three times, you have three chances of getting it wrong. With inheritance, your classes can all share the code of a superclass, and this saves you a lot of time because of fewer errors—maybe not for this fruit example, but certainly for large applications with hundreds of thousands of lines of code.

Modularity OOP encompasses the concept of modularity, which was first presented by Information & Systems Institute, Inc., at the National Symposium on Modular Programming in 1968. Modularity basically means that large applications should be built in modules that each has its own specific purpose. Further, these modules act independently within the application. The advantage to this type of programming is that modules can be reused in other applications or duplicated and used more than once in the same application. Another big advantage to this type of programming is that if you change the functionality of one module, you will not affect the functionality of any other module, as they have the ability to function independently of one another. WPF takes full advantage of this concept with classes and UserControls, which I will cover in depth later in this book.

Maintainability Because OOP makes use of objects in its applications, and because these objects use classes that are built to be modular, the code is much easier to maintain than that of a traditional, procedural application. Say, for instance, you have a class called Foo. Foo has some complex functionality, exactly what is not important for this example. Foo has total encapsulation and is completely modular. So, if you go in and change Foo and give it some additional functionality, you know that you will not "break" the application because no other object needs Foo in order to do its job. In procedural programming (i.e., non-OOP like C), it was very common for changes in one line of code in your application to cause some other part of your code to fail, because it was dependent on the line of code you changed, and thus the application would break.

I think that is a pretty adequate outline of why OOP is worth using. But I still have yet to finish telling you why C# is a great programming language. Let's continue:

Automatic garbage collection Automatic garbage collection is basically memory management. And it does exactly what the name implies: it takes out the garbage for you. I wish I had one of these in real life, just ask my wife. OK, let's break it down: objects take up memory when they are instantiated (another fancy name for "created"). Eventually, some instantiated objects will no longer be necessary. The garbage collector will automatically find and dispose of them, freeing precious memory. You can imagine how powerful this is in an application with hundreds or even hundreds of thousands of objects. It is worth noting here that some languages such as C++ don't have automatic collection of garbage, so the programmer has to manually manage his/her garbage, and this can get quite cumbersome and have devastating performance effects if not done or not done properly.

C# is portable Applications created with C# are portable or stand-alone applications that can run on multiple machines of the same operating system and do not require any installation onto that machine's hard drive. This means that C# applications can be run via a CD-ROM, flash drive, or portable hard drive.

Partial classes Partial classes represent a new feature that was introduced in .NET 2.0. This feature allows for class implementation across multiple files. So one file can have this code:

```
public partial class MyClass
{
    public void MyMethod()
    {
        // add some functionality here
    }
}

public partial class MyClass
{
    public void MyOtherMethod()
    {
        // add more functionality here
    }
}
```

This allows programmers to break up very large classes in places where it makes sense to do so.

Language Integrated Query Language Integrated Query, or LINQ, is a feature new to .NET 3.0 and allows for context-sensitive keywords such as from, select, and where. This allows the programmer to use similar syntax for managing databases, data collections, and even XML.

XML documentation C# now allows the programmer to embed XML comments right into their source files. This is done by putting /// before any line of code. C# will then treat that code as XML and can even export it to a separate XML file. This is very handy when you have many developers working on the same application, and documentation is needed to explain to the next developer how to make use of the source file.

C# possesses many more powerful features, but for the scope of this book, I think I have adequately discussed some of the major ones. This after all is a hands-on book, and I don't want to bore you with theory, but rather brush over this stuff so you can get to some real development. I think at this point it would be beneficial to go over XAML.

XAML

XAML, or Extensible Application Markup Language, is an XML (Extensible Markup Language) based declarative language developed by Microsoft. XAML originally stood for Extensible Avalon Markup Language, because Avalon was the codename for WPF. It is not uncommon to still see "WPF (formerly known as Avalon)" on pages dedicated to WPF development. XAML is basically, as I described before, the user interface language of WPF that defines objects and their properties. I say that XAML in its basic form describes how the application looks, but it can do much more than that. As a matter of fact, the number one advantage of XAML is its speed and efficiency; often a single line of XAML can represent dozens of lines of equivalent C#. Further, with only a few lines of XAML, any WPF object can be hooked up to C# code-behind classes that can contain complex functionality. It is also worth mentioning that anything that can be done in XAML can also be done in C# but usually with many more lines of code.

XAML objects are written in XML-based form and describe how the user sees the object or framework element, by setting properties in the XML. A typical XAML control looks like this:

```
<Button x:Name="spinBtn"
    HorizontalAlignment="Right"
    Margin="0,0,19.8,42.5"
    VerticalAlignment="Bottom"
    Width="186.25"
    Height="80"
    Background="Blue"
    Foreground="White"
    Content="Spin"/>
```

The preceding code creates a Button control. The Button is able to be referenced by C# code because it has an x:Name property set to spinBtn.

As you can see, it also has other properties such as the following:

- HorizontalAlignment: Controls how the Button will be aligned in the application
- Margin: Determines where in the parent grid the control will be placed
- VerticalAlignment: Controls how the Button will be aligned in the application
- Width: Sets the width of the Button
- Height: Sets the height of the Button
- Background: Sets the background color of the Button
- Foreground: Sets the color of the content (text) of the Button
- Content: Controls what the text on the Button will be

Following is the C# code that would create the exact same Button:

```
Button button = new Button();
button.Name = "spinBtn";
button.HorizontalAlignment = HorizontalAlignment.Right;
button.Margin = new Thickness(0,0,19.8,42.5)
button.Width = 186.25;
```

```
button.Height = 80;
button.Background = new SolidColorBrush(Color.FromArgb(255, 0, 0, 255));
button.Foreground = new SolidColorBrush(Color.FromARgb(255, 255, 255, 255))
button.Content = "Spin";
LayoutGrid.Children.Add(button);
```

As you can see, it is a bit more work in that you have to first create an object called button of the Button type. You then have to set each margin separately for Top, Left, Bottom, and Right. Finally, you then have to add the object as a child of the LayoutGrid.

XAML is great because it helps to separate the design of the application from the C# development. This allows for faster development by increasing the efficiency between designers and developers as discussed in Chapter 2. To reiterate, this is done by separating the design layer (XAML) from the logic layer (C#).

Another advantage to XAML is its native support of vector graphics in addition to standard bitmap graphics. What is the difference, you ask? Vector graphics are created with mathematical coordinates and have no actual pixels like bitmaps do. This allows you to scale a vector graphic to any size and still retain very good clarity of the object. If you scale up a bitmap, the quality of it reduces significantly, and it will pixelate.

XAML has one very awesome functionality feature called **binding**. That means that an object can have one of its properties "bound" to the properties of another. You will see this later on in greater depth, but just know for now that in XAML you can bind the size of a button to the value of a slider control, for instance. Therefore, when you slide the slider up, the button grows in size, and conversely, when you slide the slider down, the button size will decrease. Binding is very powerful, and I think you will understand that when we get into it later in Chapter 9.

It is important to note that any object can be created in the C# code-behind file and added to the Workspace. Also, binding can be done in C# as well because a XAML file and its C# code-behind file are *both* partial classes, connected to each other with the InitializeComponent method run in the code-behind's constructor method. They are different parts of the same object, whether it is a Page, Button, UserControl, or any other class; as such, at different times it may be more appropriate to write code for that object in the XAML file or in the C# code-behind file.

XAML also allows you to define resources for the application. Resources can include data sources, ControlTemplates, and Storyboards, among others. We will go over these in depth later on as well.

While XAML is very powerful, there is not much more to say about it on a background level, so at this point I think it would be better for you to learn about XAML through hands-on exercises, which is what you will start to do in the following chapters.

Summary

In this chapter, you learned about C# and the .NET Framework. I went over some advantages of using C# and delved into the basics of classes and OOP and some advantages of both. Finally, I covered the basics of XAML—what it is, what it can do—and some powerful features such as data binding. In the next chapter, I am going to talk about the layout controls that allow you to place content into your WPF/Silverlight applications.

Chapter 5

LAYOUT ELEMENTS

What this chapter covers:

- The Grid
- The Canvas
- The StackPanel
- The WrapPanel
- The DockPanel
- The ScrollViewer
- The Border
- The UniformGrid
- The ViewBox

As I already discussed, WPF/Silverlight use XAML to create the user interface (UI) layer that provides the "face" of any WPF or Silverlight application. In other words, XAML allows the developer to create the interface that users will see when they use your application. WPF uses layout elements in order to arrange your content such as Images, MediaElements, Buttons, and any other UI FrameWork elements. I tend to think of layout elements much like tables in HTML. Of course, as you may have already guessed, WPF controls are a lot more complex than HTML tables, but the comparison should help to provide you with a starting point of what layout elements are. In this chapter, I will discuss all of the most popular layout elements by talking about what makes them unique and when it is appropriate to use each one. I will also walk you through creating a new project that uses each one.

The Grid

Undoubtedly the most popular and most used WPF layout element is the Grid. As a matter of fact, when you first create a new WPF Windows application, Visual Studio 2008 automatically puts in a Grid layout element for you. You can see the code here:

```
<Window x:Class="LayoutControlsProject.Window1"
    xmlns="http://schemas.microsoft.com/winfx/2006/xaml/presentation"
    xmlns:x="http://schemas.microsoft.com/winfx/2006/xaml"
    Title="LayoutControlsProject" Height="300" Width="300"
    >
    <Grid>

    </Grid>
</Window>
```

This does not mean that you cannot add other layout elements; in fact, layout elements are meant to have other layout elements placed inside of them. Which one you choose depends on how you want to display your content. A Grid is very much like an HTML table in that you can define Rows and Columns and then place content inside of those Rows and Columns. This is a good time to create a new WPF Application project in Visual Studio 2008. To do that, follow these steps:

1. Open Visual Studio 2008, create a new WPF Application project, and call it LayoutControlsProject like I have done in Figure 5-1. Click OK.

Notice in the XAML that Visual Studio 2008 has created a Grid by default.

2. Leave Visual Studio 2008 open. Go ahead and start Blend 2, open LayoutControlsProject, and look at it in Design view.

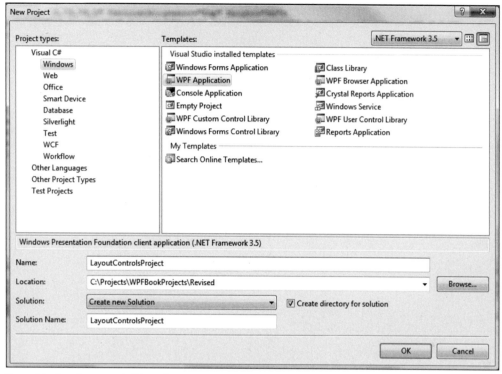

Figure 5-1. Creating a new WPF application in Visual Studio 2008

Notice around your main Grid there is a blue bar at the top and on the left. These are where you add Rows and Columns. When you place your cursor over the top bar, notice a yellow line is drawn from the top of your Grid to the bottom. If you click the blue bar, the line becomes blue and does not go away when you move your mouse off of it because you have just created a new Column (see Figure 5-2).

Figure 5-2. Creating Columns visually in Blend 2

If you place your mouse on the blue bar to the left, you will see that it too draws a yellow line, but this line is a horizontal line. If you click the blue bar, the yellow line become blue and permanent, and you have just created a Row like I did in Figure 5-3.

Figure 5-3. Creating Rows visually in Blend 2

If you switch over to the XAML view or just look at the XAML in the Split view, you can see that Blend 2 has created Column and Row definitions. You can see the code here:

```
<Grid.ColumnDefinitions>
    <ColumnDefinition Width="0.194*"/>
    <ColumnDefinition Width="0.806*"/>
</Grid.ColumnDefinitions>
<Grid.RowDefinitions>
    <RowDefinition Height="0.508*"/>
    <RowDefinition Height="0.492*"/>
</Grid.RowDefinitions>
```

Notice that the Columns and Rows have Height and Width values. If you hard-code the Height and Width values, it means that your Grid cannot scale to accommodate for content placed inside of it. For this reason, it is good practice to not hard-code these values, and instead take full advantage of the way WPF's powerful layout engine can scale objects automatically. Blend 2 has placed Height and Width values in for you because your Grid is in Canvas Layout mode as opposed to Grid Layout mode. The Blend team created the Canvas Layout mode to make it easier for designers not experienced with layout panels to get started. Fortunately for you, you are getting started with me, and I am going to teach you about the slightly more complex Grid Layout mode. At the very top left of the Grid, you can see a little button that if clicked will change the Grid's mode to Grid Layout mode as shown in Figure 5-4.

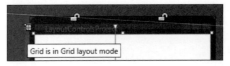

Figure 5-4. The main Grid in Grid Layout mode

Now you will see little lock icons appear where the blue Row and Column lines are. These little lock icons allow you to lock the height of a Row or the width of a Column; click one of the lock icons so that it turns to a "locked" state. If you look at the XAML code, you will see that the Row and Column definitions still have Height and Width values with an asterisk after them. If the Row or Column's lock icon is not locked, these values can change depending on the size of the content that they display or by the size of the application window. If you lock one of the icons by clicking it, you will notice that the asterisk disappears and the lock icon appears locked. Now if the content dynamically changes or the size of the application window changes, the locked Column or Row will not change. Following is a good exercise to help you understand Rows and Columns:

1. Create a WPF application in a new instance of Blend 2 called RowColEx.
2. Set the Width and Height of the window to 800 by 600, respectively.
3. Create two Rows and two Columns.
4. Click the button in the left-hand corner of the Grid to change to Grid Layout mode.
5. Place a Rectangle in each of the cells (four in total).
6. Leave the Rows and Columns unlocked (this is the default).
7. Run the application.
8. Resize the application window to make it smaller.

Notice how the Rectangles scale down. This is because the Grid Columns and Rows are changing as the application window changes in size.

9. Close the running application.
10. Click all four of the locks so that now all Columns and Rows are locked.
11. Run the application again and resize the application window so that it is smaller.

Notice now the Rectangles do not scale. This is because the Rows and Columns are not changing as the application window changes in size.

12. Close this sample application and go back to the LayoutControlsProject project.

Now that you have Rows and Columns, what can you do with them? Well, you can add controls into the Grid and then specify in the XAML what Row and Column they should be in. You'll do that now:

1. Select the TextBlock tool from the toolbar.
2. Draw a TextBlock in the Workspace.
3. Set the text to be Row 0 Column 0.

Now if you look at the XAML, you will see something that looks like this:

```
<TextBlock Margin="23,37,21.072,51.112" Text="Row 0 Column 0"
TextWrapping="Wrap"/>
```

You can see that the control does not specify what Row or Column it is in. If you do not specify a Column or Row, Blend 2 will automatically place your content into Row 0 and Column 0. So, now you'll alter the code to hard-code the TextBlock to be in Row 0 and Column 0.

4. Change your code so that it resembles the following:

```
<TextBlock Margin="23,37,21,51" Text="Row 0 column 0"
TextWrapping="Wrap" Grid.Column="0" Grid.Row="0"/>
```

5. Now copy this XAML and paste it four times, and change the values for the text as well as the Grid.Column and Grid.Row so that your code looks like this:

```
<TextBlock Margin="23,37,21,51" Text="Row 0 Column 0"
TextWrapping="Wrap" Grid.Column="0" Grid.Row="0"/>
<TextBlock Margin="23,37,21,51" Text="Row 0 Column 1"
 TextWrapping="Wrap" Grid.Column="1" Grid.Row="0"/>
<TextBlock Margin="23,37,21,51" Text="Row 1 Column 0"
TextWrapping="Wrap" Grid.Column="0" Grid.Row="1"/>
<TextBlock Margin="23,37,21,51" Text="Row 1 Column 1"
TextWrapping="Wrap" Grid.Column="1" Grid.Row="1"/>
```

6. Click the Design tab in Blend 2; you will see that your TextBlocks all place themselves into their correct Rows and Columns. Your project should look like what I have in Figure 5-5.

> *The* Rows *and* Columns *start with a value of* 0 *and not* 1.

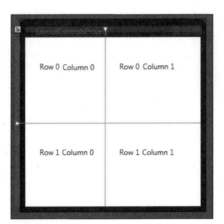

Figure 5-5. TextBlocks in different Grid Rows and Columns

Another interesting thing about the Grid is that it positions its content using margins. Basically, margins specify how far away an object is from the left, top, right, and bottom of another object and are relative to a Grid's cell's boundaries if, in fact they are inside of a Grid with ColumnDefinitions and/or RowDefinitions. Say, for example, you have a Rectangle control inside of a Grid and its VerticalAlignment is set to Top and its HorizontalAlignment is set to Left. If you give the Rectangle control a Margin property of "10,10,0,0", the Rectangle will be 10 pixels from the left and 10 pixels from the top. Conversely, if you set the Rectangle's HorizontalAlignment to Right and its VerticalAlignment to Bottom, and then give it a Margin property of "0,0,10,10", the Rectangle control will be 10 pixels from the right and 10 pixels from the bottom.

The Canvas

The next layout element I am going to talk about is the Canvas. This is one of my personal favorites because it allows the user to specify *absolute positioning* of its children. The Canvas will never change the position of child elements in it, and I find this very useful. To see how the Canvas works, you have to make some changes to the project:

1. In Blend 2, change the XAML so that Window1 is now 600 by 600 (to give you some breathing room).

2. Change each of the TextBlocks to have a Width of 150 and a Height of 20.

3. Move each of the TextBlocks up to the top left of its cell.

Your project should look something like what is in Figure 5-6.

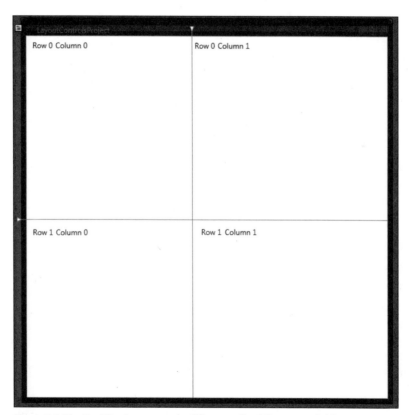

Figure 5-6. The TextBlocks are now in different cells of the parent Grid.

4. Hold down the Grid tool on the toolbar until the other layout element options become visible, and select the Canvas layout element.

5. In the Row 0 Column 1 cell, draw a Canvas. With the Selection tool, double-click the new Canvas in the Objects and Timeline panel so that it has a yellow line around it.

Now you can add some content to your Canvas because when a layout control has a yellow line around it, anything drawn in the Workspace will go into it. Add some content now by following these steps:

1. Select the Ellipse tool from the toolbar.

2. Hold down Shift and draw an Ellipse in the Row 0 Column 1 cell.

3. With the new Ellipse selected, change the Background to a gradient in the Brushes section of the Properties panel.

4. Change the gradient to a radial gradient and adjust the colors and gradient with the Brush Transform tool until you have something like what you see in Figure 5-7.

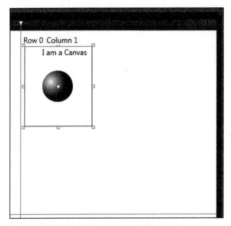

Figure 5-7. A TextBlock and Ellipse in a Canvas in your main Grid

5. Select the TextBlock tool from the toolbar.

6. Draw out a TextBlock in your new Canvas.

7. Change the text to read I am a Canvas.

If you look at the XAML, you will see the new Canvas inside of your main Grid, and inside of the Canvas you will see the Ellipse and the TextBlock. The interesting thing to see here is that the Canvas itself has a Margin property and thus its positioning can be controlled by its parent Grid. However, notice that the Ellipse and TextBlock do not have any Margin properties, but rather they have Canvas.Top and Canvas.Left properties. This means that they are overwriting the Dependency property of their parent Canvas and essentially telling the Canvas where they want to be placed. Therefore, the Canvas cannot implicitly change the position of its child objects, nor can the Grid.

Let's now move on to another very popular layout element called the StackPanel.

The StackPanel

A StackPanel is another layout element, and its claim to fame is that it will position content inside of it for you in a stacking manner (horizontally or vertically) as opposed to the Grid or Canvas, which rely on the developer to set the relative or absolute positioning of child objects. Here you'll create a StackPanel and see exactly how it does this:

1. Select the StackPanel tool from the toolbar.
2. In Row 1 Column 0, draw out a StackPanel.
3. Select the Ellipse tool again from the toolbar.
4. Draw three Ellipses in the newly created StackPanel.

Notice that the StackPanel arranges your three Ellipses vertically inside of it (see Figure 5-8).

You can override the way the StackPanel stacks its content by changing values in the XAML or by changing the Orientation property from Vertical to Horizontal in the Layout section of the Properties panel. Do that now, and you will see that the StackPanel changes from displaying its content from vertically to horizontally, as shown in Figure 5-9.

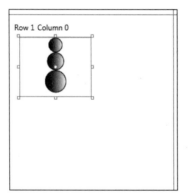

Figure 5-8. A StackPanel will position its child content automatically.

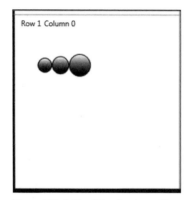

Figure 5-9. A StackPanel can position its child content horizontally or vertically.

The WrapPanel

The WrapPanel is a very cool panel in that it can dynamically reposition its child content while the application is running. This is a very new concept, not to .NET but certainly to Rich Media Applications, and one that is pretty handy. Imagine if you had an HTML table with content in it, let's say three or four rectangle bitmaps. What if the user adjusted the browser's size so that some of the rectangle bitmaps were cut off? You would be out of luck, wouldn't you? In WPF, let's take the same scenario; in this case, the user adjusts the application's Window until the Rectangles are cut off. If the Rectangles were in any other layout element, you would be out of luck again, but not if the Rectangles are inside of a WrapPanel. The WrapPanel on the fly would change the position of its child objects until adjusting their position would no longer avoid cutting them off. Let's see this in action:

1. Select the WrapPanel tool from the toolbar.

2. Draw out a WrapPanel under your StackPanel.

3. Select the Rectangle tool from the toolbar . . . to work with something other than Ellipses.

4. Draw out five Rectangles inside the WrapPanel.

Notice that, like the StackPanel, the WrapPanel automatically positions its content for you. And, like a StackPanel, you can change the orientation through the Orientation property in the XAML or the Orientation setting in the Layout section of the Properties panel. Your WrapPanel should look something like what I have in Figure 5-10 (you can see I gave my Rectangles a gradient).

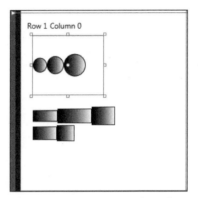

Figure 5-10. Under your StackPanel, you have drawn out a WrapPanel and placed five Rectangles into it.

5. Press F5 to run your application, and you will see that it looks just like it did in Blend's Design view.

6. Grab the lower-right corner of the window and move it so that the StackPanel and WrapPanel start to get cut off.

Did you notice that the StackPanel does not readjust its content, but the WrapPanel does? You can see my example in Figure 5-11.

I really like this layout element for this reason. It does impress many developers that are new to WPF because while this type of functionality is not new, it previously required laborious math and code writing to get it right. The WrapPanel simplifies the technical details in a way previously unseen in Rich Media Applications.

Figure 5-11. The StackPanel will not reposition its content when resized, but the WrapPanel will.

The DockPanel

The DockPanel, as its name implies, allows you to *dock* its content to the top, bottom, left, or right of the control. You'll create a DockPanel now:

1. Select the DockPanel tool from the toolbar.
2. In Row 0 Column 0, draw out a DockPanel.
3. Hold down the Pen tool and select the Pencil tool.
4. Draw four squiggly shapes in the DockPanel.

By default, the DockPanel will dock all of its content to the left of the panel, as shown in Figure 5-12.

You can change where these objects are docked in the XAML or in the Dock property of the Layout section in the Properties panel.

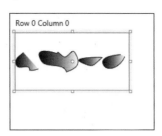

Figure 5-12. The DockPanel docks its child content to any side of the panel.

5. For the first shape, leave the default Dock value of Left.
6. Select the second shape and change its Dock property to Top.
7. Select the third shape and change its Dock property to Right.
8. Change the last shape's Dock property to Bottom.

Notice how the DockPanel rearranges its content to match your specifications (see Figure 5-13).

The DockPanel will always dock its contents to where you specify, even if the DockPanel grows in size. Try this out:

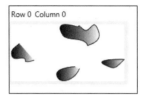

Figure 5-13. You can dock content of a DockPanel to the left, right, top, or bottom of the panel.

9. Press F5 to run the application and resize the application window.

Notice that as the DockPanel scales, its contents stay docked to their respective positions (see Figure 5-14). This is very handy in certain situations. For example, say you wanted to create a browser WPF application and you wanted the site navigation to always be at the top of the page; DockPanel would come in very handy for that because even if the user resized his browser, the navigation control would always remain at the top of the page.

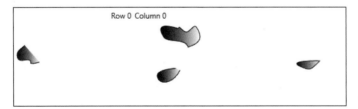

Figure 5-14. When running the project and the window is scaled, the DockPanel will grow and still dock its contents.

Let's move on and talk about the ScrollViewer.

The ScrollViewer

The ScrollViewer is a layout element that allows for only one piece of content at a time. If that content is bigger than the ScrollViewer, it will allow the user to scroll around and see the entire piece of content. So for this exercise, you'll need an image that is at least double the size of your ScrollViewer (if it is smaller or the same size, there will be no need to scroll).

1. Right-click the project in the Project panel, select Add Existing Item, and then choose your image.

2. Once it is in your project, double-click the image to add it to the Workspace inside of an Image control.

3. Select the ScrollViewer tool from the toolbar.

4. In Row 1 Column 1, draw out a ScrollViewer.

5. In the Objects and Timeline panel, drag your Image control into the ScrollViewer.

You should have something similar to what I have in Figure 5-15.

Figure 5-15. An Image control inside of a ScrollViewer in Blend 2's Design view

You are almost ready to run your application, but first you need to set your ScrollViewer control so that you have both horizontal and vertical scrollbars:

6. Set both HorizontalScrollBarVisibility and VerticalScrollBarVisibility to Visible in the Layout section of the Properties panel. Now your ScrollViewer should look something what you see in Figure 5-16.

7. Press F5 and run the application.

Figure 5-16. A ScrollViewer with visible horizontal and vertical scrollbars

You can see that you now have the ability to scroll around the ScrollViewer control to view all parts of the Image control inside of it (see Figure 5-17).

Figure 5-17. When you run the application, you can now scroll around the entire Image control nested in your ScrollViewer.

Let's keep going and explore the next layout element in WPF, the Border.

The Border

The Border is a very simple layout element that allows you to draw a Stroke around another element and then give it a Background or an actual border. The Border layout element can only have one child element, and that content can be either left, right, top, bottom, or center aligned. These properties can be set manually in the XAML or in Blend 2 in the Layout section of the Properties panel. Try making a Border element now:

1. Select the Border tool from the toolbar.

2. In Row 0 Column 1, draw a Border.

3. Copy the red Ellipse inside of your Canvas into the new Border.

4. Change the HorizontalAlignment property in the Layout section of the Properties panel to see how the child object is affected.

5. Change the VerticalAlignment property in the Layout section of the Properties panel to see how the child object is affected.

6. Change the Background of the border to a gradient in the Brushes section of the Properties panel.

7. Use the Brush Transform tool to adjust the gradient to go from top to bottom.

8. Select the BorderBrush property in the Brushes section of the Properties panel and select a solid color; I chose green.

9. In the Appearance section of the Properties panel, give the Border a BorderThickness of 3 for the left and right and 1 for the top and bottom.

Your Border should look something like that shown in Figure 5-18.

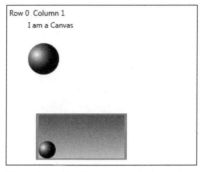

Figure 5-18. The Border layout element allows you to draw a Stroke and Background around an element.

Now let's can move on to the UniformGrid.

The UniformGrid

The UniformGrid layout element is basically just a Grid that will spread out all of its content evenly given the size of the Grid. For example, in Figure 5-19, you can see four Ellipses; the UniformGrid divides up all of its space and spreads out the Ellipses uniformly.

Now if you remove two of the ellipses, the UniformGrid will redisplay its content so that it is spread out uniformly (see Figure 5-20).

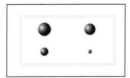

Figure 5-19. The UniformGrid divides up all of its space and spreads out the Ellipses uniformly.

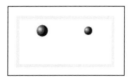

Figure 5-20. If you remove two of the ellipses, the UniformGrid divides up all of its space and spreads out the remaining Ellipses uniformly.

Now let's move on to the final layout element I am going to discuss in this chapter, the ViewBox. This is one is one of my personal favorites, because it has a special talent that is very useful and no other layout element possesses.

The ViewBox

Oftentimes I find myself wanting to be able to scale multiple objects at the same time. This is precisely what the ViewBox does; if you place any object into the ViewBox, it will scale that object so that the object takes up all available space in the ViewBox. If you place two objects in a ViewBox, it will scale those two objects until they have completely filled the available area of the ViewBox—very handy. Go ahead and make one now:

1. Right-click the project in the Project panel, select Add Existing Item, and then import an image into the project. (Alternatively, you can drag an image from your hard drive into the project in the Project panel.)

2. Double-click the image to create an Image control in the Workspace.

3. Select the ViewBox tool from the toolbar.

4. Draw a ViewBox in Row 0 Column 1; I know the project is starting to get cramped, but don't fret, as this is the last layout element you will work with in this chapter.

5. In the Objects and Timeline panel, drag the newly created Image control into the ViewBox.

Notice that the Image control scaled down to fit inside of the ViewBox (see Figure 5-21). Very cool, huh?

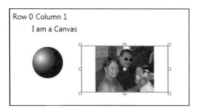

Figure 5-21. Your Image control scales to fit into your ViewBox.

6. Now make the ViewBox bigger and see what happens to the Image control.

Notice the Image control gets bigger, as shown in Figure 5-22.

Figure 5-22. When you scale the ViewBox, the Image control inside of it scales as well.

So, I think you can see that this layout element is one that can be very useful. And keep in mind it can scale multiple objects. You will be making use of this in subsequent chapters.

Summary

Layout elements allow you to easily place content into your applications. You have gone through each of the major layout elements and actually created them with hands-on exercises. You also learned that each layout element has its own special ability:

- The Grid allows you to declare Rows and Columns so that you can then position objects precisely within that Grid.

- The Canvas allows you to specify where the content inside of it is placed by using the Margin property.

- The StackPanel positions its content automatically, but you can specify whether the content is stacked horizontally or vertically.

- The WrapPanel will position its content automatically but will shift or wrap that content if the size of the application changes.

- The DockPanel will dock content placed inside of it to the top, bottom, left, and right of the DockPanel.

- The ScrollViewer will give users scrollbars that allow them to scroll around to see all of the content placed inside of it.

- The Border simply allows you to draw a Stroke around the content placed inside of it as well as a Background.

- The UniformGrid will divide up the space available to give all of its child content an equal amount of that space.

- The ViewBox will scale the content placed inside of it.

These layout elements give the developer many choices on how to display content based on the situation that the application calls for. Again, I like to think of layout elements as similar to HTML tables because they basically do the same thing, and that is specify how content is presented in an application. Becoming familiar with all of these different layout elements will make you very proficient at making WPF applications with complex, scalable UIs.

In the next chapter, I am going to talk about the MediaElement because it makes the very powerful Windows Media Player available to both WPF and Silverlight. Because video is such a large part of Rich Media Applications, I thought it best to dedicate an entire chapter to the MediaElement and even a case study chapter (Chapter 15) on how to build a Silverlight video player. With that, let's forge on.

Chapter 6

THE MEDIAELEMENT

What this chapter covers:

- What is the MediaElement
- Playback modes

WPF/Silverlight were created to develop Rich Media Applications for both online and offline use. Audio and video are a large part of any Rich Media Application, and Microsoft did not forget this when it engineered WPF/Silverlight, because Microsoft added a very powerful control called the MediaElement that can play audio as well as video. Further, Microsoft made this UserControl 100% controllable by giving the developer the ability to, among other things, play, pause, and stop the media. The MediaElement even broadcasts events when it is started, stopped, or paused, allowing the developer to hook into those events and respond to them. A good example might be the MediaElement in an application could disappear when the user stops the video. In this chapter, I will discuss the MediaElement in detail and provide examples of how to implement one in both XAML and C#. So, let's get started.

Playback modes

The MediaElement supports two modes of operation: Independent mode and Clock mode. What mode the MediaElement will play in is set when the MediaElement is created, most often in XAML, by setting the LoadedBehavior. The LoadedBehavior does as its name suggests: it describes how the MediaElement will behave once it is loaded. This is a very important part of the MediaElement, and therefore each of the two modes deserves detailed explanation. Let's start with Independent mode, as it is the mode that you as a developer will use the most because of the power it allows you.

Independent mode

Independent mode allows you to control the play behavior of the MediaElement so that controls can be added such as play, pause, stop, and SpeedRatio. The SpeedRatio is a value between zero and infinity; values less than one will make the MediaElement play its media slower, while values greater than one will result in faster playback of the media. I have used this property in the past to create a feature that would effectively allow the user to hold down a button that would speed through the media, in this case a video. Conversely, you could create a button that would play the media in slow motion; I think this used to be referred to as super slow motion (SSM) in the days of VCRs.

Independent mode also allows you to specify the Position of the MediaElement. This property specifies the amount of time since the beginning of the video or audio, which allows you to create controls that enable the user to jump from one position, in time, of the media to another. This can be used to create a control such as a scrubber. A **scrubber**, in case you don't know, is a horizontal bar that represents the total time of the media and a playhead that represents where you currently are in the media. So if you are at the very beginning of the media, the playhead will be at the beginning of the horizontal line, and if you are near the end of the media, the playhead will be at the end of the line.

Finally, Independent mode allows the developer to set the MediaElement's URI. What, you are probably asking, is a URI? Glad you asked. A URI, or **Uniform Resource Identifier**, is an address for a particular resource, much like URLs are addresses for web sites on the Internet. In fact, URIs can even be URLs for resources located on the Web. If you are confused, don't worry; URIs had me confused too until I came to think of them as URLs. They are much more complex than that, of course, but for the most part a URI allows you to specify a path to a resource such as a video file (AVI, WMV, etc.) or an audio file (MP3, WAV). The resource can either be local to the project or be an actual URL where the file is located. You do not have to use a URL to set the source of a MediaElement; you can do that by simply declaring the Source property in the XAML. But if you wanted to set the source in C#, you would have to use a URI. Why, you ask, would someone want to set the source in the C# using a URI? Say you wanted to make an application that allowed a user to drag a video file from her MyDocuments folder on her local hard drive onto your application, and once this was done the MediaElement would then get the name of that video file and play it. You would then have to listen for the Drop event in C#, turn the name of the dropped file into a URI, and tell your MediaElement to play it. You would not be able to do this in the XAML, because XAML is rendered once when it is loaded and cannot change unless told to do so by the C# code-behind. So using the code-behind and a URI, you can do exactly that. Now that you understand the Independent mode of the MediaElement, let's move on to the Clock mode.

> Technically XAML can be changed on a XAML EventTrigger, but that is beyond the scope of this book.

Clock mode

MediaTimeline is a timeline object that controls how the media is played back, much like a Storyboard (like you created in your "Hello World!" application). The MediaTimeline has a set duration that is determined by how long the source of your MediaElement is. This is called a NaturalDuration. If you tell your MediaElement to run in Clock mode, you are telling the MediaTimeline to drive the media playback. A BeginTime property is also assigned based upon the length of the media source. What this all means is that control of the MediaElement is handed over to WPF, and you cannot build controls for it. This may sound like a bad idea, but there are times when you as the developer do not want the user to have control over the MediaElement. Say, for example, before you let the user into the interface of your application, you want him to view a video explaining how to use the interface. You would not want the user to stop or pause the video, so you would not build controls for it. In this example, it would be easier for you to let the video play in Clock mode. By default, a MediaElement runs in Clock mode.

Switching between playback modes

If you were to create an application with a MediaElement and did not set what mode it would run in, it would run in Clock mode; and if you were then to create a Button that told the MediaElement to stop, it would throw a runtime error, because in order for that Button to stop the MediaElement, you would have had to specify that it runs in Independent mode. So, how do you do that? The following XAML code creates a MediaElement called myVideo, specifies a media source, and sets the Height and Width properties to Auto, which will make the MediaElement the size of the source video, in this case cap_001.avi.

```
<MediaElement x:Name="myVideo"
Source="cap_001.avi" Height="Auto" Width="Auto"/>
```

Now if you were to add a stop Button like this:

```
<Button x:Name="stopBtn" Content="Stop" Width="100" Height="50"/>
```

and give it an EventHandler in the C# like this:

```
void stopBtn_Click(object sender, RoutedEventArgs e)
    {
        myVideo.Stop();
    }
```

when you run the application and try to click the stop Button, you would get a runtime error like you see in Figure 6-1.

A **runtime error** is an error that occurs when the application is running as opposed to a compile error, which is thrown when the application is compiling.

If you set the LoadedBehavior of the MediaElement to Manual as shown in the following code and run the application, you will see that clicking the stop Button will no longer throw an error. This is very good, but if you were paying close attention you will have noticed that the video is no longer playing. Why is that? Because you told the MediaElement that you want to control it *manually*, and because you never told it to play, it will not.

```
<MediaElement x:Name="myVideo" Source="cap_001.avi"
Height="Auto" Width="Auto" Loaded Behavior="Manual"/>
```

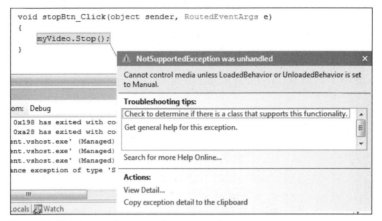

Figure 6-1. This is a runtime error that occurs when you try to stop a MediaElement that is in Clock mode.

So now that the MediaElement is set to Manual and thus to run in Independent mode, you need to tell it to play. In order to do that, you need to go into the code-behind C# file and tell it to play. Following is the code that will allow you to do that:

```
public Window1()
    {
        InitializeComponent();
        stopBtn.Click += new RoutedEventHandler(stopBtn_Click);
        myVideo.Play();
    }
```

Now if you run the application, you will see that the video plays and the stop Button works as well.

Creating your first MediaElement project

I think now would be a good time for me to run you through an exercise that

- Creates a MediaElement
- Specifies a Source video for the MediaElement
- Creates play, stop, and pause controls for the MediaElement
- Creates a switch video Button that creates a URI and plays another video

1. Open Visual Studio 2008. Create a new WPF Application project and call it MyMediaElementProject like I have done in Figure 6-2. Click OK.

2. Now open Blend, navigate to where the project was saved, and open MyMediaElementProject.sln.

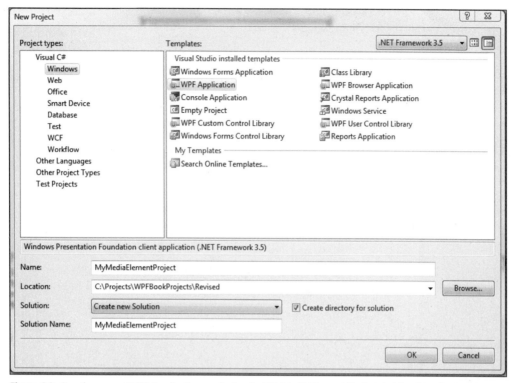

Figure 6-2. Creating a new WPF Application project called MyMediaElement Project in Visual Studio 2008

> *Once you close the MyMediaElement project in Visual Studio 2008, it will appear at the top of the list in the* Recent Projects *section. In order to open it, all you have to do is single-click it.*

3. With the project opened in Blend, I like to change the Height and Width to 500 by 500 just to give a little breathing room. I find it very quick and easy to do this in the XAML view as shown in Figure 6-3.

Figure 6-3. Manually setting the Height and Width to 500 by 500 in XAML view in Blend

Coming from a background of Flash as well as .NET, I like to give my projects a little bit of design by giving them a gradient background. To do this yourself, continue with these steps:

4. Select the Window in the Objects and Timeline panel and then click the Gradient brush button in the Brushes section of the Properties panel.

5. Create a gradient that goes from white to dark blue.

6. Use the Brush Transform tool to make the gradient go from top to bottom as opposed to the default left to right.

If you forgot how to do any of these steps, I suggest you refer back to Chapter 3, as I cover all of this in depth. Play around with your Background gradient until you are satisfied with it. You can see my project background in Figure 6-4.

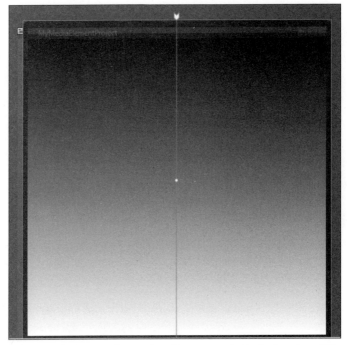

Figure 6-4. This is my Background gradient as seen in the Design view of Blend.

7. Next you want to add a MediaElement to the project. Because you are going to control the MediaElement a lot with code, it's easier to switch over to Visual Studio 2008 to do this. Save the project in Blend 2 and switch back to Visual Studio 2008. When you do that, you should be prompted by Visual Studio 2008 to reload the project because it has been modified (see Figure 6-5). Click Yes to All to reload the project.

Figure 6-5. Visual Studio 2008 realizes that your project has been modified by Blend and asks whether you want to reload your project.

8. Now that the project has been updated in Visual Studio 2008, open Window1.xaml and inside the Grid create a MediaElement with the name of MyMediaElement. Give it a LoadedBehavior of Manual so that it will run in Independent mode and you can control it (see Figure 6-6).

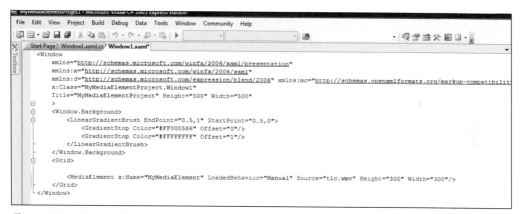

Figure 6-6. Creating a MediaElement with the name of MyMediaElement and a LoadedBehavior of Manual in Visual Studio 2008

9. Next, you need to add a video to the project. To do this, right-click the project name (MyMediaElementProject) in Visual Studio 2008's Solution Explorer (shown in Figure 6-7) and click Add ➤ Existing Item. Then navigate to a video you have stored on your machine. If you do not have an AVI or WMV, you can download one off the Internet easily.

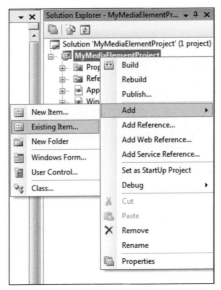

Figure 6-7. Selecting Add ➤ Existing Item in Visual Studio 2008's Solution Explorer in order to add a video file to your project

> By default, Visual Studio 2008 will not be looking for video file types, so make sure you change the type of file to Video Files (*.avi, *.mpg, *.mpeg, *.mov, *.qt).

10. Before you can use this video file, there are a couple of things you need to do to it. Because this video is eventually going to be set as the source of the MediaElement using a URI, you need to right-click it and select Properties. Change its Build Action setting to Content and set the Copy to Output Directory property to Copy always like I have done in Figure 6-8.

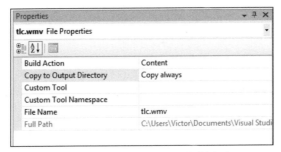

Figure 6-8. Setting your MediaElement's Build Action property to Content and its Copy to Output Directory property to Copy always

The Properties *panel in Visual Studio 2008 is located under Solution Explorer. If it is not visible, select your media in Solution Explorer and press F4 (or click* Menu View ➤ Properties Window*) and the* Properties *panel will appear.*

11. Now that that's done, you can change the source of the MediaElement named MyMediaElement to your video file. Also set the Height and Width to 300 by 300. The code should now look like this (note that my video source happens to be tlc.wmv; yours should be the name of your video):

```
<MediaElement x:Name="MyMediaElement"
  LoadedBehavior="Manual" Source="tlc.wmv" Height="300" Width="300"/>
```

12. Now in your Window1.xaml.cs code-behind file, set the MediaElement to play by using this code:

```
public Window1()
        {
            InitializeComponent();
            MyMediaElement.Play();
        }
```

13. Press F5 and run the application. You should see the video playing, as shown in Figure 6-9.

Figure 6-9. When you run the application, you should see the MediaElement playing your video.

14. Close the running application.

Blend 2's Make a Button feature

At this point, you are going to want to start to add some controls. You are going to add three controls:

- Stop
- Play
- Pause

You could use Blend's prebuilt Button control to create these MediaElement controls, but I like to create my buttons using shapes and then let Blend 2 turn them into Button controls. This is a good time to show you my approach, starting with the play Button.

In order to do this, it's easiest to switch over to Blend 2 and make the Buttons and then switch back to Visual Studio 2008 to wire them up. So do that now:

1. Switch over to Blend 2, and it should ask you to reload the project. Click Yes. Once the project reloads, you should see your MediaElement in the Design Workspace, as shown in Figure 6-10.

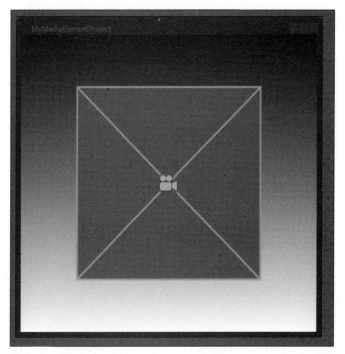

Figure 6-10. The MediaElement shows up in the Design Workspace of Blend 2.

> When you run the application in either Blend 2 or Visual Studio 2008, it is saved automatically.

2. Select the Rectangle tool from the toolbar.

3. Draw a Rectangle in the Workspace (roughly the size of a standard video control button) and use the radius handles to give it slightly rounded corners like I have done in Figure 6-11.

Figure 6-11. Using the Rectangle tool and the Brush Transform tool to create a button background Rectangle

4. Give it a linear gradient fill through settings in the Brushes section of the Properties panel.

5. Use the Brush Transform tool to rotate and shrink the gradient so that it now goes from top to bottom until it looks something like what I have done in Figure 6-11.

6. With that done, select the button background Rectangle, duplicate it three more times, and place them next to each other so that you have something like what I have in Figure 6-12.

Figure 6-12. Duplicating your button background Rectangle three times for the other controls that you have yet to build

Now you need to add a foreground play symbol to the play Button. I like to use a sideways triangle like you commonly see in most video players. You could make one in Photoshop and save it as a PNG with a transparent background, but here I am going to have you use the Pen tool to create it right in Blend.

7. Select the Pen tool from the toolbar. Then click once for what will be the top left of the triangle. Click again for the right side of the triangle, and finally click once for what will be the bottom-left corner of the triangle (see Figure 6-13).

Figure 6-13. Using the Blend Pen tool to click three times to make a sideways triangle symbol

8. Place the new triangle play symbol over the first button background Rectangle.

9. Select both the button background Rectangle and the play symbol's Path, right-click, click Group Into, and choose Canvas (you can also select them in the Objects and Timeline panel by selecting one and then holding down the Ctrl key and selecting the other one).

10. Blend then wraps the two elements into a Canvas. Now select Tools ➤ Make a Button from the menu.

11. Blend now asks you to give your new resource a name. Use the default of ButtonStyle1 and click OK.

> When I use the Pen tool to make shapes, I find it helpful to click the Show snap grid button located just above the Results panel at the bottom of the Blend 2 IDE so I can see the snap grid.

12. You now have a Button, but you may have noticed that Blend put text (called a ContentPresenter) in your Button that reads "Button". You don't want that, so with the new Button selected, go to the Properties panel, and in the Common Properties section, remove the text Button from the Content property box.

13. Go ahead and run the application by pressing F5. You should see that you now have a play Button. But the problem is the MediaElement is already playing, and the play Button doesn't do anything yet.

14. To solve this problem, switch back to Visual Studio 2008. Select Yes to All to reload the project and remove the play command.

15. Give your play Button a name so you can code against it with C# code. To do that, go into the XAML and find the play Button; it will be easy to find as it is your only actual Button control in the XAML (remember, you have not yet turned the other Rectangles into Button controls). Give it a name of playBtn following my well-formatted code (note that some of your values will be different from mine such as those for the Margin, Height, and Width properties):

```
<Button x:Name="playBtn"
        HorizontalAlignment="Left"
        Margin="135,0,0,52"
        Style="{DynamicResource ButtonStyle1}"
        VerticalAlignment="Bottom"
        Width="41" Height="30"
        Content=""
    />
```

> I find it much easier to read my XAML if I format it like I have done here rather than the default of all code on one line. I like to keep the x:Name on the same line as the control type, and then every other property has its own line, except for Height and Width, as I feel they are so closely related they can be together. I then place the closing bracket directly under the opening bracket, much like curly brackets in C#.

Objects added to the XAML file are not detectable in the C# code-behind file until the application is built. It can be built (with the F6 key) or built and run (with the F5 key). After the application has been built with the new object (in this case the playBtn), IntelliSense should be aware of it and provide code completion for it. It is entirely possible to go right ahead and write the necessary C# without pre-building the project. You will simply need to type all the C# in by hand instead of relying on IntelliSense to finish your lines for you. For this reason, I suggest you compile and run the application. Once you finish, you will wire up your playBtn after the InitializeComponent(); code. To do so, follow these steps:

1. Press F5 to compile and run your application.

2. Stop your application and go into the Window1.xaml.cs code-behind page.

3. Place your cursor after InitializeComponent(); and start to type playBtn. Once IntelliSense shows you playBtn as an option, select it.

4. Place a dot after playBtn and choose Click from IntelliSense.

5. Type += and Visual Studio will understand you want to create an EventHandler.

6. Press the Tab key twice, and Visual Studio will create the method stub for you, as shown in the following code:

```
public Window1()
        {
InitializeComponent();
            playBtn.Click += new RoutedEventHandler(playBtn_Click);
        }

        void playBtn_Click(object sender, RoutedEventArgs e)
        {
            throw new NotImplementedException();
        }
```

7. Now you can erase the default code that Visual Studio puts in the new method that reads throw new Exception("The method or operation is not implemented."); and add your own code. The code you want to add will tell the MediaElement to play. You do that with this code:

```
void playBtn_Click(object sender, RoutedEventArgs e)
        {
            MyMediaElement.Play();
        }
```

> The InitializeComponent *method is something that needs to be called to render the XAML of the application. Never put any code before it or remove it, or you will get errors.*

8. Press F5 to run the application and test out your new play Button.

Pretty cool, huh? Now go back into Blend to prepare for creating your stop Button. When you go back into Blend, you will be prompted to reload the application; do so.

Creating the stop Button

Now you are going to create your stop Button. The first thing you need to do is create your stop symbol. This is very easy as it is usually just a square. To do this, follow these steps:

1. Grab your Rectangle tool and create a small Rectangle that is just big enough to fit within your second button background Rectangle.

2. Place the stop symbol Rectangle over your second button background Rectangle.

3. Select both objects in the Objects and Timeline panel or in the Workspace itself.

4. Right-click and select Group Into ➤ Canvas.

5. Click Tools ➤ Make Button.

6. Click OK.

7. Remove the text Button from the Content property box in the Common Properties section of the Properties panel.

8. Save your project.

9. Go back into Visual Studio 2008.

10. Click Yes to All to reload project.

> If you like to select objects directly in the Workspace, I find it convenient to "lock" items I do not want to select to keep them from getting in the way. This is done in the Objects and Timeline panel. If you do not remember how to lock an object, refer back to Chapter 3.

That was a lot, but I would wager that you got through it very quickly and with little to no troubles. That is what WPF was intended to do, that is, to give the developer a very easy-to-use set of tools to create applications easily and quickly. Now you need to give your new stop Button a name. You do this in the XAML by adding the x:Name property to the Button. I also like to format the Button's XAML so that it is easier to read.

1. Add the following code in XAML view to give your stop Button a name:

```
<Button x:Name="stopBtn"       HorizontalAlignment="Left"
     Margin="177,0,0,43"
     Style="{DynamicResource ButtonStyle2}"
     VerticalAlignment="Bottom"
     Width="55" Height="30"
     Content=""
/>
```

2. Now compile the application by either running it by pressing F5 or compiling it without running it by pressing F6 so IntelliSense will know about your new Button.

3. You are now ready to wire your stop Button up in Window1.xaml.cs. Under the playBtn code, start tying stopBtn and select stopBtn when it appears in IntelliSense.

4. Type .Click and a += and press the Tab key twice to create the method stub.

5. Erase the default text in the method stub.

6. Here is the code you need to stop the MediaElement from playing:

```
void stopBtn_Click(object sender, RoutedEventArgs e)
        {
                MyMediaElement.Stop();

        }
```

7. Run your application again and press the play Button. Once it starts to play, press the stop Button, and you will see that the video will stop.

But wait, doesn't that look more like a pause than a stop? It does because the video stops, but the MediaElement displays the very last frame it played. You can actually see that it does stop the video if you click the play Button again, as the MediaElement will start the video over again from the beginning. Well, that is not acceptable for your application. You need this piece of code that will tell the MediaElement to position itself at the beginning of the video. You can do that by setting the position of the MediaElement to a TimeSpan of zero, which will essentially put the source video of the MediaElement to its beginning position:

```
MyMediaElement.Position = new TimeSpan(0);
```

You would think that you could just add it to the stopBtn_Click EventHandler like this:

```
void stopBtn_Click(object sender, RoutedEventArgs e)
        {
                MyMediaElement.Position = new TimeSpan(0);
                MyMediaElement.Stop();
        }
```

Unfortunately, this will not work because the two events occur almost at the same time, and the MediaElement does not have enough time to react and perform both requests. For that reason, you need to call two events on the stop Button. The first one will set the media to the 0 position, and the second will actually stop the media. To do this, you can listen for the PreviewMouseDown event. This will fire prior to the MouseLeftButtonDown event (hence the word "Preview") and prior to the Click event (which your stop Button is currently listening for).

8. Add a new event under the current stopBtn.Click like this:

```
stopBtn.Click += new RoutedEventHandler(stopBtn_Click);
stopBtn.PreviewMouseDown += new
MouseButtonEventHandler(stopBtn_PreviewMouseDown);
```

9. Now in the stopBtn_PreviewMouseDown EventHandler, set the TimeSpan of the MediaElement to 0 like this:

```
void stopBtn_PreviewMouseDown(object sender, MouseButtonEventArgs e)
        {
                MyMediaElement.Position = new TimeSpan(0);
        }
```

10. Run the application again. You will see that it behaves exactly as you would expect when you press the stop Button.

Creating the pause Button

Let's move on and create your pause Button.

1. Return back to Blend and reload the project.

2. Use the Rectangle tool to create two slim bars to mimic the pause symbol commonly displayed on video players (see Figure 6-14).

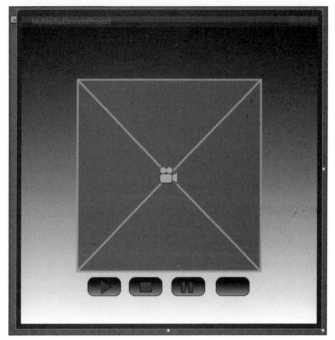

Figure 6-14. Two red rectangles mimic the pause symbol commonly displayed on video players.

3. Select the two Rectangles and the button background Rectangle.

4. Select Group Into ➤ Canvas, and then select Tools ➤ Make a Button.

5. Remove the text Button from the Content property box in the Common Properties section of the Properties panel.

6. Save your application and switch back to Visual Studio 2008 and reload your application.

7. Go into the XAML and name the new Button pauseBtn and format the code to match the specifications of your previous Buttons.

8. Compile your application and then in the Window1.xaml.cs constructor create the Click EventHandler by typing the name pauseBtn.Click+= and pressing the Tab key twice.

9. In the new pause method, simply tell your `MediaElement` to pause as I did in the following code:

```
void pauseBtn_Click(object sender, RoutedEventArgs e)
        {
              MyMediaElement.Pause();
        }
```

10. Run your application and press the play Button. Once the video plays, click the pause Button, and your video should pause. If you press the play Button again, you will see that the video resumes where it left off, unlike the stop Button, which causes play to restart the video.

Now at this point I think it would be good to talk a little about user experience. When I am playing with video controls in someone else's application, I myself get frustrated if I press a pause button and the video pauses, but nothing happens when I press it again (that is, it is not a toggle switch). I think that provides for a bad user experience. So, let's fix that now.

What you are going to do is make a private variable. A **private variable** is a variable that is only accessible to the class that created it. In this case, your variable will only be accessible to Window1. You are going to call this variable _isPaused. If the video is playing, _isPaused will be false, and if the video is paused, it will be true. This type of variable is called a **Boolean variable**. When your pause Button is clicked, your method will look to see whether _isPaused is true or false. If it is true, the video is paused, and you will play the video; but if it is false, the video is not paused, and then the application will pause it. So let's do that now:

1. Above your Window1 constructor, create a private Boolean variable and set it to true because when the application starts the video is not playing:

```
namespace MyMediaElementProject
{
    /// <summary>
    /// Interaction logic for Window1.xaml
    /// </summary>
    public partial class Window1 : Window
    {
        private Boolean _isPaused = true;
        public Window1()
        {
            InitializeComponent();
            playBtn.Click += new RoutedEventHandler(playBtn_Click);
            stopBtn.Click += new RoutedEventHandler(stopBtn_Click);
            stopBtn.PreviewMouseDown += ➡
new MouseButtonEventHandler(stopBtn_PreviewMouseDown);
            pauseBtn.Click += new RoutedEventHandler(pauseBtn_Click);
        }
```

> It is a common naming convention to use an underscore for private variables.

2. When the play Button is clicked, set _isPaused to false:

```
void playBtn_Click(object sender, RoutedEventArgs e)
        {
            _isPaused = false;
            MyMediaElement.Play();
        }
```

3. When the pause Button is clicked, you will use an if/then conditional to check to see whether _isPaused is true or false and then act accordingly:

```
void pauseBtn_Click(object sender, RoutedEventArgs e)
        {
            if (_isPaused == true)
            {
                _isPaused = false;
                MyMediaElement.Play();
            }
            else
            {
                _isPaused = true;
                MyMediaElement.Pause();
            }

        }
```

4. Run your application and play the video. Pause it by clicking the pause Button. Now click the pause Button again. Ahhh! Much better, now your pause Button is a toggle Button.

Creating the video toggle Button

At this point, your application is almost done. Now let's add a Button that toggles between two videos. To do this, you need to add another video into your project:

1. Right-click Solution Explorer in Visual Studio 2008 and select Add Existing Item. Navigate to your video and double-click it.

2. Once your video is in the project, right-click it and go to its properties (or select it and press F4). Set the Build Action to Content and the Copy to Output Directory to Copy always.

3. Compile your project and switch over to Blend and reload the application.

4. Now style up your video toggle Button.

In Blend, I basically made two little play triangles for the video toggle Button; if you can think of a better way to represent a video toggle Button, be my guest. You can see what I did in Figure 6-15.

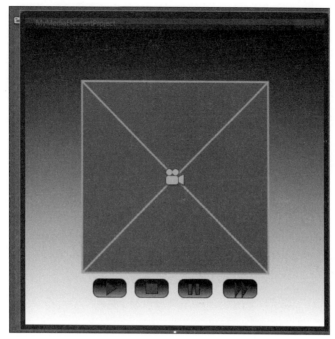

Figure 6-15. Here you can see how I styled my video toggle Button.

5. Select all of the Button components (one button background Rectangle and two triangle Paths, if you are following the method I used), right-click, and select Group Into ➤ Canvas.

6. Select Tools ➤ Make a Button like you have done three times before, and remove the text Button from the Content property box in the Common Properties section in the Properties panel.

7. Run and close your application, and then switch back over to Visual Studio 2008 and reload the application.

Now the first thing you need is a private String variable to tell you what video is currently the source of your MediaElement. You will use the video that you declared in the XAML as the first video as it is already loaded. You will call it _videoVar.

8. Code your video variable (be sure to use the name of your video; here, I'm using babyUsingiPhone.AVI for this example):

```
private String _videoVar = "babyUsingiPhone.AVI";
        private Boolean _isPaused = true;
        public Window1()
        {
            InitializeComponent();
            playBtn.Click += new RoutedEventHandler(playBtn_Click);
            stopBtn.Click += new RoutedEventHandler(stopBtn_Click);
            pauseBtn.Click += new RoutedEventHandler(pauseBtn_Click);
        }
```

9. Now you need to wire up your video toggle Button. So give it an x:Name of videoToggle in the XAML and press F6 to compile the application so IntelliSense can pick up your toggleVideo Button.

10. Create the event for the toggleVideo Button by typing its name under your other events. When IntelliSense picks it up, press Enter, and then type .Click+= and press the Tab key twice so Visual Studio 2008 will create the EventHandler for you.

11. In the EventHandler, you now need to run a conditional that will check what the current source is from your _videoVar variable. It will then set the _videoVar to the next video, create a URI variable, and set MyMediaElement to that URI. Here is the code:

```
void videoToggle_Click(object sender, RoutedEventArgs e)
        {
            // if _videoVar is babyUsingiPhone
            if (_videoVar == "babyUsingiPhone.AVI")
            {
                // set _vdieoVar to the next video
                _videoVar = "MVI_1205.AVI";
                // create a var called src of the type Uri
                // set the source of the Uri to the new video
                // inform it that the Uri is a Relative path...
as opposed to an Absolute path
                Uri src = new Uri("MVI_1205.AVI", UriKind.Relative);
                // set MyMediaElement's Source to the new src
Uri variable
                MyMediaElement.Source = src;
                // Tell the MediaElement to play
                MyMediaElement.Play();

            }
            else
            {
                _videoVar = "babyUsingiPhone.AVI";
                Uri src = new Uri("babyUsingiPhone.AVI",
UriKind.Relative);
                 MyMediaElement.Source = src;
                MyMediaElement.Play();
            }
        }
```

So there you have it, a fully functional MediaElement video player complete with play, stop, pause, and toggle video controls. Pretty cool and not very difficult, huh? Figure 6-16 shows my completed WPF video player.

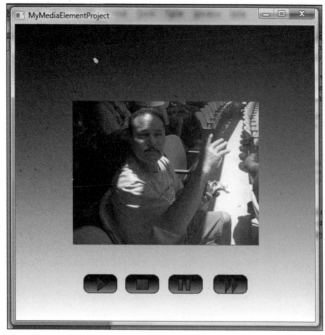

Figure 6-16. My completed WPF `MediaElement` video player with video controls for play, stop, pause, and toggle video

It is worth mentioning here that audio works much the same way as video with the ability to add controls similar to the ones you just created. A good exercise would be for you to go off now and create your own MP3 player using the principles and concepts discussed in this chapter. Feel free to send me an e-mail if you get stuck. Watch this book become a best-seller, and then I will be getting 39,000 e-mails per day asking me how to build an MP3 player. Oh well, never let it be said I don't love my readers: wpfautho@gmail.com.

> *You can build (or compile) the application without running it. But I have found that to be a little inconsistent when it comes to IntelliSense being able to find objects, so I like to just run the application.*

> *A compressed file containing a finished version of the application without the video assets (to reduce download size) can be found at* www.windowspresentationfoundation. com/bookDownloads/MyMediaElementProject.zip.

Summary

In this chapter, I discussed the very powerful and easy-to-code MediaElement. You learned about the two modes of the MediaElement, Clock and Independent. You also learned that if you set your LoadedBehavior to Manual, you can run your MediaElement in the Independent mode and thus control how the MediaElement plays your video. This allows you to create custom video player controls such as play, stop, pause, and toggle video. You now know that you can set the source of a MediaElement in XAML or you can do it in the code-behind file using what is called a URI. In order to use a URI, you know now that you have to set certain properties on your video file in Solution Explorer. Finally, you actually went through and built a custom WPF MediaElement video player by switching between Visual Studio for the code-behind and Blend to create the visual control Buttons. You also learned how to use conditional if statements to turn your Buttons into toggle Buttons to enhance user experience.

In the next chapter, I will delve into ControlTemplates, Styles, and even custom UserControls.

Chapter 7

CONTROLTEMPLATES, STYLES, AND CUSTOM USERCONTROLS

What this chapter covers:

- Understanding ControlTemplates
- How Styles work with ControlTemplates
- Creating a Button ControlTemplate
- Creating Styles and using them to overwrite WPF controls
- Using Styles to mandate how controls display their content
- Using ResourceDictionaries
- Applying resources to WPF controls
- Using Styles and ControlTemplates to create your own custom WPF UserControls
- How to create and use custom UserControls

A very important concept in object-oriented programming is one that says you can create something once and then reuse it over and over again. Of course, this means you can reuse a resource in one application, but in WPF you can take this further and reuse a resource over and over again in other applications. ControlTemplates and UserControls allow you to do just that. I have been working with WPF now for well over a year, and in that time I have been able to create my own libraries of resources that I am now able to reuse in new applications that I create. This allows me to develop new applications faster because I don't have to re-create new resources, but rather add a reference to them in my new applications and then simply make use of them. In this chapter, you are going to create a Style for a WPF Button control that will contain a ControlTemplate, and then change that ControlTemplate to have the Button show an Image control. You are then going to create a ResourceDictionary and move the Button Style to it. Finally, you are going to take everything you have learned and create a custom UserControl.

The ControlTemplate

A ControlTemplate is nothing more than a resource, defined in a Style that allows you to specify the way a control is displayed in the Visual Tree. It literally allows you to build a template for a WPF control, hence the name ControlTemplate. You can create ControlTemplates for a host of WPF controls such as Buttons, ListBoxes, StackPanels, etc. Further, once you create a ControlTemplate, say for a Button, you are then able to make use of that resource throughout your application. Let's move forward and create a new WPF project, create a ControlTemplate, and then apply that ControlTemplate to other controls.

A Button ControlTemplate

You'll start off by creating a new WPF Application project in Visual Studio 2008:

1. Open Visual Studio 2008.
2. Select WPF Application from the Visual Studio installed templates.
3. Enter a project name of ControlTemplateProject (see Figure 7-1) and click OK.

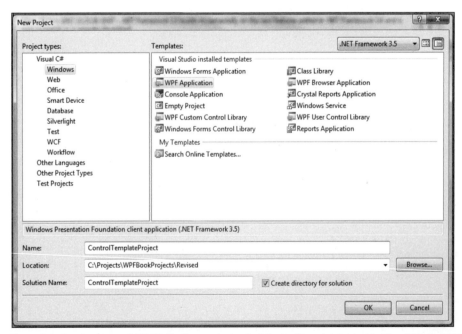

Figure 7-1. Creating a new WPF Application project called ControlTemplateProject in Visual Studio 2008

In this project, you are going to create a ControlTemplate for a WPF Button control. You are then going to create a few WPF Buttons and apply your new ControlTemplate to them to see how simple it is to reuse a ControlTemplate resource. So start by opening your new project in both Visual Studio 2008 as well as Blend.

4. Open Blend 2 and navigate to where you saved your project, and then open the .sln (solution) file.

Now you should have your project open in both Visual Studio 2008 and Blend 2. As you probably know by now, this is the typical workflow for me, as I like to do my design work in Blend 2 and then use Visual Studio to create my functionality (EventHandlers, etc.). With that in mind, you'll use Blend 2 to design your new Button ControlTemplate.

Figure 7-2. Selecting [Window] in the Objects and Timeline panel

5. Give yourself a little breathing room by selecting [Window] in the Objects and Timeline panel (see Figure 7-2).

6. Change the Height and Width of the [Window] to 600 by 600 in the Layout section of the Properties panel (see Figure 7-3).

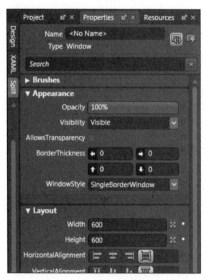

Figure 7-3. Changing the Width and Height settings to 600

7. Select the Rectangle tool in the toolbar, and draw a Rectangle control in the Workspace. Use the radius handles to give your new Rectangle rounded edges (see Figure 7-4).

Now you have the basis for what will be your Button control. But it does look a little simple, does it not? Go ahead and give it a quick gradient.

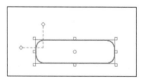

Figure 7-4. Using the radius handles to give the Rectangle rounded edges

143

8. Make sure the Rectangle is selected, and then in the Brushes section of the Properties panel, click Fill and select a Gradient brush (see Figure 7-5).

Figure 7-5. Giving your Rectangle a Gradient brush fill in the Brushes section of the Properties panel

Go ahead and play with the gradient fill colors as well as the Brush Transformation tool until you have something you are pleased with or something like I have done, as shown in Figure 7-6.

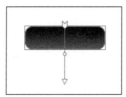

Figure 7-6. I created this gradient fill by adjusting the colors in the Brushes section of the Properties panel and by adjusting the gradient with the Brush Transformation tool.

Now that you have a Rectangle that you are happy with, you need to tell Blend that you want to use this as a ControlTemplate for a Button. The easiest way to do this is by using Blend's Make a Button feature as follows:

9. Make sure your Rectangle is selected, and then click Tools ➤ Make a Button.

10. Blend 2 will ask you to name your new control. Name it BlueButtonControl and then click OK.

Now let's see what Blend 2 has done for you. The first thing to notice is that the Rectangle now has letters over it that read "Button" (see Figure 7-7).

Figure 7-7. When you turn your Rectangle into a Button control, Blend places text over your Rectangle.

What Blend also did was turn the Rectangle in the Objects and Timeline panel into a Button control (see Figure 7-8)—very cool!

Figure 7-8. Blend turns your Rectangle into a Button control.

So now, the newly created Button control, formerly a Rectangle, has all of the capabilities of a normal WPF Button control, but the difference is that instead of using WPF's basic Button ControlTemplate, it uses yours. Pretty cool, huh? You'll give your new Button a little functionality to prove it is just like any other WPF standard Button control, but before you do, I think it would be good to delve into the XAML and see exactly what Blend 2 did for you "under the hood," so to speak.

11. Before you take a look at the XAML, give the new Button control a name. Name your Button myButton in the Name field of the Properties panel like I have done in Figure 7-9.

Figure 7-9. Naming your Button control in the Name section of the Properties panel

12. Now click the XAML tab (or look in the XAML view in Blend 2's Split view) to see the XAML that Blend 2 has created for your myButton control, and you will see something very similar to, if not exactly like, what I have here:

```
<Window
    xmlns="http://schemas.microsoft.com/winfx/2006/xaml/presentation"
    xmlns:x="http://schemas.microsoft.com/winfx/2006/xaml"
    x:Class="ControlTemplateProject.Window1"
    Title="ControlTemplateProject" Height="600" Width="600"
```

```
        >
    <Window.Resources>
        <Style x:Key="BlueButtonControl" BasedOn="{x:Null}"
TargetType="{x:Type Button}">
            <Setter Property="Template">
                <Setter.Value>
                    <ControlTemplate TargetType="{x:Type Button}">
                        <Grid>
                            <Rectangle Stroke="#FF000000" RadiusX="11.5"
RadiusY="11.5">
                                <Rectangle.Fill>
                                    <LinearGradientBrush EndPoint="0.5,2.292"
StartPoint="0.5,0.111">
                                        <GradientStop Color="#FF0C024C"
Offset="0"/>
                                        <GradientStop Color="#FFFFFFFF"
Offset="1"/>
                                    </LinearGradientBrush>
                                </Rectangle.Fill>
                            </Rectangle>
                            <ContentPresenter SnapsToDevicePixels=
"{TemplateBinding SnapsToDevicePixels}" HorizontalAlignment=
"{TemplateBinding HorizontalContentAlignment}" VerticalAlignment=
"{TemplateBinding VerticalContentAlignment}"
RecognizesAccessKey="True"/>
                        </Grid>
                        <ControlTemplate.Triggers>
                            <Trigger Property="IsFocused" Value="True"/>
                            <Trigger Property="IsDefaulted" Value="True"/>
                            <Trigger Property="IsMouseOver" Value="True"/>
                            <Trigger Property="IsPressed" Value="True"/>
                            <Trigger Property="IsEnabled" Value="False"/>
                        </ControlTemplate.Triggers>
                    </ControlTemplate>
                </Setter.Value>
            </Setter>
        </Style>
    </Window.Resources>
    <Grid>

        <Button HorizontalAlignment="Left" Margin="138,148,0,0"
x:Name="myButton" Style="{DynamicResource BlueButtonControl}"
VerticalAlignment="Top" Width="129" Height="36" Content="Button"/>

    </Grid>
</Window>
```

Notice that in the main Grid there is only one UI FrameWork element, and that is a Button control with the x:Name of myButton.

> *For easier-to-read XAML, I like to reformat my code with line breaks like I have done here:*
>
> ```
> <Button x:Name="myButton"
>         HorizontalAlignment="Left"
>         Margin="138,148,0,0"
>         Style="{DynamicResource BlueButtonControl}"
>         VerticalAlignment="Top"
>         Width="129" Height="36"
>         Content="Button"
>         />
> ```

Let's break down exactly what Blend 2 did:

- Blend 2 created a Windows.Resources section.
- In the Windows.Resources section, Blend created a Style for you called BlueButtonControl (the name you provided in the Make a Button dialog box).
- Blend then created a Setter that defines a Template. Setters are how ControlTemplates set properties for the object they are defining.
- In that Template, Blend created a ControlTemplate with the TargetType of Button.
- In that ControlTemplate, Blend defined how the Button will be displayed by creating the following:
  - A Grid
  - A Rectangle
  - A Rectangle.Fill
  - A ContentPresenter (this is the text that reads "Button")
  - ControlTemplate.Triggers to define how interaction is handled
- Blend then bound the Style of your Button control to the DynamicResource of your BlueButtonControl Style.

Because you just created a Style that holds your ControlTemplate, I feel this would be a good time to take a closer look at Styles.

Styles

Styles allow you to set properties for controls. In a project, say you have a lot of ListBoxes that have to look very different from an ordinary ListBox (with the default style). You could create a Style that defines how a ListBox should look and then apply that Style to any other ListBox you wish; however, what if you want to reuse your Style in another XAML file other than Window1.xaml? To reuse a Style in another XAML file, you can define it in a file called a ResourceDictionary that is accessible to your entire application, not just Window1.xaml. In fact, it is best practice to put all of your Styles in a ResourceDictionary. I'll walk you through the steps for creating a ResourceDictionary for your ControlTemplateProject project now:

1. On the toolbar, click the Asset Library button and do a search for listbox.

2. When you see the ListBox control appear, click it.

3. Draw a ListBox in the Workspace.

4. Right-click the ListBox and select Edit Control Parts (Template) ➤ Edit a Copy.

5. In the Create Style Resource dialog box, give the new Style resource a name of MyListBoxStyle.

6. In the Define section of the dialog box, find where it says Resource Dictionary. Notice it is grayed out. That is because there is no ResourceDictionary yet, so to create one click the New button.

7. Blend then opens a Resource Dictionary dialog box and asks what name you want to give to your new ResourceDictionary. Name the ResourceDictionary applicationResourceDict and click OK.

8. Notice now Blend has ungrayed the Resource Dictionary option, selected it for you, and entered the name of the newly created ResourceDictionary, applicationResourceDict. Click OK.

Blend opens the newly created applicationResourceDict.xaml file. Here you can edit the Style of MyListBoxStyle to change the way the ListBox is displayed. Do that now:

1. Select Bd (a Border control) from the Objects and Timeline panel.

2. In the Properties panel under the Layout section, change the HorizontalAlignment property from the default Stretch to Center (see Figure 7-10).

Figure 7-10. Changing the way the ListBox displays its content by changing the HorizontalAlignment setting Center

Notice now the ListBox contents change to center alignment. Now if you go back to Window1.xaml, by clicking the Window1.xaml tab at the top of Blend and looking at the ListBox, you see . . . wait, nothing! That is because the ListBox does not have any content yet. To add items, continue with these steps:

3. Right-click the ListBox and click Add ListBox Item.

4. Repeat one time to add a total of two generic ListBoxItems.

Now you can see that the ListBoxItems are positioned in the center of the ListBox, as shown in Figure 7-11.

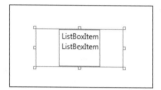

Figure 7-11. Changing the ListBox Style will affect the way your ListBox displays its content.

Now, what if you wanted to create a new ListBox and apply your new Style to it? Here is how that is done:

5. Select the Last Used tool on the toolbar and draw a ListBox on the Workspace.

6. Right-click the new ListBox and click Add ListBox Item.

7. Repeat the previous step twice to add two more generic ListBoxItems.

8. Right-click the new ListBox, click Edit Control Parts (Template) ➤ Apply Resources, and left-click MyListBoxStyle.

Notice right away the new ListBox displays its content exactly the same way as the first ListBox, that is, center justified (see Figure 7-12).

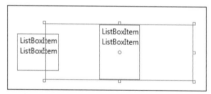

Figure 7-12. Styles can easily be applied to other controls of the same type.

Overriding default Styles for controls

You may be thinking to yourself, "Big deal!" I would not blame you because this is a pretty boring example of applying Styles. In order to show you the real power of Styles, let me present you with a scenario that I recently faced. In an application I was working on, I had to populate a ListBox with PNG images. That was easy enough to do with Styles, but the problem was that when one of the ListBox items (a PNG image) was selected, the background of that ListBoxItem turned blue. This is the default behavior of a ListBox. If you want to see this behavior for yourself, press F5 to run the application, and click one of the ListBox items; you will see that its background will turn blue. This presented a problem for me in my application, because the designer thought it looked horrible and was not what he had in mind when conceptualizing the application. So, I was tasked with getting rid of the blue background. After some thought, I eventually came up with the idea to use Styles to override the default behavior. This, to me, *did* seem like a big deal. I feel it would be a good exercise for you to duplicate the steps I followed. You'll override the default behavior of the ListBox in your application now:

1. In Window1.xaml, select a ListBoxItem in the Objects and Timeline panel (see Figure 7-13).

Figure 7-13. Selecting any ListBoxItem in the Objects and Timeline panel

2. Right-click the ListBoxItem and select Edit Control Parts (Template) ➤ Edit a Copy.

3. Leave the default name of ListBoxItemStyle1 and select the ResourceDictionary that you created earlier.

Blend 2 opens up the ResourceDictionary and shows you a ListBoxItem as you can see in Figure 7-14.

Blend does not allow you to override this style visually, so I am going to explain how to do it in the XAML.

Figure 7-14. Blend allows you to visually edit your new ListBoxItem control.

4. Click the XAML tab to show the XAML or edit it right in the XAML of the Split view.

5. Find the Style with the x:Name of ListBoxItemStyle1.

Notice that there are ControlTemplate.Triggers inside of your Style. These are Triggers that respond to user interaction. The Trigger that you want to work with is the IsSelected Trigger, as this is what occurs when the ListBoxItem is selected. The particular XAML you want to change is this:

```
<Trigger Property="IsSelected" Value="true">
    <Setter Property="Background" TargetName="Bd"
Value="{DynamicResource {x:Static SystemColors.HighlightBrushKey}}"/>
    <Setter Property="Foreground" Value="{DynamicResource
{x:Static SystemColors.HighlightTextBrushKey}}"/>
</Trigger>
```

So, what the preceding code is saying is that when an item is selected, change the Background and Foreground properties.

6. You don't want to change the Background property, so just remove that line of XAML so that your code looks like this:

```
<Trigger Property="IsSelected" Value="true">
    <Setter Property="Foreground" Value="{DynamicResource
{x:Static SystemColors.HighlightTextBrushKey}}"/>
</Trigger>
```

7. Run the application by pressing F5, and click the ListBoxItem for which you created the Style.

Wait a tick! That is not what you wanted now, is it? Your background does remain white, but now your text disappears. Why is that? That is because of the remaining line of XAML in the setter, specifically the one that addresses the Foreground color property:

```
<Setter Property="Foreground" Value=
"{DynamicResource {x:Static SystemColors.HighlightTextBrushKey}}"/>
```

Say you want to see what this color is. To do that, in the Design view of Blend, you would click [Window] in the Objects and Timeline panel. Next, in the Properties panel, click the Brush resources button in the Brushes bucket like I am doing in Figure 7-15.

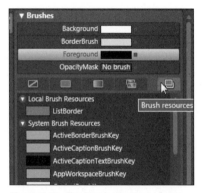

Figure 7-15. The Brush resources button

Notice that in Figure 7-15 you can see a list of System Brush Resources. Now, look for HighlightTextBrushKey because that is what was set in the color in the Setter code earlier. Notice that it is white. That's right, all system color values are resources as well the ones that you create. That being the case, you can use these System color resources instead of making your own.

8. So now, remove the line of XAML shown earlier after step 7, run the application again, and see the new results.

What did you see? What is that you say? Nothing happens? Well, you are somewhat correct if you assumed that nothing is occurring. What *is* happening is the ListBoxItem is, in fact, being selected, but because there is nothing in the IsSelected Setter, you are not seeing any changes when the item is being selected. In order to correct this, you'll need to replace the line of XAML you just removed, but change the Value setting to your own value and not the one that Blend 2 chose for you, namely SystemColors.HighlightTextBrushKey, which, as you just learned, is white.

9. Replace the value of Value with Red as shown here:

```
<Trigger Property="IsSelected" Value="true">
<Setter Property="Foreground" Value="Red"/>
</Trigger>
```

10. Run the application once again and see what results you get.

Ah, much better! This is the exact result you wanted. When you select your ListBoxItem, it turns red and has no blue background. When you select another item, it turns back to its default state of black. But now, you have to tell all of the other ListBoxItems to make use of the same Style, or they will use their default.

11. Select each additional ListBoxItem, right-click it, select Edit Control Parts (Template) ➤ Apply Resource and select ListBoxItemStyle1.

12. Recompile the application by pressing F5 and test it by selecting different ListBoxItems.

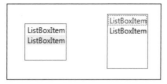

Figure 7-16. The ListBoxItems now turn red when selected.

Notice that every ListBoxItem in each ListBox responds exactly how you had hoped by turning red when selected and black when unselected. Further, you don't see that annoying blue background when an item is selected (see Figure 7-16).

Now you know what a Style is and how to create one. You also now know how to apply a Style to a control of the same type, and how to create a ResourceDictionary that contains your Styles that will be available to all XAML pages of your project. Finally, you have seen how Styles can be very useful in a real-world situation by giving you the ability to override a control's default behavior by using Setters to set the control's properties such as the IsSelected property of a ListBox control. Now that you understand Styles, you can get back to your Button control and do some really fun stuff.

Adding your Button Style to your ResourceDictionary

So you now understand the way that the Button control you have made is displayed inside of a Style. If you look at Window1.xaml, you can see the Button control Style called BlueButtonControl defined in a section called Window.Resources. Earlier in this section, you learned that it is best practice to put all of your Styles in a ResourceDictionary, and you even learned how to do that. So, why did I have you create your Button control Style inside of your Window1.xaml if it is not best practice to do so? Did I make a mistake? Actually, yes I did, but this mistake will allow me to show you how to fix a common error that I find many developers tend to make, and that is defining resources such as Styles in the XAML page they are working on rather than in a ResourceDictionary. So next you'll move your BlueButtonControl resource from Window1.xaml to ApplicationResourceDictionary.xaml:

1. Open Window1.xaml in XAML view.

2. Select the following code for the BlueButtonControl Style and cut it out of the XAML (by right-clicking and clicking Cut, or by holding Ctrl+X, or by clicking Edit ➤ Cut).

```
<Style x:Key="BlueButtonControl" BasedOn="{x:Null}"
TargetType="{x:Type Button}">
  <Setter Property="Template">
```

```xml
        <Setter.Value>
          <ControlTemplate TargetType="{x:Type Button}">
           <Grid>
                <Rectangle Stroke="#FF000000" RadiusX="11.5"
RadiusY="11.5">
                    <Rectangle.Fill>
                      <LinearGradientBrush EndPoint="0.5,2.292"
StartPoint="0.5,0.111">
                          <GradientStop Color="#FF0C024C" Offset="0"/>
                          <GradientStop Color="#FFFFFFFF" Offset="1"/>
                      </LinearGradientBrush>
                    </Rectangle.Fill>
                </Rectangle>
                <ContentPresenter SnapsToDevicePixels="{TemplateBinding
SnapsToDevicePixels}" HorizontalAlignment="{TemplateBinding
HorizontalContentAlignment}" VerticalAlignment="{TemplateBinding
VerticalContentAlignment}" RecognizesAccessKey="True"/>
           </Grid>
           <ControlTemplate.Triggers>
                <Trigger Property="IsFocused" Value="True"/>
                <Trigger Property="IsDefaulted" Value="True"/>
                <Trigger Property="IsMouseOver" Value="True"/>
                <Trigger Property="IsPressed" Value="True"/>
                <Trigger Property="IsEnabled" Value="False"/>
           </ControlTemplate.Triggers>
          </ControlTemplate>
        </Setter.Value>
      </Setter>
    </Style>
```

3. Now open ApplicationResourceDict.xml and paste the Style right above the MyListBoxStyle Style.

4. Run the application again by pressing F5.

Notice that the Button looks exactly the way it did before, but rather than getting its Style from the Window1.xaml's Window.Resources, it is getting it from ApplicationResourceDict.xaml. That was very simple indeed, but now that you have done this, you can use this Style all across your application. This would come in handy if you created a custom UserControl, which is defined in a separate XAML file, and wanted to use a Style defined in the ResourceDictionary. You will be doing this later in the section "Custom User Controls."

Replacing text with an image via your Button Style

So, at this point, you still have that pesky "Button" text on your Button. Say you want to have an icon on your button rather than text. You can set that up in the Style you have created for your Button. You'll do that next.

First you need to import an image into your project:

1. In Blend 2, right-click the project in the Project panel and click Add ➤ New Folder.

2. Name the new folder Images.

3. Right-click the Images folder you just created and click Add ➤ Existing Item (or simply drag an image from your hard drive to the new Images folder).

4. Navigate to an image you would like to use and select it. (I suggest an image with a height of around 300 pixels, because this image is going to have to fit into a Button control, and you don't want it too big.)

> *You could use a large image and scale it down, but the application may run slowly and act sluggish because even though the image has been scaled down, a large image will still have a large amount of pixel information that has to be processed.*

Now that you have a new image file imported into the project, you need to edit the Button Style so that the Button will display the new image. But first, you'll get rid of the "Button" text:

5. Delete the text Button from the Content property in the XAML so that the code now looks like this:

```
<Button x:Name="myButton"
    HorizontalAlignment="Left"
    Margin="138,148,0,0"
    Style="{DynamicResource BlueButtonControl}"
    VerticalAlignment="Top"
    Width="129" Height="36"
/>
```

You can also remove this text in Blend 2 visually by removing the text Button in the Content property box of the Common Properties section of the Properties panel. I only had you do it in the XAML because you are going to change the Button Style to incorporate the image in XAML.

6. Now that you have that done, open the ApplicationResourceDictionary.xaml file and find the Style named BlueButtonControl.

If you look, you will see the ControlTemplate section. This is where the layout of the Button is defined, and it is here you are going to want to add an Image control. So do that now:

1. Open the ResourceDictionary in Visual Studio 2008, as you want to make use of its IntelliSense feature.

Below the ContentPresenter is where you are going to add the Image control because, remember, controls nearer the bottom of the XAML (and Visual Tree) show up at the top visually (i.e., if you declare your Image before the Rectangle in the XAML, you will never see it because it will be behind the Rectangle visually).

2. Start typing <Image until IntelliSense gives you the option of Image and press Enter.

3. Start typing source, and when IntelliSense shows Source, press Enter, and for the source specify the path to your imported image (mine is Images/shay.tif).

4. There are many other attributes you could add, but for the purposes of this exercise, this is sufficient. Run your application, and you should see your Image over your Button as shown in Figure 7-17.

Figure 7-17. The ControlTemplate for the Button control contains an Image control.

Pretty cool, huh?

Using your Style and ControlTemplate on multiple Button controls

So, now let's see the real power of a ControlTemplate by creating a regular Button in the Workspace in Blend 2 and then applying your ControlTemplate to it. Close the running application, switch back to Blend 2, and reload the project.

1. Select the Button tool on the toolbar and draw a Button control in the Workspace.

2. Right-click the new Button control, select Edit Control Parts (Template) ➤ Apply Resource, and choose your BlueButtonControl ControlTemplate.

Notice that in an instant the new Button now looks just like the original Button (see Figure 7-18).

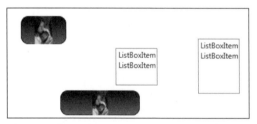

Figure 7-18. In an instant, you can apply a Button Style with a ControlTemplate to a new Button.

You should be able to see the usefulness of ControlTemplates especially in applications that have many items that look similar such as Buttons. For example, say you wanted a navigation bar that has many instances of BlueButtonControl, but each has different text. You could make many instances of generic Button controls and apply the BlueButtonControl Style (which contains the ControlTemplate) to them all and set different Text properties for each. You'll do that now:

1. Erase the current Button controls you have in the Workspace.

2. Select the Button tool from the toolbar.

3. Draw one Button control in the Workspace.

4. Select that Button and apply the BlueButtonControl Style to it.

5. Copy that Button and paste in three more instances so that you have four Buttons in the Workspace (see Figure 7-19).

6. Select all four Buttons, right-click, and select Group Into ➤ ViewBox. This allows you to move the navigation around as a group. Further, if you scale the ViewBox, all items inside of it will scale as well. As you learned in Chapter 5, this is the only control that will allow for this.

Figure 7-19. Four Buttons in a ViewBox, all using the BlueButtonControl Style

You have a problem; if you look closely, you will notice that the text is behind your image. That is not good because you want to be able to see it. You solve this problem by following these steps:

7. Go into ApplicationResourceDictionary.xaml.

8. Find the BlueButtonControl Style.

9. Change the order in the ControlTemplate so that the Image control appears before the ContentPresenter (the ContentPresenter is the control that displays text). Your code should now look like this:

```
<ControlTemplate TargetType="{x:Type Button}">
    <Grid>
        <Rectangle Stroke="#FF000000" RadiusX="11.5" RadiusY="11.5">
            <Rectangle.Fill>
                <LinearGradientBrush EndPoint="0.5,2.292"
StartPoint="0.5,0.111">
                    <GradientStop Color="#FF0C024C" Offset="0"/>
                    <GradientStop Color="#FFFFFFFF" Offset="1"/>
                </LinearGradientBrush>
            </Rectangle.Fill>
        </Rectangle>
        <Image Source="Images/shay.tif"/>
        <ContentPresenter SnapsToDevicePixels="{TemplateBinding
SnapsToDevicePixels}" HorizontalAlignment="{TemplateBinding
HorizontalContentAlignment}" VerticalAlignment="{TemplateBinding
VerticalContentAlignment}" RecognizesAccessKey="True"/>
```

Now look at Window1.xaml in Blend's Design view, and you will see that the text is in front of the image, as shown in Figure 7-20.

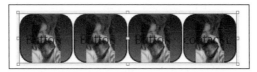

Figure 7-20. Move the ContentPresenter to follow the Image control in the XAML, so the text now appears in front of the Image control in Blend's Design view.

This is looking better, but you still have a little ways to go. Now the text is showing up as you had hoped, but it is black and not very legible when it is over a somewhat dark Image as in Figure 7-19.You could change the Foreground color for each Button, but that would get a bit tedious, so you are going to change the color of the text in the Style so that it will change the text color for all Buttons in one swift move. Do that now:

1. Open ApplicationResouceDictionary.xml.

2. Find the BlueButtonControl Style.

3. In the ControlTemplate, find the ContentPresenter.

4. Add the property TextBlock.Foreground="Aqua" as shown in the following code:

```
<ContentPresenter
    SnapsToDevicePixels="{TemplateBinding SnapsToDevicePixels}"
    HorizontalAlignment="{TemplateBinding HorizontalContentAlignment}"
    VerticalAlignment="{TemplateBinding VerticalContentAlignment}"
    RecognizesAccessKey="True"
    TextBlock.Foreground="Aqua"
/>
```

5. Run the application.

You will see that all of the navigation Buttons have a Foreground color that is legible against a dark background (see Figure 7-21).

Figure 7-21. Changing the way that every Button that uses your BlueButtonControl displays its text

Now, all you need to do is change each Button's Content property to reflect what the text for that Button should be. This is something you don't want to set in the ControlTemplate because each Button obviously will have a different Content attribute. This can be done right in the XAML for each Button or by selecting each Button in the Workspace and modifying its Content property in the Common Properties section of the Properties panel.

6. Set the text of your Buttons to be home, about us, links, and contact us (common navigation buttons for most small web sites), as shown in Figure 7-22.

Figure 7-22. Setting the Content property (i.e., text) for each Button to have a different name

Imagine now if you had to create each Button by hand. You would have to create a Rectangle and match the gradient to be like the other Buttons. You would then have to turn it into a Button using Blend's Make a Button feature. You would then have to add an Image control and set the Foreground property of the ContentPresenter. Sounds like a lot of work, doesn't it? Indeed it is, and that is why Styles with ControlTemplates are so powerful. It takes a bit of time to set up the Style with a ControlTemplate, but once it is built, it is very easy to implement on other controls of the same type.

Wiring up the home Button

So, now just to keep your event handling skills sharp and to make this project actually *do* something, you'll wire up the home Button:

1. Select the home Button.

2. Give it a name in the Name section of Blend's Properties panel of myButton.

Now that you have given this Button a name, you can control it via code. But first, you'll put an Image control in the Workspace and make it hidden. Then when the home Button is clicked, it will toggle the visibility of the Image control.

1. In Blend 2 in the Project panel, double-click the image in the Images directory; this will place an Image control in the Workspace with the Source property set to that of the image you just clicked.

2. Give the new Image control a name of myImage.

3. Set the Visibility of myImage to Hidden in the Appearance section of the Properties panel.

4. Save the project and switch to Visual Studio 2008 to code the logic.

5. Reload the project in Visual Studio 2008 when prompted to do so.

In order to create a toggle button, you are going to need a variable that knows whether or not myImage is Hidden or Visible You can do that by continuing with these steps:

6. Open Window1.xaml.cs.

7. Above the constructor, declare a private Boolean called _isHidden, as shown in the following code, and declare it as true because myImage by default is Hidden:

```
public partial class Window1 : System.Windows.Window
    {
        private Boolean _isHidden = true;
```

```
public Window1()
{
    InitializeComponent();

}

}
```

8. Now in the constructor, you need to create an EventHandler for the home Button:

```
public partial class Window1 : System.Windows.Window
    {
        private Boolean _isHidden = true;
        public Window1()
        {
            InitializeComponent();
            this.myButton.Click += new
RoutedEventHandler(myButton_Click);

        }

        void myButton_Click(object sender, RoutedEventArgs e)
        {
            throw new Exception("The method or operation is not
implemented.");
        }

    }
```

> To let Visual Studio 2008 help you to create an EventHandler, click the name of the control, type .Click+= and press the Tab key twice. Visual Studio 2008 will create an EventHandler for you.

9. In the EventHandler, remove the following default code:

```
throw new Exception("The method or operation is not implemented.");
```

10. Now you need to create a conditional statement that checks to see whether _isHidden is true or false and turn on or off the Visibility of myImage depending upon the value of that variable. You also need to set the _isHidden variable to false if it is true and to true if it is false:

```
void myButton_Click(object sender, RoutedEventArgs e)
        {
            if (_isHidden == true)
            {
                _isHidden = false;
                this.myImage.Visibility = Visibility.Visible;
            }
            else
```

```
            {
                _isHidden = true;
                this.myImage.Visibility = Visibility.Hidden;
            }
        }
```

11. Run the application.

Now you will see that your home Button does in fact toggle the visibility of your myImage control as shown in Figures 7-23 and 7-24.

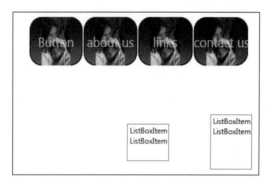

Figure 7-23. The application before you click the home Button.

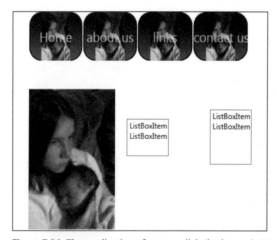

Figure 7-24. The application after you click the home Button

Custom UserControls

A UserControl in WPF allows developers to create custom controls much like controls that ship with Blend 2, such as the Button control. You can specify how your custom controls look as well as

EventHandlers for their behavior. In the preceding exercises, you used a Style with a ControlTemplate to make your navigation Buttons look a certain way, that is, a Rectangle with an Image control. What if you wanted to simplify that process, that is, avoid having to create a Button in the Workspace and then tell that Button to use the Style resource with your ControlTemplate in it? What if you wanted to have a BlueButton UserControl that allowed you to draw a BlueButtonControl right in the Workspace just like you did when you created a plain old Button control? The answer is you can take all of the resources that you have already created in this chapter and make a BlueButton UserControl that does in fact allow you to just draw a BlueButtonControl in the Workspace much like you do for the standard WPF Button control. I'll show you how to do that now!

1. In Blend 2, right-click the project and select Add New Item.

2. Under installed templates, select UserControl.

3. Give your new UserControl the name of BlueButtonUserControl.

4. Make sure the Include Code File option is selected, because this is where you can add EventHandlers.

5. Click OK.

Blend 2 creates a BlueButtonUserControl.xaml file as well as a code-behind BlueButtonUserControl. xaml.cs file. Blend immediately opens up BlueButtonUserControl.xaml and allows you to start designing your new UserControl. Do that now:

6. Select the Button tool on the toolbar (this is the last time you will have to do this to create a BlueButtonControl).

7. Right-click the new Button control and select Edit Control Parts (Template) ➤ Apply Resource of BlueButtonControl.

You can see that immediately your new Button control looks just like your BlueButtonControl. But notice the UserControl is much bigger than your BlueButtonControl. Follow these steps to remedy this:

8. Move the BlueButtonControl up to the very top left of the UserControl by dragging it in the Workspace.

9. Select the UserControl in the Objects and Timeline panel.

10. Adjust the height and width to be just about the same size as the BlueButtonControl by using the Selection tool to scale the UserControl.

11. Hold down the Ctrl+Shift keys and press the B key (or click Project ➤ Build Solution in the menu bar) to compile (not run) the application.

12. Go back to Window1.xaml.

So that is it, you have created a custom UserControl that you can use just like a built-in control such as a WPF Button. I guess at this point you would like me to show you how to use this new custom control. Oh ye of little faith. OK, to see the new BlueButtonUserControl in action, follow these steps:

1. In Blend, click the Asset Library button in the toolbar.

2. Click the Custom Controls tab, and you will see your BlueButtonUserControl (see Figure 7-25).

3. Select your BlueButtonUserControl.

4. Draw a `BlueButtonUserControl` in the Workspace.

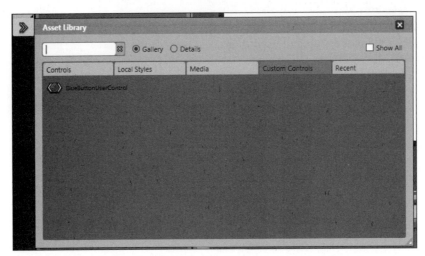

Figure 7-25. Under Custom Controls in the Asset Library, you can see your custom UserControls.

That is all there is to it. You can see in Figure 7-26 that I drew a bunch of them out, all with different sizes.

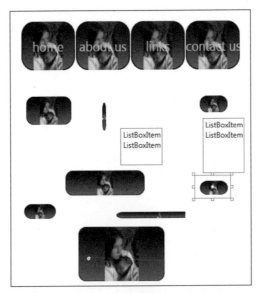

Figure 7-26. You can use your new UserControl just like the Button control and draw out as many BlueButtonControls in the Workspace as you like.

But now, say you want to give the new UserControl you just drew in the Workspace some functionality. You would have a hard time doing that because the Button, which has a Click event, is wrapped inside a UserControl, which does not have the Click event. However, the Button you drew inside of the UserControl does. So, in order to get the Click event of the Button inside the UserControl, you need to name both the UserControl you just drew in the Workspace as well as the Button inside of the UserControl. So do that now.

1. Open BlueButtonUserControl.xaml and select the Button in the Objects and Timeline panel.

2. In the Properties panel, name the Button InsideButton.

3. Press F5 to compile the application.

4. Close the file.

5. Now in Window1.xaml, name the UserControl at the very bottom of the Workspace myBlueButtonUC ("UC" for UserControl).

6. Press F5 again to compile the application, stop the application, and switch over the Visual Studio 2008.

Now you are ready to give myBlueButtonUC functionality. To make it easy, you will just give it the same functionality that you gave to the home Button:

7. Under your myButton code, type myBlueButton and a dot.

8. Find InsideButton in the IntelliSense list, click it, and type another dot.

9. Find Click in the IntelliSense list and click it.

10. Type += and click the Tab key twice, and you should see something like this code here:

```
public Window1()
        {
            InitializeComponent();
            this.myButton.Click
+= new RoutedEventHandler(myButton_Click);
            myBlueButtonUC.InsideButton.Click
+= new RoutedEventHandler(InsideButton_Click);

        }

        void InsideButton_Click(object sender, RoutedEventArgs e)
        {
            throw new Exception
("The method or operation is not implemented.");
        }
```

11. Delete the new EventHandler called InsideButton_Click and change the method that is invoked to the same one that myButton uses so that myButton and myBlueButtonUC both run the same method when clicked. Your code should look as follows:

```
private Boolean _isHidden = true;
        public Window1()
        {
            InitializeComponent();
            this.myButton.Click
```

```
        += new RoutedEventHandler(myButton_Click);
                myBlueButtonUC.InsideButton.Click
  += new RoutedEventHandler(myButton_Click);

        }

        void myButton_Click(object sender, RoutedEventArgs e)
        {
            if (_isHidden == true)
            {
                _isHidden = false;
                this.myImage.Visibility = Visibility.Visible;
            }
            else
            {
                _isHidden = true;
                this.myImage.Visibility = Visibility.Hidden;
            }
        }
}
```

12. Now press F5 to compile and run the application, and click myBlueButtonUC. It will have the same functionality as the home Button in the ViewBox. Also, the functionality of the home Button is not affected at all, as both controls are using the same method.

So now you can see how easy it is to make your own custom UserControl and use it very quickly.

> *A compressed file containing a finished version of the application you just created can be found at* www.windowspresentationfoundation.com/bookDownloads/ ControlTemplateProject.zip.

Summary

This was a very exciting chapter in that you have now been exposed to some very powerful features that WPF incorporates to promote reusability, encapsulation, and the capability to not rely only on built-in WPF controls. In this chapter, you learned what a ControlTemplate is and how to create one inside of a Style for a Button control. You then explored Styles and how they work with ControlTemplates. You then saw how to use Styles to do things like overwrite the default properties of a control such as a ListBox or to make a Button control display an Image control. You also learned how and why to put Styles in ResourceDictionaries. I showed you how you can create simple WPF controls such as Buttons and apply your Style resources to them quickly and easily to save time. Finally, you took everything you learned and made your very own custom UserControl, which you were then able to use like a regular WPF Button control, complete with functionality that makes use of a method that you had created earlier in the chapter.

In the next chapter, I am going to go into more detail about events and EventHandlers and teach you about the many different ones there are and how they work.

Chapter 8

EVENTS AND EVENTHANDLERS

What this chapter covers:

- What are events and EventHandlers
- Creating a project and exploring and creating some different events

All WPF objects have a set of events that fire when users interact with them. You have already seen some events in earlier chapters. For example, in the previous chapter, you saw how a Button has an event called Click. This event is exclusive to the Button class in WPF. You listened for the Click event and then created a method (sometimes mistakenly referred to as a function) to "handle" that event, and thus you created an EventHandler. So you now know that objects have events. You also know that any method or function that is called when an event is fired is called an EventHandler. In this chapter, I am going to discuss the many different events that objects have, from the Click event you have already encountered to the MouseWheel event. You are going to create EventHandlers for all of these different events as well. So let's get started and create a new WPF project.

Creating an EventAndEventHandlers project

As I have stated so many times before, this is a very hands-on book, so now would be a great time to create a new WPF Application project and start exploring events and

EventHandlers with hands-on examples because, as you might have guessed, I am of the opinion that people learn best by doing rather than just reading. So let's do that now:

1. Open Visual Studio 2008.

2. Select File ➤ New Project, and choose WPF Application.

3. Give the project the name of EventsAndEventHandlers. Choose a location to save the project, and click OK (see Figure 8-1).

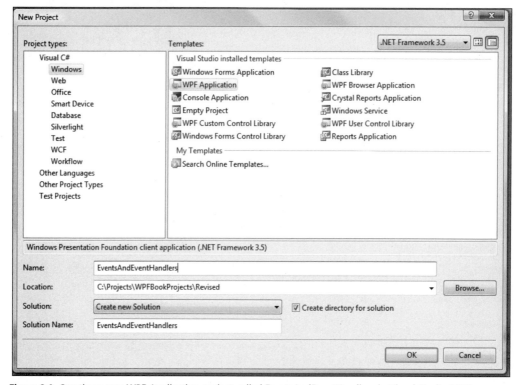

Figure 8-1. Creating a new WPF Application project called EventsAndEventHandlers in Visual Studio 2008

4. Make a mental note of where the project was created, as we are about to open it in Blend 2.

5. Now, open Blend 2, navigate to where you saved the project, and then open it.

6. Now that you have your project created in Blend 2, select the Button tool from the toolbar and draw a Button control in the Workspace like I have done in Figure 8-2.

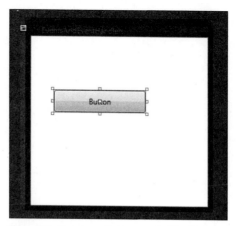

Figure 8-2. Drawing a Button control in the Workspace in Blend

7. Now save the project and switch back to Visual Studio 2008, and when prompted to reload the project, select Yes.

8. Now that you have a Button in the XAML, you need to give it a unique name so that you can control it programmatically in the C# of Window1.xaml.cs. So in Window1.xaml, locate the XAML of your Button and give it the name of MyButton as shown in the following code:

```
<Button x:Name="myButton"
Margin="37,84,101,0"
VerticalAlignment="Top"
Height="34"
Content="Button"
/>
```

> For easier-to-read XAML, you can restructure your code so that each property is on its own line.

9. Press F6 to recompile the project without running it. Remember, this is a handy feature that Blend does not yet have.

10. So now that you have named your Button and recompiled the application, open Window1.xaml.cs and in the constructor below the code that reads InitializeComponent();, type the Button name and type a . (dot). You will see an IntelliSense drop-down menu of the events that your Button has.

> *Quite a list of events for a* Button *will appear in the IntelliSense drop-down menu; however, many of these are very advanced and out of the scope of this book. If you would like to know more about each of these events, the Microsoft Windows Software Development Kit for Windows Vista and .NET Framework 3.0 Runtime Components would be a great place to learn more about them. You can download this SDK from Microsoft directly here:* www.microsoft.com/downloads/details. aspx?familyid=C2B1E300-F358-4523-B479-F53D234CDCCF&displaylang=en.

Let's go over the events that you would commonly use for a Button.

Click

You have actually coded for the Click event in the last chapter, but since it is the first event listed in the IntelliSense list, let's review it here. You'll code for it again, as you can never practice too much when it comes to coding.

1. After you click the Click event in IntelliSense, type += and press the Tab key twice. Visual Studio 2008 creates the event and the EventHandler method stub for you.

2. In the new method stub, remove the default text of throw new NotImplementedException();. Replace it with a MessageBox as shown here:

```
public partial class Window1 : Window
    {
public Window1()
        {
            InitializeComponent();
            myButton.Click += new RoutedEventHandler(myButton_Click);
        }

        void myButton_Click(object sender, RoutedEventArgs e)
        {
            MessageBox.Show("I was Clicked");
        }
    }
```

3. Press F5 to compile and run the application.

Now you can click the Button and see a MessageBox with the message "I was Clicked."

That was simple enough, so let's move on to the next event in the IntelliSense list, DragEnter. Delete the code you just created before you try the next exercise.

DragEnter

The DragEnter event will occur when you drag an item from your desktop, say a JPEG image you have, over another object. You'll see an example of this now. The first thing you need to do is to tell your application that you want to be able to drag items onto it. In order to do that, you need to set the AllowDrop property in Window1 to true.

1. Set the `AllowDrop` property to true now so that your code looks like the following code.

> *The following code in bold may have been added by Blend and will crash the application in Visual Studio. If Blend has added the bold code, delete it.*

```
<Window
xmlns="http://schemas.microsoft.com/winfx/2006/xaml/presentation"
xmlns:x="http://schemas.microsoft.com/winfx/2006/xaml"
xmlns:Microsoft_Windows_Themes="clr-namespace:Microsoft.Windows.
Themes;assembly=PresentationFramework.Aero"
x:Class="EventsAndEventHandlers.Window1"
Title="EventsAndEventHandlers"
Height="300" Width="300"
AllowDrop="True"
>
```

2. Now you have to add the DragEnter EventHandler into `Window1.xaml.cs` just below the constructor as shown here:

```
public Window1()
        {
            InitializeComponent();
            myButton.DragEnter += new
DragEventHandler(myButton_DragEnter);


        }

        void myButton_DragEnter(object sender, DragEventArgs e)
        {
            MessageBox.Show("DragEnter");
        }
```

3. Compile and run the application by pressing F5, and drag an item from your personal hard drive into the application window, and you will see the MessageBox shown in Figure 8-3.

Erase the DragEnter code, and let's move on to the next event, DragLeave.

Figure 8-3. A MessageBox for the DragEnter event

DragLeave

The DragLeave event is fired when you drag an item from your personal folders over your Button and then drag that item off of the Button. The simple code for this follows.

1. Use the following code to have MyButton respond to the DragLeave event:

```
public Window1()
    {
        InitializeComponent();
        myButton.DragLeave += new
DragEventHandler(myButton_DragLeave);



    }

    void myButton_DragLeave(object sender, DragEventArgs e)
    {
        MessageBox.Show("DragLeave");
    }
```

2. Run the application and test it. Figure 8-4 shows the results of this new code.

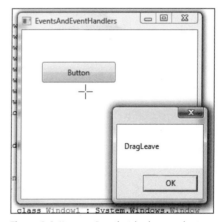

Figure 8-4. MessageBox that is shown when an item is dragged from your personal folders over the Button and then off it again

Erase the code before you move on to the next event, DragOver.

DragOver

The DragOver event behaves much like the DragEnter event in that it will fire when you drag an item from your personal folders over your Button. The difference is that DragOver will fire every time the mouse moves and it is over the target, while DragEnter will only fire when the mouse moves over the target regardless of whether the mouse moves again. The code for the DragOver event follows.

1. Use the following code as a guide and code MyButton to respond to the DragOver event:

```
public Window1()
    {
        InitializeComponent();
        myButton.DragOver += new
DragEventHandler(myButton_DragOver);


    }

    void myButton_DragOver(object sender, DragEventArgs e)
    {
        MessageBox.Show("DragOver");
    }
```

2. Run your application and test it. Figure 8-5 shows the behavior for the DragOver event.

Figure 8-5. The MessageBox that is shown when an item from your personal folders is dragged over your Button

Erase the code and let's move on to the Drop event.

Drop

The Drop event is a very cool one, and I use it to make applications that allow the user to drop content such as images, video, or audio onto the application, where I can then grab that content and display it. For example, I recently made a video player that has a list of videos the user can play, but the user can also drag a personal video and drop it onto the application, and the video will start playing.

I decided it would be a lot of fun and great practice to have you try this out yourself—you'll build an application that allows users to drag and drop a video from their personal folders onto your application, which will then play that video.

You can use the same project to create this functionality. First, delete any code you have for your Button, press F6 to recompile your application, and then switch over to Blend 2 and reload the project. Now let's create your MediaElement:

1. Delete MyButton from the Workspace.

2. Click the Asset Library button on the toolbar and find the MediaElement by typing MediaElement into the search box.

3. Draw a MediaElement control in the Workspace that is roughly 300 by 300 like I have done in Figure 8-6.

4. Give the MediaElement control a name of myME in the Properties panel.

5. Press Ctrl+S to save the application.

6. Switch back to Visual Studio 2008.

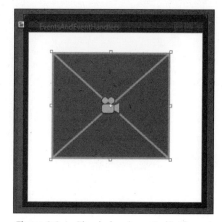

Figure 8-6. In Blend, drawing a MediaElement control in the Workspace

You have already set Window1.xaml to allow for a drop by setting the AllowDrop property, so that is taken care of. Because you don't want the user to have to drop the video or image file directly onto the MediaElement, you are going to put the Drop event on Window1 itself. Before you can control Window1, however, you have to give it a unique name:

7. In the XAML, change Window1 to mainWindow as shown here:

```
<Window x:Name="mainWindow"
xmlns="http://schemas.microsoft.com/winfx/2006/xaml/presentation"
 xmlns:x="http://schemas.microsoft.com/winfx/2006/xaml"
 x:Class="EventsAndEventHandlers.Window1"
Title="EventsAndEventHandlers"
Height="300" Width="300"
AllowDrop="True"
 >
```

8. Now that the main window has the name of mainWindow, you can go into the Window1.xaml.cs code-behind and listen for the Drop event. Change your code so it matches the following:

```
public Window1()
        {
            InitializeComponent();
            mainWindow.Drop += new DragEventHandler(mainWindow_Drop);
        }

        void mainWindow_Drop(object sender, DragEventArgs e)
        {
            throw new Exception
("The method or operation is not implemented.");
        }
```

9. Go into the new `mainWindow_Drop` method and delete the default text that reads `throw new Exception("The method or operation is not implemented.");`.

Now you can add the functionality:

10. The first thing you need to do is to get the path of the file that was dropped onto the window. Here is the code that does this:

```
void mainWindow_Drop(object sender, DragEventArgs e)
    {
        String[] filePathInfo =
(String[])e.Data.GetData("FileNameW", true);
        String draggedImgStr = filePathInfo[0];
        MessageBox.Show(draggedImgStr.ToString());
    }
```

What this code does is

- Create a `String` array called `filePathInfo` that gets the full `Path` of the file that was dropped onto `mainWindow`

- Create a string called `draggedImgStr` and sets its value to the first array in the `filePathInfo` array

- Create a `MessageBox` that shows the value of `draggedImgStr` converted into a `String`

11. Run the application by pressing F5, and then drag an image from your personal folders onto your application. You see the exact results you would expect—that is, the full path of the image that you dragged onto your application (see Figure 8-7).

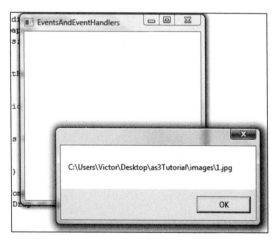

Figure 8-7. A `MessageBox` with the full path of the image dropped onto the application

So far so good. Now that you have the full path, you need to actually do something with it other than to merely display it in a `MessageBox`. What you need to do is to set the source of the `MediaElement` to the path of the value of your `draggedImgStr` variable.

12. To set the source of the MediaElement to the path of the draggedImgStr variable's value, alter your code so it looks like this:

```
void mainWindow_Drop(object sender, DragEventArgs e)
{
    String[] filePathInfo =
(String[])e.Data.GetData("FileNameW", true);
    String draggedImgStr = filePathInfo[0];
    MessageBox.Show(draggedImgStr.ToString());
    Uri uri = new Uri(draggedImgStr);
    myME.Source = uri;
}
```

What you did was to create a new URI variable named, simply enough, uri. You can think of a URI basically as a URL (I covered URIs in greater detail back in Chapter 6). You set that new URI named uri to use the draggedImgStr variable, and you then set the source of the MediaElement named myME to the new uri variable. Pretty simple, wouldn't you say?

13. Now run the application and drag a video file (or an image file if you don't have a video file on your machine) from your personal folders onto the window, and you can see that the MediaElement now plays your video or shows your image depending on what type of content you dropped onto the application window (see Figure 8-8).

Figure 8-8. A video will play when dragged and dropped onto the application.

Cool, huh? You can do this with many media types such as WMV, AVI, MPEG—basically any media type that can play in the Windows Media Player.

Of course, in a real-world application, you would want to make sure that the type of file that was dragged can actually be the source of a MediaElement. For example, a SWF or a Word document would not be a good source for a MediaElement, so you would want to do some checking, and if a file other than an image, video, or audio file were dropped, you would exit out of the method. But for our purposes, I think that this exercise has more than adequately explained the Drop event. Let's forge ahead!

Mouse events

In C#, there are many ways to handle events that involve users interacting with objects using their mouse. I am now going to discuss some of these events. It is also important to note that you are going to create examples of these events using a Button control, but most of these events can just as easily be applied to other objects such as a simple Rectangle, a MediaElement, or even the main application Window itself.

Before I start talking about these events, you'll need to do some maintenance to your application to give you some breathing room and add back a Button control:

1. Make sure your application is saved and switch back to Blend 2.

2. Change the width and height of your application to 800 by 600, respectively. I find the easiest way to do this is to alter the XAML in the Split view and just change the Height and Width properties in the mainWindow node to 800 and 600 (by default, Visual Studio made my mainWindow 300 by 300).

3. The preceding step probably scaled up your MediaElement. Switch to Design view by clicking the Design tab. If needed, rescale your MediaElement to roughly the size it was before by using the Selection tool to select it and scale it back.

I find it is easier to develop visually in Blend 2 with the Design view rather than the Split view, as I do most of my XAML coding in Visual Studio 2008, primarily because it has IntelliSense and Blend 2 does not.

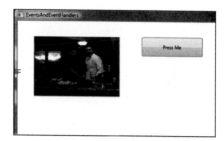

4. Click the Button tool on the toolbar and draw out a Button so that your application looks close to what you see in Figure 8-9.

5. Select the new Button control and give it a name of myButton in the Properties panel.

6. In the Common Properties bucket of the Properties panel, change the Content property to read Press Me.

Figure 8-9. After changing the size of the application, rescaling your MediaElement, and adding a Button control, your application should resemble this.

7. In XAML view, your code should look similar to this:

```
<Window
  xmlns="http://schemas.microsoft.com/winfx/2006/xaml/presentation"
  xmlns:x="http://schemas.microsoft.com/winfx/2006/xaml"
  xmlns:Microsoft_Windows_Themes="clr-namespace:Microsoft.Windows.
Themes;assembly=PresentationFramework.Aero"
  x:Name="mainWindow"
  x:Class="EventsAndEventHandlers.Window1"
  Title="EventsAndEventHandlers"
Height="600" Width="800"
AllowDrop="True"
  >

    <Grid>
     <Button x:Name="myButton"
      Content="Press Me"
      Margin="316,38,313,0"
      VerticalAlignment="Top"
      Height="46"
     />

     <MediaElement x:Name="myME"
      Margin="42,38,0,0"
      HorizontalAlignment="Left"
       VerticalAlignment="Top"
```

```
        Width="218" Height="171"
    />

    </Grid>
</Window>
```

8. Press F6 to compile the application and switch back to Visual Studio so you can explore more events.

MouseDoubleClick

As you can probably guess, a MouseDoubleClick event is fired when the user double-clicks an object. To see how this works, you'll add the MouseDoubleClick event and EventHandler to the myButton control.

1. Use the following code as a guide to wire your myButton control up to listen for and handle the MouseDoubleClick event:

```
public Window1()
        {
            InitializeComponent();
            mainWindow.Drop += new DragEventHandler(mainWindow_Drop);
            myButton.MouseDoubleClick += new MouseButtonEventHandler
(myButton_MouseDoubleClick);
        }

        void myButton_MouseDoubleClick
(object sender, MouseButtonEventArgs e)
        {
            MessageBox.Show("Button was double-clicked");
        }
```

> *I have you leave in the code for the drop functionality and just add to it so that when this application is done, it will still have the drop functionality, and thus will be a little fun.*

2. Press F5 to compile and run the application. You will see a MessageBox appear when you double-click the button (see Figure 8-10).

Erase the event and EventHandler you just coded, and let's move on to looking at the MouseDown event.

Figure 8-10. The MouseDoubleClick event was fired.

MouseDown

The MouseDown event is fired when you click your mouse on an object. This seems pretty straightforward, but there is a catch: if you were to listen for the MouseDown event on your Button, you would not get any results, because a Button control has a Click event. So, you may be asking, why would you want to use a MouseDown event on a Button? Good question; the simple answer is you wouldn't because the MouseDown event is primarily used for controls that do not have a Click event such as the Window. That being said, let's code for a MouseDown event on the Window control named mainWindow:

1. Add a MouseDown event for your mainWindow control. The code is as follows (don't be confused by the Drop event, as you left it in from the previous section):

```
public Window1()
        {
            InitializeComponent();
            mainWindow.Drop += new DragEventHandler(mainWindow_Drop);
            mainWindow.MouseDown += new
MouseButtonEventHandler(mainWindow_MouseDown);
        }

        void mainWindow_MouseDown
(object sender, MouseButtonEventArgs e)
        {
            MessageBox.Show("mainWindow MouseDown");
        }
```

2. Run the application and try it out. As you can see in Figure 8-11, you get the results that you would expect.

> *If you wanted to use a MouseDown-like event on a Button control, you could use a PreviewMouseDown event, because any event with the word "Preview" in front of it will occur before an event without the word "Preview" before it. For example, PreviewMouseDown will fire before MouseDown. In the case of a Button control, PreviewMouseDown will fire before the Click event.*

Figure 8-11. Your MessageBox appears when you MouseDown on mainWindow.

PreviewMouseDown and PreviewMouseUp

PreviewMouseDown and PreviewMouseUp, and Preview events in general, are events that will fire before the actual event, in this case the MouseDown event. This is useful if you want two events to fire one after another. For example, say I wanted to change the color of the background of the window first and then I wanted to change the Content property of myButton. Instead of putting that functionality into one method or function, I could put them into two separate EventHandler methods.

For the purposes of this book, this feature is not very useful; however, just to give a real-world example of applying this functionality, it would prove useful for traffic analysis tools, which require their methods be called isolated from any other action. So, on the PreviewMouseDown, you would make a call to the traffic analysis software that would tell the software you just clicked a Button, and then on the MouseDown event, you can actually do something in the application. Following is the code that changes the Content of the Button on PreviewMouseDown and then changes the color of the mainWindow on MouseDown:

```
public Window1()
        {
            InitializeComponent();
            mainWindow.Drop += new DragEventHandler(mainWindow_Drop);
myButton.PreviewMouseDown +=
new MouseButtonEventHandler(myButton_MouseDown);
myButton.PreviewMouseUp +=
new MouseButtonEventHandler(myButton_PreviewMouseUp);
        }

        void myButton_PreviewMouseUp
(object sender, MouseButtonEventArgs e)
        {
            myButton.Content = "background is now blue";
        }

        void myButton_MouseDown(object sender, MouseButtonEventArgs e)
        {
            mainWindow.Background = new SolidColorBrush
(Color.FromRgb(0,0,100));
        }
```

So what happens in the preceding code is the PreviewMouseDown is fired first when you click the Button, and that is where the background color is set to a SolidColorBrush with the FromRgb values of 0, 0, and 100 (red = 0, green = 0, blue = 100). Then the PreviewMouseUp EventHandler changes the Content property of myButton to read "background is now blue." If you were to compile and run the application by pressing F5, clicking the Button would in fact turn the background blue and change the Content property of myButton to read "the background is now blue" (see Figure 8-12).

Figure 8-12. Now when the Button is clicked, the background turns blue and the Button changes its content.

If you wanted to get even more fancy, you could sandwich a Click event in between the PreviewMouseDown and PreviewMouseUp events so that when myButton is clicked, a sequence of events would occur like this:

- PreviewMouseDown fires.
- Click fires.
- PreviewMouseUp fires.

MouseEnter and MouseLeave

MouseEnter and MouseLeave are two very important events. Most Rich Media Applications have buttons that do *something* when your mouse is over them and then do *something else* when you mouse is not over them, and these events enable you to provide this type of functionality. For example, navigation buttons commonly glow when your mouse is over them, and then the glow will disappear when your mouse moves off of them. In Flash and HTML, this is commonly known as RollOver and

RollOut states, but in Blend, they are known as MouseEnter and MouseLeave, respectively. Try these events out yourself:

1. Add the following MouseEnter and MouseLeave events to your application:

```
public Window1()
    {
        InitializeComponent();
        mainWindow.Drop += new DragEventHandler(mainWindow_Drop);
        myButton.MouseEnter +=
  new MouseEventHandler(myButton_MouseEnter);
        myButton.MouseLeave +=
 new MouseEventHandler(myButton_MouseLeave);
    }

        void myButton_MouseLeave(object sender, MouseEventArgs e)
        {
            myButton.Content = "You are Not Over me";
        }

        void myButton_MouseEnter(object sender, MouseEventArgs e)
        {
            myButton.Content = "You are Over me";
        }
```

2. Run the application and test it. You will see the Content of myButton change when the mouse rolls over the Button and when the mouse rolls off of the Button (see Figures 8-13 and 8-14).

Figure 8-13.
The MouseEnter state

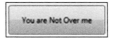

Figure 8-14.
The MouseLeave state

Now erase this code, and let's move on to some more mouse events, starting with MouseLeftButtonDown.

MouseLeftButtonDown

MouseLeftButtonDown is another way to capture when a user clicks an object. But again, like MouseDown, this event will not work for a Button control, because when you click a Button control, the Click event is fired. You can see how this event works by listening for it in the mainWindow.

> *Because many of these mouse events cannot be used on a Button control, they may seem quite limiting; but the fact is that these events are primarily made for those controls that do not have a Click event. When thought of in this context, these events become very powerful.*

1. Add the following MouseLeftButtonDown event to your application:

```
public Window1()
        {
              InitializeComponent();
              mainWindow.Drop += new DragEventHandler(mainWindow_Drop);
              mainWindow.MouseLeftButtonDown += new
MouseButtonEventHandler(mainWindow_MouseLeftButtonDown);
          }

        void mainWindow_MouseLeftButtonDown
(object sender, MouseButtonEventArgs e)
        {
              MessageBox.Show("MouseLeftButtonDown");
        }
```

2. Run your application and test it. You should get the results that you would expect, as shown in Figure 8-15.

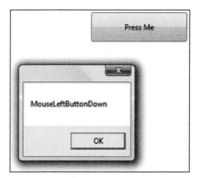

Figure 8-15. When you click your application, you get the MouseLeftButtonDown event to fire.

Erase that code, and let's move on to the next mouse event, MouseLeftButtonUp.

MouseLeftButtonUp

There are times when you don't want an event to fire until the user releases the mouse button. A good example would be a game where the user clicks and holds the mouse to build up, say, fire power. Only when the button is released do you want the event to fire; in this case, a cannon would shoot when the user finally lets go of the mouse. MouseLeftButtonUp allows you to do just this.

1. Add the following code, which listens for and handles the MouseLeftButtonUp event, to your application:

```
public Window1()
        {
              InitializeComponent();
              mainWindow.Drop += new DragEventHandler(mainWindow_Drop);
              mainWindow.MouseLeftButtonUp += new MouseButtonEventHandler
```

```
(mainWindow_MouseLeftButtonUp);
        }

        void mainWindow_MouseLeftButtonUp
(object sender,
 MouseButtonEventArgs e)
        {
            MessageBox.Show("MouseLeftButtonUp");
        }
```

Figure 8-16. When you click your application and then let go, you get the MouseLeftButtonUp event to fire.

2. Run and test your application. You should get the results you would expect when you release your mouse, as shown in Figure 8-16.

Erase that code, and let's keep going.

MouseRightButtonDown and MouseRightButtonUp

MouseRightButtonDown and MouseRightButtonUp are the same as MouseLeftButtonDown and MouseLeftButtonUp except, as I am sure you can guess, these events work for the right mouse button instead of the left. This functionality can also be very useful in a game. For example, you could have a car racing game that added speed when you clicked your mouse and reduced speed when you right-clicked your mouse. This can also be very useful in desktop applications where users have expectations of context-sensitive right-click menus.

1. Add a MouseRightButtonUp event to your application by including the following code:

```
public Window1()
        {
            InitializeComponent();
            mainWindow.Drop += new DragEventHandler(mainWindow_Drop);
            mainWindow.MouseRightButtonUp += new
MouseButtonEventHandler(mainWindow_MouseRightButtonUp);
        }

        void mainWindow_MouseRightButtonUp
(object sender, MouseButtonEventArgs e)
        {
            MessageBox.Show("MouseRightButtonUp");
        }
```

2. Press F5 to compile and run the application, and you will see a MessageBox like the one in Figure 8-17.

Figure 8-17. When you right-click your application and then let go, you get the MouseRightButtonUp event to fire.

3. Add a MouseRightButtonDown event to your application by including the following code:

```
public Window1()
        {
            InitializeComponent();
            mainWindow.Drop += new DragEventHandler(mainWindow_Drop);
            mainWindow.MouseRightButtonDown+=new
MouseButtonEventHandler(mainWindow_MouseRightButtonDown);
        }

        void mainWindow_MouseRightButtonDown
(object sender, MouseButtonEventArgs e)
        {
            MessageBox.Show("MouseRightButtonDown");
        }
```

4. Compile and run the application, and you will see a MessageBox like the one in Figure 8-18.

Figure 8-18. When you right-click your application, you get the MouseRightButtonDown event to fire.

Go ahead and erase that code, and let's move forward to the last mouse event I'll discuss, MouseWheel.

MouseWheel

Another mouse event that is very handy for game or desktop application development is the specialized event called MouseWheel. This event is fired whenever the user scrolls the mouse wheel. You'll try this out now:

1. Add a MouseWheel event to your application by adding this code:

```
public Window1()
    {
        InitializeComponent();
        mainWindow.Drop += new DragEventHandler(mainWindow_Drop);
        mainWindow.MouseWheel +=
new MouseWheelEventHandler(mainWindow_MouseWheel);
    }

        void mainWindow_MouseWheel
(object sender, MouseWheelEventArgs e)
        {
            MessageBox.Show("MouseWheel");
        }
```

2. Compile the application and test it. You will see that you get a MessageBox that reads "MouseWheel" when you scroll the mouse (see Figure 8-19).

You might be saying, "What good is a MouseWheel event if I am not looking to see what direction the mouse wheel is being scrolled?" I hadn't even thought of this until my editor was kind enough to point it out. So, can you determine the direction of the mouse wheel? The answer is yes. You can use something called the Delta of the value to determine this. When the method is fired, MouseWheelEventArgs are passed into the method in a variable named e. The event arguments are variables that are passed into a method, one of which is Delta. The value for this method can be either a negative number or a positive number. If the mouse wheel is moving in the up direction, the Delta will be positive, and if the mouse wheel is moving in the down direction, it will be negative. The following code will pop up a MessageBox that will alert you if the mouse wheel is scrolled up or down:

Figure 8-19. When you scroll the mouse wheel over your application, you get the MouseWheel event to fire.

```
void mainWindow_MouseWheel(object sender, MouseWheelEventArgs e)
    {
        if (e.Delta > 0)
        {
            MessageBox.Show("Mouse Wheel Up");
        }
        else
        {
            MessageBox.Show("Mouse Wheel Down");
        }
    }
```

There are other mouse events, but I have already covered more than will be needed in this book. Again, if you are interested in finding out more about available events, check out the Microsoft Windows Software Development Kit for Windows Vista and .NET Framework 3.0 Runtime Components, as mentioned earlier in the chapter.

> *A compressed file containing a finished version of the application you just created can be found at* www.windowspresentationfoundation.com/bookDownloads/ ControlTemplateProject.zip.

Summary

In this chapter, you learned about some of the most-used EventHandlers such as the various drag events, Drop, Click, and mouse events. You also learned how to use MouseEnter and MouseLeave to create rollover effects for buttons. Finally, you learned about some events that are not used often but can be very handy for game, UI, and desktop application development: MouseRightButtonDown, MouseRightButtonUp, and MouseWheel. There are many other very useful ones, and I would encourage you to use IntelliSense and the .NET 3.0 SDK and play around with some of them.

In the next chapter, you are going to learn about ObservableCollections, binding, and DataTemplates to create a cool image viewer!

Chapter 9

OBSERVABLECOLLECTIONS AND THE DATA FACTORY

What this chapter covers:

- How to import resources such as images into a WPF application
- Understanding the Abstract factory pattern, a common design pattern
- How to use an Abstract factory pattern to create an ObservableCollection of image paths
- How to use an ObservableCollection to create a DataSource
- Using a DataSource to populate a ComboBox
- Creating a DataTemplate that describes to WPF how to display the content of a ComboBox as an Image control and a TextBlock control
- Using an ImageBrush to set the background of a StackPanel in the Workspace to the SelectedItem of your ComboBox

An ObservableCollection is a collection of data that can be watched so that when the collection changes, when items are added or removed, for example, controls bound to that data are updated automatically. In this chapter, I am going to show you how to create an ObservableCollection of images, or rather the path on the hard drive of where the images are located. You will then make use of that ObservableCollection to populate a ComboBox that will have a DataTemplate that tells the ComboBox to show the image and the path of the image. In order to create an ObservableCollection, you are going to make use of a common design pattern called an **Abstract factory pattern**. A **design pattern** is a general repeatable solution to a commonly occurring problem in software design. A design pattern is not code, per se, but rather a template for how to design code to solve problems with many different solutions. Object-oriented design patterns most often show relationships and interactions between classes and objects. Later in this chapter, you are going to create an Abstract factory pattern called an ImageFactory. With that, let's get started.

Creating the ObservableCollection project

Now you are going to create a new project named ObservableCollection. In this project, you are going to create an ImageFactory class that gives you an ObservableCollection of image paths you can then use to populate a ComboBox. Go ahead and create the project now.

1. Open Visual Studio 2008 and create a new project by either clicking Create Project or by selecting File ➤ New ➤ Project. Make certain that WPF Application is selected and give the project the name of ObservableCollection. Make sure to make a mental note of where the project is being saved and click OK (see Figure 9-1).

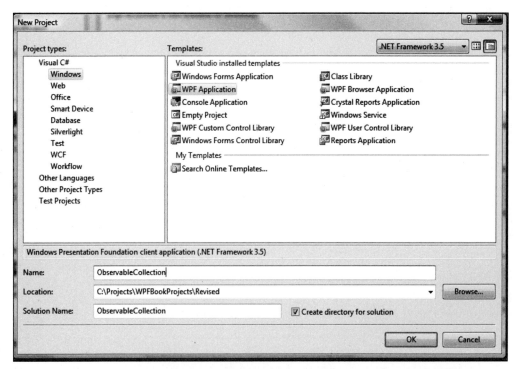

Figure 9-1. Creating a new WPF Application project called ObservableCollection in Visual Studio 2008

2. In Window1.xaml, set the Height and Width of the Window to a 600 by 800, respectively.

Importing the images

Now you need to import images from your local hard drive into the project. It would be a good idea to edit your images in a program such as Photoshop so that they are around 500 by 500. Large images will make the application run very slow and sluggish. Once you know what images you want to use, you can follow these steps to import them into the project:

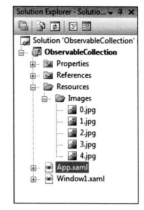

1. In Visual Studio 2008, right-click Solution Explorer, click Add ➤ New Folder, and create a folder called Resources.

2. Right-click the Resources folder, click Add ➤ New Folder, and create a new folder called Images.

3. Now right-click the Images directory and click Add Existing Item. Navigate to where your images are stored on your computer and select them. Your Solution Explorer should look something like what I have in Figure 9-2.

Figure 9-2. My Solution Explorer after importing images

> You can accomplish the same task by creating the folders in Blend 2 and dragging and dropping the images from your local directory right onto the Images folder. This is a brand new feature to Blend 2.

Creating the ObservableCollection with an Abstract factory pattern

The Abstract factory pattern is a design pattern for a common way that programmers structure classes to get data into their applications. An Abstract factory pattern is basically just a class that contains other classes that you are going to create in order to create an ObservableCollection. You'll create your data factory now:

1. Right-click Solution Explorer and click Add New Item.

2. Make sure Class is selected and give it the name ImageFactory as shown in Figure 9-3.

3. Click OK.

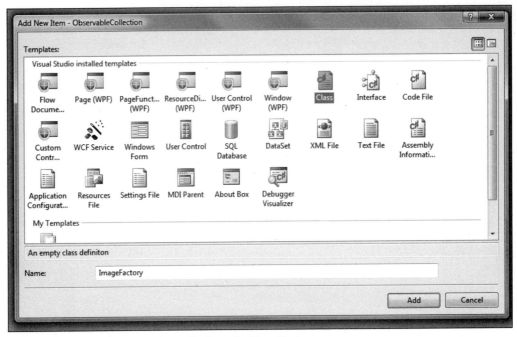

Figure 9-3. Adding a new class to the application called `ImageFactory`

Visual Studio 2008 creates the `ImageFactory` class and opens it up so you can start to develop. The first thing you need to do is to create a couple of variables that you will use inside your class.

1. First, you need to create a public static integer called count. You will use this variable to keep track of how many items you have in your `ObservableCollection`. You may not even use it, but it is good to have in case you decide to make use of it at a later time. Declare this variable right below your class declaration.

```
class ImageFactory
    {
        public static int count = 0;
```

2. Next, you need to declare a private variable that will hold your actual data. It is private because it will not be used by anyone other than the `ImageFactory` class. You are going to instantiate this new private variable as a new Image, which is a class that you will create inside the `ImageFactory` class shortly.

```
class ImageFactory
    {
        public static int count = 0;
private static Images _myactualdata = new Images();
```

3. Now you have to declare `MyImages`, which is going to be part of the Images class that you have yet to create, and give it a return value of _myactualdata.

```
public static Images MyImages
    {
        get
        {
            return _myactualdata;
        }
    }
```

4. Now you can close off the ImageFactory. Your code should look like this for your ImageFactory class:

```
using System;
using System.Collections.Generic;
using System.Text;
using System.Collections.ObjectModel;

namespace ObservableCollection
{
    class ImageFactory
    {
        public static int count = 0;
        private static Images _myactualdata = new Images();
        public static Images MyImages
        {
            get
            {
                return _myactualdata;
            }
        }
    }

}
```

5. Now in the same namespace, i.e., right under your ImageFactory class, you can add the Images class. As shown in the following code, under the ImageFactory class you declare the Images class as a type of ObservableCollection, and you also create the Images constructor with no return type:

```
using System;
using System.Collections.Generic;
using System.Text;
using System.Collections.ObjectModel;

namespace ObservableCollection
{
    class ImageFactory
    {
        public static int count = 0;
        private static Images _myactualdata = new Images();
        public static Images MyImages
        {
            get
```

```
        {
            return _myactualdata;
        }
    }
    public class Images : ObservableCollection<ImageData>
    {
        public Images()
        {
        }
    }

}
```

> *Yes, that is right, a class file can have more than one class declared in it. If you are coming from a background of Flash, your head is probably spinning right now and your heart is pounding with excitement. I know mine was when I learned I could do this.*

6. At this point, your ImageFactory class does not know what an ObservableCollection is, so in order to make use of the set of classes in the .NET System.Collections.ObjectModel, you need to do one of two things: you can either right-click the ObservableCollection and click Resolve ➤ Using System.Collections.ObjectModel; or you can manually add using System.Collections.ObjectModel; below the other using statements at the top of the ImageFactory class. I find it much easier to use the former technique. Once you have correctly accomplished this, you will notice that the code for ObservableCollection becomes a greenish color rather than the default black, and the using statement appears at the top of the class (see the following bolded code).

```
using System;
using System.Collections.Generic;
using System.Linq;
using System.Text;
using System.Collections.ObjectModel;
using System.ComponentModel;
```

7. Now you need to add your images into the ObservableCollection like this:

```
public class Images : ObservableCollection<ImageData>
    {
        public Images()
        {
            this.Add(new ImageData(@"Resources\Images\0.jpg"));
            this.Add(new ImageData(@"Resources\Images\1.jpg"));
            this.Add(new ImageData(@"Resources\Images\2.jpg"));
            this.Add(new ImageData(@"Resources\Images\3.jpg"));
            this.Add(new ImageData(@"Resources\Images\4.jpg"));
        }
    }
```

What this does is to add the image path into your ObservableCollection by calling ImageData, which is a class you are about to define of the type INotifyPropertyChanged; this will take each item in your ObservableCollection and push it into a public string called ImageName. This new class will go directly under the Images class.

8. Add the ImageData class code now:

```
public class ImageData : INotifyPropertyChanged
    {
        private String _sImageName = "";
        public ImageData(string sImageName)
        {
            ImageFactory.count++;
            ImageName = sImageName;
        }
        public String ImageName
        {
            get
            {
                return _sImageName;
            }
            set
            {
                _sImageName = value;
                NotifyPropertyChanged(ImageName);
            }
        }
        public event PropertyChangedEventHandler PropertyChanged;
        protected void NotifyPropertyChanged(String sProp)
        {
            if (PropertyChanged != null)
            {
                PropertyChanged(this, new
PropertyChangedEventArgs(sProp));
            }
        }
    }
```

9. Again, just like with ObservableCollection, the application does not know what INotifyPropertyChanged is, so right-click it and click Resolve ➤ Using System. ComponentModel; and it should change to the greenish color from black.

At this point, your **ObservableCollection** is complete; all you need to do now is close off the ObservableCollection namespace (ObservableCollection is the namespace because it is the name of your project). **Namespaces** define a mechanism for uniquely naming objects, classes, and methods so that these collections can be mixed in XAML without name conflicts. For example, say I have a class that lives in a namespace called Automobiles. In that namespace, I have a class called Tires. That class returns four tires. Now say I have a class called Motorcycles. In that class, I also have a class named Tires, but this class returns only two tires. If I try and run the Tires method, .NET will not know which Tires method I want, the one in Automobiles or the one in Motorcycles, and thus I would have a name collision and a broken application. Namespaces allow the developer in XAML to explicitly target which Tires class to run.

Your project is called ObservableCollection, so your external classes live in the namespace of ObservableCollection. Here is the code in total for ImageFactory:

```csharp
using System;
using System.Collections.Generic;
using System.Text;
using System.Collections.ObjectModel;
using System.ComponentModel;

namespace ObservableCollection
{
    class ImageFactory
    {
        public static int count = 0;
        private static Images _myactualdata = new Images();
        public static Images MyImages
        {
            get
            {
                return _myactualdata;
            }
        }

    }

    public class Images : ObservableCollection<ImageData>
    {
        public Images()
        {
            this.Add(new ImageData(@"Resources\Images\0.jpg"));
            this.Add(new ImageData(@"Resources\Images\1.jpg"));
            this.Add(new ImageData(@"Resources\Images\2.jpg"));
            this.Add(new ImageData(@"Resources\Images\3.jpg"));
            this.Add(new ImageData(@"Resources\Images\4.jpg"));
        }
    }
    public class ImageData : INotifyPropertyChanged
    {
        private String _sImageName = "";
        public ImageData(string sImageName)
        {
            ImageFactory.count++;
            ImageName = sImageName;
        }
        public String ImageName
        {
```

```
        get
        {
            return _sImageName;
        }
        set
        {
            _sImageName = value;
            NotifyPropertyChanged(ImageName);
        }
    }
    public event PropertyChangedEventHandler PropertyChanged;
    protected void NotifyPropertyChanged(String sProp)
    {
        if (PropertyChanged != null)
        {
            PropertyChanged(this, new
PropertyChangedEventArgs(sProp));
        }
    }
  }
}
```

At this point, you want to make use of your new ObservableCollection. So, press F5 to compile the application to make sure you get no errors, close the application, and then you can switch over to Blend 2 and reload the application.

Opening ObservableCollection in Blend 2

Follow these steps to begin using your ObservableCollection:

1. Oftentimes when a project is reloaded in Blend 2, you will have to click the Project tab and double-click Window1.xaml to reopen it. Do that now.

2. From the Blend 2 toolbar, click the Asset Library tool, search for ComboBox, and click it. Draw a ComboBox out in the Workspace like I have done in Figure 9-4.

Figure 9-4. Drawing a ComboBox in the Workspace

3. Put a nice gradient on the Window1 background like I have done in Figure 9-5. Refer back to Chapter 2 if you have forgotten how to do this.

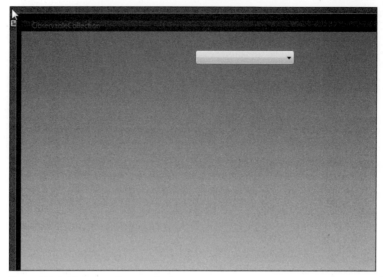

Figure 9-5. Adding a gradient to Window1

Now that you have that set up, you need to create a DataSource that uses your ImageFactory class. This can be coded by hand in Visual Studio or visually in Blend 2. Because it is so much easier to do in Blend 2, I will explain how to do it that way.

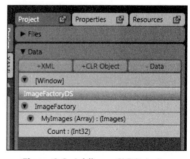

Figure 9-6. Adding a CLR DataSource visually in Blend 2

4. Click the Project tab. Notice the Data section at the bottom of the panel. Click +CLR Object in that section, and Blend 2 will give you a list of CLR objects.

5. Find and double-click ImageFactory, and then click OK (see Figure 9-6).

That's it, you now have a DataSource! Notice, if you will, that in the XAML, Blend has made a Window.Resource node and in it is your new DataSource:

```
<Window.Resources>
    <ObjectDataProvider x:Key="ImageFactoryDS"
d:IsDataSource="True" ObjectType="{x:Type
ObservableCollection:ImageFactory}"/>
</Window.Resources>
```

Pretty cool, huh? Now you need to wire up your ComboBox so that it will display the images held in your ObservableCollection. If you were to simply bind your ComboBox to your ImageFactoryDS DataSource, your ComboBox would simply display the text paths to your images. You want the ComboBox to display the actual image as well as the path of the image. In order to do that, you have to create a DataTemplate that tells the ComboBox how to display its content. To do that, follow these steps:

1. Because Visual Studio 2008 has IntelliSense and you are going to be working right in the XAML, save the project in Blend 2, switch back over to Visual Studio 2008, and reload the project when prompted.

2. In the `Window.Resources` node of your `Window1.xaml`, create a new `DataTemplate` under your `DataSource` node and call it `dtImages` (dt stands for `DataTemplate`).

```
<Window.Resources>
    <ObjectDataProvider x:Key="ImageFactoryDS"
    d:IsDataSource="True"
    ObjectType="{x:Type ObservableCollection:ImageFactory}"
/>

<DataTemplate x:Key="dtImages">
</DataTemplate>
</Window.Resources>
```

3. Now inside here is where you are going to tell WPF how to display your content. The first thing you want to do is to create a `StackPanel` that will house both an `Image` control as well as a `TextBlock` control.

```
<DataTemplate x:Key="dtImages">
    <StackPanel Orientation="Horizontal">
</StackPanel>
</DataTemplate>
```

4. Next you want to add an `Image` control and bind its `Source` property to the `ImageName` value of your `ImageFactoryDS` DataSource.

```
<Image
Source="{Binding Path=ImageName}"
Height="50" Width="50"/>
```

5. This takes care of displaying the image, but now you also want to add a `TextBlock` that will display the path of your `Image`. So under your `Image` control, you are going to add a `TextBlock` control and bind its `Text` property to the same variable as your `Image` control, `ImageName`:

```
<TextBlock Text="{Binding Path=ImageName}"/>
```

So now here is the code for your `DataTemplate` called `dtImages`, located in the `<Window.Resources>` node:

```
<DataTemplate x:Key="dtImages">

    <StackPanel Orientation="Horizontal">

    <Image Source="{Binding Path=ImageName}" Height="50" Width="50"/>

    <TextBlock Text="{Binding Path=ImageName}"/>

    </StackPanel>

</DataTemplate>
```

Simple enough, right? If these concepts seem to be making your head pound, don't fret, as they were very frustrating to me when I first started using them. After doing them time and time again, they start to become second nature, much like any programming language.

So, now what? Now, all you have to do is to tell the ComboBox to use the ImageFactoryDS DataSource, seen in the Windows.Resources section of your XAML, as its ItemSource property and tell it to use dtImages DataTemplate for its ItemTemplate property. Sounds a little confusing, but the following code should make it all clear:

```
<Grid>

    <ComboBox
        Margin="284,29,340,0"
        VerticalAlignment="Top"
        Height="22"
        ItemsSource="{Binding Source={StaticResource ImageFactoryDS},
Path=MyImages}"
        ItemTemplate="{StaticResource dtImages}"/>

    </Grid>
```

Not too difficult, right? But the results are quite cool and powerful. Further, you can reuse your dtImages DataTemplate and ImageFactoryDS DataSource in other places or even other projects. In fact, if you were to move these two resources to a ResourceDictionary (you created one of these in Chapter 7), you would be able to make use of these resources through the entire application time and time again. That being said, let's take a look at your application now.

6. Add the preceding code, and then compile and run the application by pressing F5. Click the ComboBox, and see how it displays the images from your data factory as well as the text paths to them (see Figure 9-7).

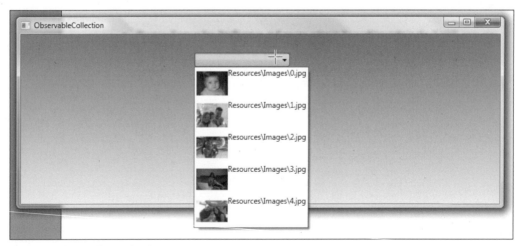

Figure 9-7. The running application

Now this pretty much sums up how to create ObservableCollections and make use of it; but this is a pretty lame application at this point, because you have a ComboBox that allows you to select an image, but you never make use of it. So, in the next section, you'll change it so you will have an application that is kind of cool and useful to you as a reference for future WPF applications.

> *If you were to remove an image from the* ImageFactory *class and recompile, you would see that it is no longer in the* ComboBox.

Doing something with the selected image

So now that you have a ComboBox, you should really have the application do something when you select an image. You'll make it so that when you select an image, the application shows a larger version of that image.

1. Switch back over to Blend 2, reload the application, click the StackPanel tool from the toolbar, and draw a StackPanel on the page under the ComboBox, like I have done in Figure 9-8.

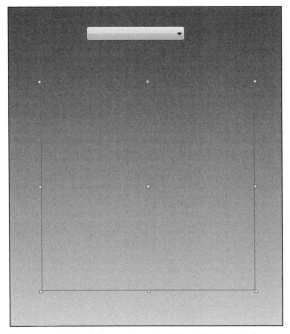

Figure 9-8. In Blend 2, drawing a StackPanel in the Workspace

2. Save the project in Blend 2, switch back over to Visual Studio 2008, and reload the application so you can wire up the functionality in the XAML that will brush the selected image onto the StackPanel.

3. In the XAML, you will see that Blend created a StackPanel that looks something like what I have here:

```
<StackPanel Margin="198,147,238,120"/>
```

What you are going to want to do is change it so that it does not close itself off but rather uses a </StackPanel> tag to close off the control. Change your code to look like this:

```
<StackPanel Margin="198,147,238,120">

</StackPanel>
```

Before you go on, it's important for you to understand what an ImageBrush is. Everything visible in your application was painted by a brush. For example, when you draw a Button in the Workspace, a brush is used to define how the Button's background and foreground are displayed. There are different types of brushes such as SolidColorBrush or a LinearGradientBrush. The one you are interested in here, the ImageBrush, basically paints an area with an ImageSource. And guess what? Your ObservableCollection is just that. With that, you'll paint the background of the StackPanel you just added with an ImageBrush.

Because the ComboBox is bound to the ObservableCollection, you can bind the ImageBrush of the StackPanel to the selected item of the ComboBox. But before you do that, you need to give the ComboBox a unique name.

4. Give your ComboBox the name myCB as shown here:

```
<ComboBox x:Name="myCB"
          Margin="284,29,340,0"
          VerticalAlignment="Top"
          Height="22"
          ItemsSource="{Binding Source={StaticResource ImageFactoryDS},
    Path=MyImages}"
          ItemTemplate="{StaticResource dtImages}"/>
```

5. Now you can go back to the StackPanel and give it a background that is bound to the selected item of the myCB ComboBox. Create a StackPanel.Background node like this:

```
<StackPanel Margin="198,147,238,120">
        <StackPanel.Background>

        </StackPanel.Background>

</StackPanel>
```

6. Inside of that node, create an ImageBrush node.

```
<StackPanel Margin="198,147,238,120">
        <StackPanel.Background>
                <ImageBrush/>
        </StackPanel.Background>

</StackPanel>
```

7. Bind the ImageSource property of the ImageBrush to the SelectedItem of your ComboBox.

```
<StackPanel Margin="198,147,238,120">
    <StackPanel.Background>
    <ImageBrush ImageSource=
"{Binding Path=SelectedItem.ImageName, ElementName=myCB}"/>
    </StackPanel.Background>
</StackPanel>
```

8. Now the background of your StackPanel will be whatever image you have selected in your ComboBox. Press F5 to compile the application, select an image from your ComboBox, and watch the background of your StackPanel change to that image (see Figure 9-9).

Figure 9-9. The running application shows the StackPanel's background is bound to the selected item.

Pretty cool, huh? You might have noticed two issues though. If you look at Figure 9-9, you will see that the ComboBox is too short to accommodate the image thumbnail, and it is not long enough to accommodate the full text path of your image.

9. To fix these problems, switch over to Blend 2, reload the project, and increase the height and width of your ComboBox by selecting it and pulling on the scale handles like I have done in Figure 9-10.

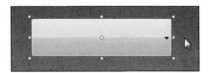

Figure 9-10. Changing the size of the ComboBox in Blend 2

203

10. Press F5 to compile and run the application. When you select an image from the ComboBox, you will see that the ComboBox now has the correct height and width to show both the image thumbnail as well as the full text path (see Figure 9-11).

Figure 9-11. The running application with a scaled ComboBox

So now you have a cool little application that has some fun functionality.

> *You can download the source application at* www.windowspresentationfoundation. com/bookDownloads/3DImage.zip.

Summary

In this chapter, you learned how to import image resources into your project, and then you learned about a common data pattern called an Abstract factory pattern. You used this pattern to create an ImageFactory class that is a series of image paths stored in an ObservableCollection. You then used that ObservableCollection to create a DataSource called ImageFactoryDS. You then used this DataSource to populate a ComboBox that makes use of a DataTemplate that describes to WPF how to show the content in your ComboBox, an Image control and a TextBlock control to be more precise. Finally, you gave your application some further functionality by creating a StackPanel in the Workspace and then used an ImageBrush bound to the SelectedItem of your ComboBox to set the background of your StackPanel to the image you selected in your ComboBox.

Later in Chapter 12, you are going to create an application that starts off like this one but gets *much* more fancy with 3D and Storyboards. I bet you can hardly wait, but before you can do that, you have to learn about 3D in WPF. The next chapter should prepare you adequately, so read on!

Chapter 10

WPF AND 3D

What this chapter covers:

- How to create a 3D image in Blend 2
- Working with ZAM 3D
- Using OBJ files in WPF
- The 3D Tools library

One of the most powerful features of Windows Presentation Foundation is its ability to make use of 3D objects. 3D objects are created in the XAML in what is known in WPF as a Viewport3D. However, trying to create a XAML Viewport3D by hand would be very impractical, if not impossible; you could spend a lot of time at it and still end up with something that looked only somewhat attractive. So for almost all of the XAML Viewport3Ds in this chapter, I am going to show you how to use third-party software such as ZAM 3D by Electric Rain to create your models. You are going to download that program and make use of it in this chapter. Blend 2 at this time has very limited capabilities for creating 3D objects, and I will cover what it can do in this chapter as well. Then I am going to show how to import and make use of OBJ, or object, files. Object files are a common file type for 3D objects that all of the major 3D software programs have the ability to export. Finally, I am going to teach you how to make use of a library called 3D Tools that will allow you to "paint" 2D WPF controls such as a MediaElement onto a 3D object and interact with it. Without this library, you could still "paint" 2D controls onto 3D objects, but you would then lose the ability to inter-act with those controls. By "interact," I mean you would no longer be able to click the buttons. With that, let's get started and make some 3D magic!

Blend and the 3D image

As I just stated, Blend 2 in its current form has very limited capability for creating 3D objects. In order to create a 3D image in Blend 2, follow these steps:

1. Open Visual Studio 2008, create a new WPF Application and call it 3DImage, and take note where Visual Studio is saving the project so you can open it in Blend 2 (see Figure 10-1).

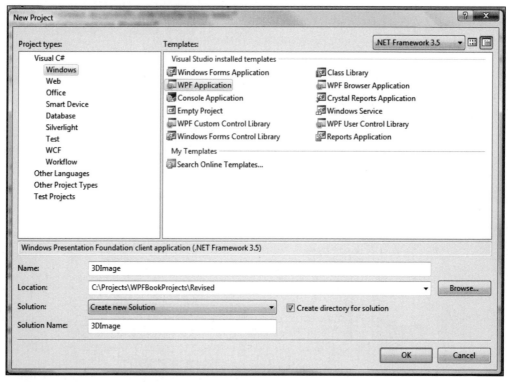

Figure 10-1. Creating a new project called 3DImage in Visual Studio

2. Open Blend 2, navigate to the project, and open it.

3. In the XAML in the Split view, set the Width and Height to 800 by 600, respectively, and click the Design tab to switch to Design view.

4. Now in the Project panel, right-click the 3DImage project and click Add Existing Item (see Figure 10-2).

Figure 10-2. Adding an existing item through
Blend 2's Project panel

5. Now navigate to an image located on your hard drive. If you do not have an image on your
hard drive, you can always go to Google Image Search, find images there, and then save them
to your hard drive.

> Obviously, you should only use these "found images" for personal work. If you're
> doing anything commercial, you'll need to get permission to use them.

6. Once you add an image to your project, you will see it in your Project panel. Double-click the
image, and it will appear in an Image control in your Workspace (see Figure 10-3).

Figure 10-3. Double-click an image in the Project panel, and
Blend 2 will place it in the Workspace.

7. Now with the image selected, choose Tools ➤ Make Image 3D as shown in Figure 10-4.

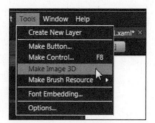

Figure 10-4. Selecting Tools ➤ Make Image 3D

It doesn't look much different, right? But if you look in your Objects and Timeline panel, you will see that your Image control is no longer an Image control but rather a Viewport3D control (see Figure 10-5).

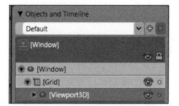

Figure 10-5. Blend has turned your Image control into a Viewport3D control.

So, what is different? Well, you're about to find out:

8. Double-click the Viewport3D control, and you will see the gimbal control, shown in Figure 10-6, that gives you handles that allow you to rotate your Viewport3D.

Figure 10-6. The Viewport3D gimbal control

9. Start to rotate your Viewport3D. You may notice that it is being cut off and bound by the original size of the image, as shown in Figure 10-7.

Figure 10-7. The Viewport3D is being bound by the original size of the image.

10. In order to fix this, double-click an empty space in the Workspace so you no longer see the rotation gimbal control. Click the Viewport3D to select it, and in the Properties panel search for and unselect the ClipToBounds property as I have done in Figure 10-8.

Figure 10-8. If you uncheck ClipToBounds, your Viewport3D will no longer be bound by the original size of your image.

Ahh, now that is better (see Figure 10-9).

Figure 10-9. The Viewport3D is no longer bound by the original size of the image.

11. Now double-click the Viewport3D and play around with the gimbal control to see all of the interesting ways you can now show your image.

Currently, this is the only 3D object that you can create in Blend 2, so once you have had your fill of playing with your application, let's move on and start to use some third-party software to create some cool 3D objects, and then pull them into WPF and add animations to them.

> *Currently this is the only 3D object you can build in Blend 2. You can build 3D objects by hand, but unless it is a very basic 3D primitive, this is not practical.*

Working with Electric Rain's ZAM 3D

Currently the only 3D software program that exports directly into XAML is Electric Rain's ZAM 3D. Electric Rain became well known for its Flash 3D software tool, Swift 3D, and that company is trying to achieve the same thing in the Blend world with ZAM 3D. In order to get ZAM 3D, simply go to www.erain.com/Products/ZAM3D/DefaultPDC.asp and you will see the free download link. You will be asked to register with your e-mail address. Once you confirm your e-mail address, you will be redirected back to the ZAM 3D download page. Once you download, install, and run the program, you will see the ZAM 3D integrated development environment (IDE).

Now that you've got ZAM 3D set up and open, you'll next create some 3D content that you will later bring into Blend.

At the time this book was written, ZAM 3D is/was in a Community Technology Preview (CTP) state, and it is free to download and use.

1. Click the Create Text button in the ZAM 3D toolbar as shown in Figure 10-10.

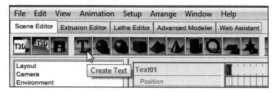

Figure 10-10. Activating the Text primitive tool in the ZAM 3D toolbar

On the ZAM 3D stage, you will see a 3D text primitive that reads "Text," as shown in Figure 10-11.

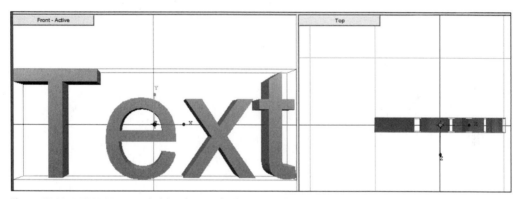

Figure 10-11. A ZAM 3D text primitive that reads "Text"

2. Change that text to read "WPF" by changing the word in the Text box from Text to WPF as I have done in Figure 10-12, and then press Enter.

Figure 10-12. Changing the Text property from Text to WPF

Now you'll give some style to the 3D primitive by applying a material to it:

3. Click the Show Materials button and select the Glossy tab as shown in Figure 10-13.

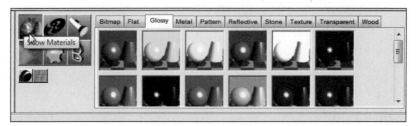

Figure 10-13. Clicking Show Materials and selecting the Glossy tab

4. Select a color and drag it onto your 3D text object, which will change colors as a result (see Figure 10-14).

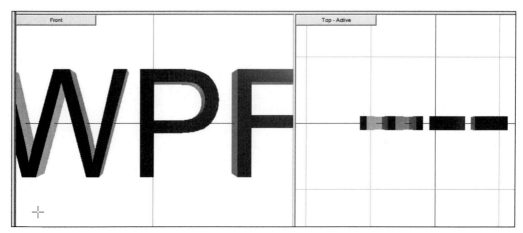

Figure 10-14. Dragging a glossy material onto your 3D text object

Notice only the front of your 3D text object has the material applied to it. You'll fix this now:

5. Drag and drop a glossy material onto the edges of the object as well. In Figure 10-15, you can see I have applied a black glossy material to my 3D text object.

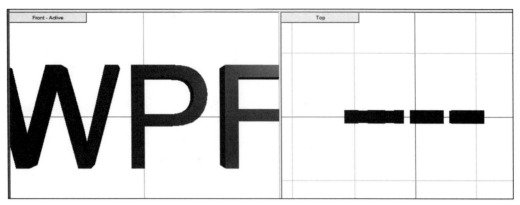

Figure 10-15. Dragging a black glossy material to the edges of the 3D object

6. Now add another object by clicking the Create Torus button on the ZAM 3D toolbar like I have done in Figure 10-16.

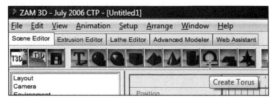

Figure 10-16. Clicking the Create Torus button in the ZAM 3D toolbar

Now you can see a torus on the stage as shown in Figure 10-17.

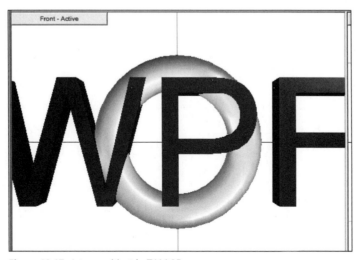

Figure 10-17. A torus object in ZAM 3D

215

But wait, this is not good; your 3D text object and your 3D torus are occupying the same space. You need to place one in front of the other:

7. Select your torus in the Top view and move it behind your text object (see Figure 10-18).

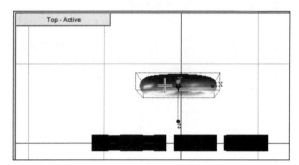

Figure 10-18. In ZAM 3D's Top view, you can select your torus and drag it so that it is now behind your text object.

Ahh, now that looks better. Now you'll add a material to your torus.

8. Select the Show Materials button and click the Stone tab. Drag a stone material onto your torus (see Figure 10-19).

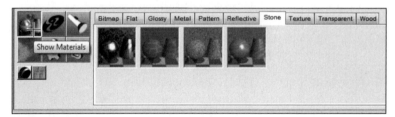

Figure 10-19. Applying a stone material to your torus primitive

Now you have two 3D objects, both with materials applied to them (see Figure 10-20).

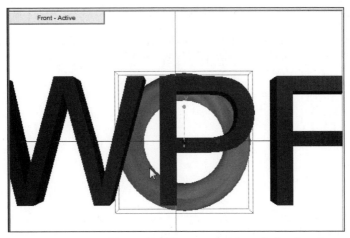

Figure 10-20. Two 3D objects with different materials applied to them in ZAM 3D

Currently, both objects have a default lighting scheme, and you could change this as well as add animations; but for the purposes of this exercise, this will suffice. However, I do suggest you look for tutorials for ZAM 3D online, as you can do some really cool things with it.

So now, export your 3D objects into XAML so you can pull them into Blend 2:

9. Click the front viewport menu to activate it. Click and hold the button that says Front - Active and then click Perspective as shown in Figure 10-21.

Figure 10-21. Choosing Perspective from Front - Menu

10. Click Edit ➤ Copy XAML to copy the XAML to your clipboard (see Figure 10-22).

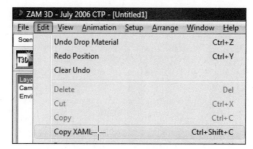

Figure 10-22. Clicking Edit ➤ Copy XAML to copy the XAML for your scene to the clipboard

Now you need to create a new project. You can do this right in Blend 2:

11. In Blend 2, click File ➤ New Project and create a WPF Application (.exe) project called ZAM3DWPF (see Figure 10-23). Click OK.

Figure 10-23. In Blend, creating a new project called ZAM3DWPF

Now in the XAML portion of the Split view, you will see some code like this:

```
<Window
    xmlns="http://schemas.microsoft.com/winfx/2006/xaml/presentation"
    xmlns:x="http://schemas.microsoft.com/winfx/2006/xaml"
    x:Class="ZAM3DWPF.Window1"
    x:Name="Window"
    Title="Window1"
    Width="640" Height="480">
    <Grid x:Name="LayoutRoot"/>
</Window>
```

You can see that Blend 2 created a default Grid with the name of LayoutRoot for you to display your content in. However, Blend 2 also closed off your Grid so that you cannot place anything inside of it.

In order for you to manually place content in this Grid, you need to change it so that it does not self-close, and then add a closing tag for your Grid:

12. Change your XAML code so that it now looks like this:

```
<Window
    xmlns="http://schemas.microsoft.com/winfx/2006/xaml/presentation"
    xmlns:x="http://schemas.microsoft.com/winfx/2006/xaml"
    x:Class="ZAM3DWPF.Window1"
    x:Name="Window"
    Title="Window1"
    Width="640" Height="480">
    <Grid x:Name="LayoutRoot">
        <!-- place content here -->
    </Grid>
</Window>
```

You are now ready to place your cursor between the opening Grid tag and the closing Grid tag and paste in your 3D objects.

13. Select the entire comment line `<!-- place content here -->` (be sure to include the angle brackets) and press Ctrl+V to paste the XAML from ZAM 3D into your project.

I would normally show you any code you pasted in so you could see what it looks like, but if I did so in this case, you would see about 350 lines of code that describes to WPF how to draw the Viewport3D. Since that doesn't make for very good reading, I have decided to not include it here.

Take a look at the code that you pasted in—yes, that is a *lot* of code. But did you notice that right away, in less than a second, Blend 2 displayed your 3D objects in the Design portion of the Split view? How cool is that? Also, do you now see what I meant about trying to create a 3D object by hand in XAML? Looking at the code it generated, it's not really feasible, is it?

One thing that ZAM 3D does that I do not like is it places the Viewport3D into a Viewbox. If you remember, a Viewbox when resized will scale its content. You don't really want that.

14. In the XAML portion of the Split view, delete the following line of code at the top:

```
<Viewbox x:Name="ZAM 3DViewbox"
ClipToBounds="true"
 xmlns="http://schemas.microsoft.com/winfx/2006/xaml/presentation"
xmlns:x="http://schemas.microsoft.com/winfx/2006/xaml"
xmlns:d="http://schemas.microsoft.com/expression/
interactivedesigner/2006"
xmlns:c="http://schemas.openxmlformats.org/markup-compatibility/
2006" c:Ignorable="d">
```

and delete this line of code at the bottom:

```
</Viewbox>
```

Great! Now your WPF project looks just like your ZAM 3D project (see Figure 10-24).

Figure 10-24. Your WPF project in Blend now contains your 3D objects from ZAM 3D.

Working with Viewport3Ds in Blend 2

Before I explain what is going on here, you'll take care of a couple of housekeeping issues with your WPF project:

1. Select the Viewport3D, and in the Layout section of the Properties panel, click the Auto size buttons for Width and Height so that your Viewport3D fills your project (see Figure 10-25).

2. Select the Window in the Objects and Timeline panel. Under the Brushes section of the Properties panel, select the No brush button for the Background property as shown in Figure 10-26.

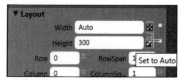

Figure 10-25. Clicking the Auto size buttons for Width and Height

Figure 10-26. Setting the Background property to No brush

Now you are almost ready to start playing around with your Viewport3D. You just need to do one more thing:

3. Uncheck the ClipToBounds property in the Appearance section of the Properties panel. (Remember how it messed up your 3D image earlier?)

Here's where the fun begins:

4. With the Viewport3D selected, select the Camera Orbit tool from the toolbar as shown in Figure 10-27.

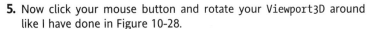

Figure 10-27.
The Camera Orbit tool

5. Now click your mouse button and rotate your Viewport3D around like I have done in Figure 10-28.

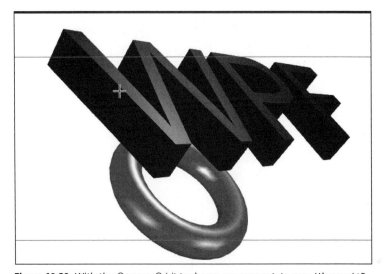

Figure 10-28. With the Camera Orbit tool, you can now rotate your Viewport3D.

6. Hold down the Alt key, and click-hold and drag your mouse to zoom in and out on your Viewport3D as shown in Figure 10-29.

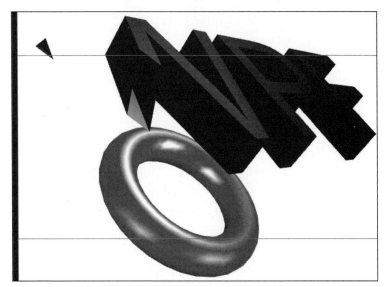

Figure 10-29. Using the Camera Orbit tool to manipulate your 3D objects

221

Hold it, do you see how when you zoom in, your objects start to clip or disappear? This is because you need to change the Near Clipping Plane and Far Clipping Plane properties for the Viewport3D. These properties basically control how close to or far away from the camera an object can get before it disappears from the rendered view. You can fix that as follows:

7. Turn down the Viewport3D arrow in the Objects and Timeline panel, turn down the Camera arrow, and select Perspective like I have done in Figure 10-30.

Figure 10-30. Selecting Camera inside of the Viewport3D.

8. In the Camera bucket of the Properties panel, change the Near Clipping Plane value to a very low number like .01. Now you can see that in Figure 10-31 you can zoom in as close as you want to your Viewport3D.

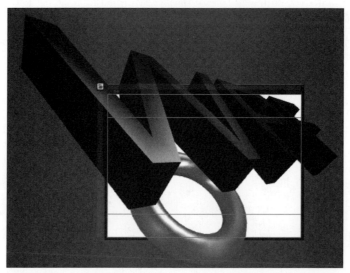

Figure 10-31. Changing the Near Clipping Plane value allows you to zoom in close on your Viewport3D.

9. Later you are going to make your Viewport3D very small, so it would be a good idea to set the Far Clipping Plane to a high number like 100. Go ahead and do that now.

Next, you'll put your Viewport3D to use by making a flyby animation of it!

> *I press Ctrl+Z to undo everything since I first put my* Viewport3D *on stage. Because I did this, I have to again uncheck* ClipToBounds *and also select* No brush *for my window background.*

Creating a flyby animation

Now that you have a Viewport3D, you'll make it do something. I suggest you start off very small and then animate it so that it looks like it is flying toward you and then disappears. Here's how to do that:

1. In Blend 2, select your Viewport3D and select the Camera Orbit tool.

2. Hold down the Alt key, and click-hold and drag your mouse from the top of the Workspace to the bottom until your Viewport3D is very small as shown in Figure 10-32.

Figure 10-32. Making your Viewport3D very small with the Camera Orbit tool

3. Press F7 in Blend 2 to bring up the Animation Workspace.

4. At the bottom of the screen, click the > button to bring up the Create Storyboard dialog box (Figure 10-33).

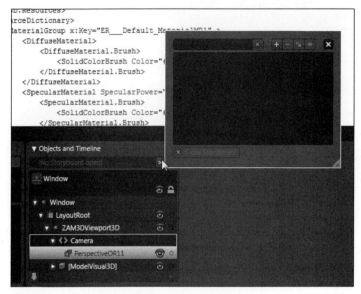

Figure 10-33. Blend 2's Create Storyboard dialog box

5. In the Create Storyboard dialog box, click the + button to create a new Storyboard (see Figure 10-34).

Figure 10-34. Click the + button to create
a new Storyboard

6. A Create Storyboard dialog box will pop up. Name your Storyboard FlyBy and click OK (see Figure 10-35).

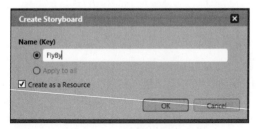

Figure 10-35. Naming your Storyboard FlyBy

Now you will notice that a red line appears around your Workspace indicating that Blend 2 is recording everything you do from this point forward into your new FlyBy Storyboard.

7. On your timeline, move your playhead out to 2 seconds like I have done in Figure 10-36.

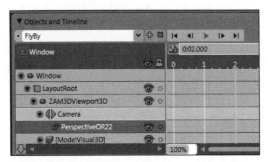

Figure 10-36. Moving your playhead out to 2 seconds

8. Now select your Viewport3D and select the Camera Orbit tool. With the Alt key held down, click-hold your mouse and drag it from the bottom to the top of the Workspace.

9. Do this several times until your Viewport3D is as big as it can get (see Figure 10-37).

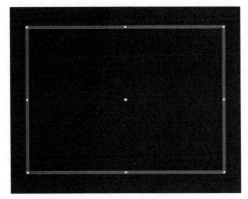

Figure 10-37. Using the Camera Orbit tool to make your Viewport3D as big as it can be

10. Next, move your playhead on your timeline out about a tenth of a second.

11. Double-click anywhere on the window so that your Viewport3D is no longer selected.

12. Press the V key to use your Selection tool.

13. Select the Viewport3D.

14. In the Appearance section of the Properties panel, change the Visibility property of your Viewport3D to Hidden. This will simulate the Viewport3D getting so big that it passes you.

15. Click the red dot at the top of the Workspace that says Timeline recording is on so that it now reads Timeline recording is off.

16. Open the Create Storyboard dialog box again and click the Close Storyboard button as shown in Figure 10-38.

Figure 10-38. Closing the FlyBy Storyboard

17. Press F6 to change from the Animation Workspace back to the Design Workspace.

18. Press F5 to run the application.

Oh yeah, now is that too cool for school, or what? As a challenge to you, I want you to try the following tasks on your own:

1. Remove the Trigger that tells the Storyboard to run when the Window is loaded.

2. Create a Button in the Workspace that is labeled Play Flyby.

3. Use Visual Studio 2008 to run the FlyBy Storyboard when the Play Flyby button is clicked.

4. Make the Viewport3D not become hidden, but rather get larger and then very quickly shrink back down to its starting size.

5. If you want to get fancy, make your Viewport3D rotate so that at its largest point, you are looking at the back of it, and when it shrinks back down, it will also appear to flip back around. You can see this type of logo animation in broadcast graphics.

I suggest you download my example application at www.windowspresentationfoundation.com/bookDownloads/ZAMDWPF.zip so that you can see what the final application should do. Also, if you get stuck with any of the preceding suggested exercises, you can look at my application to see how I did it. Good luck! And, feel free to e-mail me your samples at wpfauthor@gmail.com.

> *As a hint, the following code allows you to run a* Storyboard *from C#:*
>
> ```
> Storyboard board = (Storyboard)TryFindResource("FlyBy");
>
>         if (board != null)
>         {
>             board.Begin(this);
>         }
> ```

Importing and working with OBJ files

Wikipedia describes OBJ files (files with the `.obj` extension) as a geometry definition file format first developed by Wavefront Technologies for its Advanced Visualizer animation package. The OBJ file format is open source and has been adopted by other 3D animation vendors such as 3ds Max, Maya, Poser, Softimage, and Blender, among others. Because the OBJ file format is a data format file, it is perfect for importing into XAML, and you will try that now.

1. In Visual Studio 2008, create a new WPF Application and call it OBJImport like I have done in Figure 10-39.

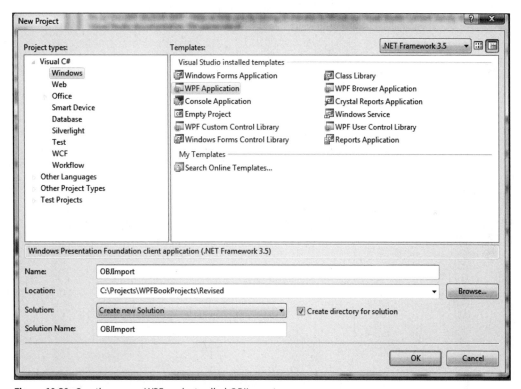

Figure 10-39. Creating a new WPF project called OBJImport

2. Start up Blend 2 and open the project.

Now you need to import an OBJ file. But wait, you don't have one yet do you? Well, if you have a 3D modeling package such as 3ds Max, you can just export any model you like as an OBJ file. Or head on over to this site, www.3dchaya.com, which allows you to download royalty-free OBJ models. I chose one of Ginkakuji temple (www.3dchaya.com/dlrank/dlranklog.cgi?dl=gin00obj) for the exercises in this chapter. Once you save an OBJ model to your hard drive, you can import it into Blend 2.

3. In Blend 2, right-click the project in the Project panel and select Add Existing Item. **Navigate to** where you saved your OBJ model and double-click it. Notice now that in the Project panel you can see your OBJ file (see Figure 10-40).

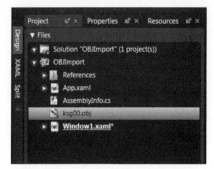

Figure 10-40. The OBJ model now appears in your Project panel.

4. To bring this OBJ model into the Workspace, simply double-click it in the Project panel.

5. Set the size of your project to a Height of 600 and a Width of 800 in the XAML portion of Blend 2's Split view to give you some breathing room.

6. Resize your OBJ model by clicking it and pulling the scale handles so that it is now a pretty good size (see Figure 10-41).

Figure 10-41. My resized Ginkakuji temple OBJ model in Blend 2's Design view

In the tutorial that follows, I use the word "Temple" to refer to my OBJ model. If your model is something different from what I am using, just substitute the appropriate term for your OBJ model wherever you see the term "Temple."

Now you'll do something with your OBJ model: you'll create a button that says Animate Temple that, when clicked, will give you a 360 degree view of the object.

1. Select the Button tool from the toolbar and draw a Button in the Workspace.

2. In the Properties panel, change the Content property from Button to Animate Temple so that you have something that looks like what I have in Figure 10-42.

Figure 10-42. Creating an Animate Temple button

3. In order to program against this Button, you need to give it a unique name. In the Properties panel, give your new Button the name of AnimateButton.

4. With your Button selected, press F7 to show Blend 2's Animation Workspace.

5. Add an event Trigger by clicking the + Event button in the Interaction panel (see Figure 10-43).

Figure 10-43. Adding an event Trigger in Blend 2

Now you will see something that should closely, if not exactly, resemble what I have in Figure 10-44.

Figure 10-44. Creating a new event Trigger

You need to make some changes for this Trigger to do what you want, so do that now:

6. Currently, the Interaction panel is saying this Trigger will occur **When** Window Loaded **is raised**, but you don't want that; you want the event to occur when the AnimateButton button is clicked. So use the drop-downs for When and is raised to select AnimateTemple and Click, respectively, just like I have done in Figure 10-45.

Figure 10-45. Specifying that the event will fire when your Animate Temple button is clicked

> AnimateButton *will not appear in the* When *drop-down unless it is selected.*

Now that you have your Trigger, you need to add an action that will occur once that Trigger is raised.

7. Click the + button next to the Is Raised drop-down menu as shown in Figure 10-46.

Figure 10-46. Adding an action by clicking the + button next to the Is Raised drop-down menu

8. Once you click the Add new action button, Blend will tell you in a dialog box that you need a timeline. Click OK.

Blend 2 then takes the liberty to give you a timeline and name it for you, something like OnClick1.

9. Because this name is not at all intuitive, right-click OnClick1 and select Rename.

10. Change the name to TempleAnimation (see Figure 10-47).

Figure 10-47. Changing the name of the Storyboard from OnClick1 to TempleAnimation

Now in the Objects and Timeline panel, you can see all objects in your Workspace on the left and the timeline Blend has provided on the right (see Figure 10-48).

Figure 10-48. Blend has provided you with a timeline so you can create your animation.

Notice too that Blend 2 has placed a red line around your Workspace; this indicates any changes you make will be recorded into a Storyboard called TempleAnimation.

Here I think it is important to talk about how Blend 2 handles animation. You could place your playhead out at 2 seconds and then rotate your temple. Then when you run your project and click your AnimateButton button, it would work just as you expected it to. However, if you click your AnimateButton button a second time, it would not do anything. Why is this? It is because your Storyboard is just a set of instructions that tell the temple object to spin. If it has already spun to the position you specified (because you already clicked your AnimateButton button and spun it), it will realize this and do nothing. But there is a simple solution: if at the very beginning of your Storyboard you specify a start position, and then move out to 2 seconds and spin the temple object, your AnimateButton button will work every time you click it. So do that now:

11. Leave the playhead at the default position of 0 seconds. Double-click the temple object until you see the gimbal tool as shown in Figure 10-49.

Figure 10-49. Double-clicking the temple object brings up the gimbal tool.

12. Click the Record Keyframe button to record the default axis of the Viewport3D as I have done in Figure 10-50.

Figure 10-50. Recording the default axis of the Viewport3D

13. *Now* you can move your playhead out to 2 seconds, as shown in Figure 10-51.

Figure 10-51. Moving the playhead out to 2 seconds

14. Click the Rotate tab of the Transform bucket in the Properties panel, as shown in Figure 10-52.

Figure 10-52. Clicking the Rotate tab in the Transform bucket

15. With the playhead at 2 seconds, change the Y property to 90 so the model will rotate 90 degrees over a 2-second time span.

16. Move the playhead out to 4 seconds, and set the Y rotation to 180 so the model will rotate to 180 degrees over 2 seconds.

17. Move the playhead out to 6 seconds, and set the Y rotation property to -90 so the model will rotate to –90 degrees over 2 seconds.

18. Move the playhead out to 8 seconds, and set the Y rotation property to 0 to rotate the model to 0 degrees over 2 seconds.

19. Click the close (X) button next to the name of the Storyboard to close the Storyboard.

20. Press F6 to get back to the Design Workspace and out of the Animation Workspace.

21. Press F5 to compile and run your application. When you click the AnimateButton button, your 3D object will spin a perfect 360 degrees over 8 seconds. Very cool!

> *The project you just created can be downloaded here:* windowspresentationfoundation.com/bookDownloads/OBJImport.zip.

Using the 3D Tools library

As I mentioned in the introduction of this chapter, WPF allows you to paint controls onto 3D objects. However, one huge drawback is that those objects, once painted onto a 3D object, can no longer be interacted with. For example, if you painted a MediaElement video player onto a 3D surface, you could no longer interact with its play, stop, or pause buttons. Not good. However, I learned about a library created by the WPF team called 3D Tools at www.contentpresenter.com, a site created by Lee Brimelow that has many wonderful WPF tutorials. I suggest that at some point you go to this site and study some of his tutorials, as they will help you to master WPF.

The first thing you need to do is download the 3D Tools library:

1. In your browser, navigate to www.codeplex.com/3DTools/.

2. Click the Releases button at the top of the page.

3. Download the 3DTools-1.01-bin file.

4. Select I agree to accept the end user license agreement.

5. Save 3DTools-1.01-bin.zip to your hard drive.

6. Unzip the contents.

In Lee Brimelow's tutorial, he shows you how to use the 3D Tools library to put a MediaElement custom UserControl onto the 3D plane mesh. Unfortunately, he does not show how to create a MediaElement custom UserControl. So some who work through the tutorial end up stuck there. Fortunately for you, I *will* show you how to create one, and then, just like I learned from Lee's tutorial, I will show you how to paint it onto a 3D interactive object.

Building a new 3DMediaElementProject

You learned how to build a MediaElement project in Chapter 6. As a refresher, or in case you have not yet read Chapter 6, I am going to once again show you how to create a simple MediaElement with basic stop and play controls.

1. Open Visual Studio 2008 and create a new WPF Application project called 3DMediaElementProject as shown in Figure 10-53.

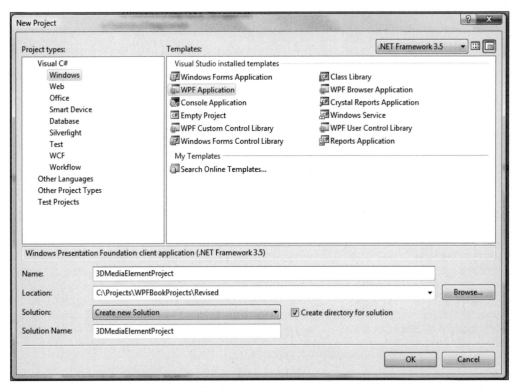

Figure 10-53. Creating a new WPF project called 3DMediaElementProject

2. Open the project in Blend 2. Click Asset Library on the toolbar, select MediaElement, and draw in the Workspace like I have done in Figure 10-54.

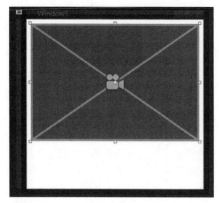

Figure 10-54. Drawing a MediaElement in the Workspace

3. Give the MediaElement the name of ME in the Name field of the Properties panel.

4. Select the Button tool from the toolbar and draw two Buttons under the MediaElement as shown in Figure 10-55.

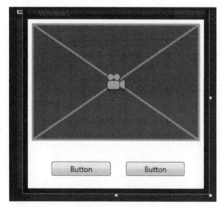

Figure 10-55. Drawing two Button controls under your MediaElement

5. In the Name field of the Properties panel, name the Button control on the left PlayBtn and the one on the right StopBtn.

6. Select PlayBtn, and in the Common Properties bucket of the Properties panel, change the Content property from Button to Play.

7. Select StopBtn, and in the Common Properties bucket of the Properties panel, change the Content property from Button to Stop (see Figure 10-56).

Figure 10-56. Changing the Buttons to read Play and Stop

At this point, you are almost ready to start wiring up your buttons, but you first need to add a video into the project and set it as the source of the MediaElement named ME. Do that now:

8. Locate a video file (WMV or AVI) on your local hard drive.

9. Click the Project tab in Blend 2.

10. Drag the video file from your local hard drive and drop it on the folder named 3DMediaElementProject so that the video appears in your project like mine does in Figure 10-57 (my video is named MVI_1211.AVI).

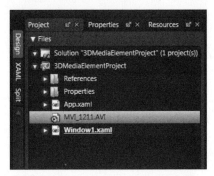

Figure 10-57. Dragging a video file into your project

11. Select your ME MediaElement and in the Media bucket set the Source property to the name of your video file.

12. Press F5 to compile and run the application, and ensure your video plays as shown in Figure 10-58.

Figure 10-58. Running the application to ensure the video plays

Wiring up the buttons in Visual Studio 2008

Great, the video plays like expected. Now you need to switch back over to Visual Studio 2008 to wire up the play and stop buttons. Remember from Chapter 6 that if you want to control a MediaElement with code, you have to set its LoadedBehavior to Manual. When Blend 2 creates a MediaElement, it sets its LoadedBehavior to Play by default. So the first thing you are going to do is set your MediaElement named ME to Manual. Then you will go ahead and wire up the buttons.

1. Close the running application. Switch back to Visual Studio 2008 and reload the project when prompted to do so.

2. Open Window1.xaml.cs.

3. In the constructor under the InitializeComponent statement, set the MediaElement's LoadedBehavior to Manual as shown in the following code:

```
namespace _DMediaElementProject
{
    /// <summary>
    /// Interaction logic for Window1.xaml
    /// </summary>
    public partial class Window1 : Window
    {
        public Window1()
        {
            InitializeComponent();
            ME.LoadedBehavior = MediaState.Manual;
        }
    }
}
```

Now, you have overridden the default LoadedBehavior set by Blend 2.

4. Go ahead and wire up your simple play and stop buttons as I have done in the following code:

```
using System;
using System.Collections.Generic;
using System.Linq;
using System.Text;
using System.Windows;
using System.Windows.Controls;
using System.Windows.Data;
using System.Windows.Documents;
using System.Windows.Input;
using System.Windows.Media;
using System.Windows.Media.Imaging;
using System.Windows.Navigation;
using System.Windows.Shapes;

namespace _DMediaElementProject
{
    /// <summary>
```

```
/// Interaction logic for Window1.xaml
/// </summary>
public partial class Window1 : Window
{
    public Window1()
    {
        InitializeComponent();
        ME.LoadedBehavior = MediaState.Manual;
        PlayBtn.Click += new RoutedEventHandler(PlayBtn_Click);
        StopBtn.Click += new RoutedEventHandler(StopBtn_Click);
        ME.Play();
    }

    void StopBtn_Click(object sender, RoutedEventArgs e)
    {
        ME.Stop();
    }

    void PlayBtn_Click(object sender, RoutedEventArgs e)
    {
        ME.Play();
    }
}
}
```

Notice that under the Stop event, you also tell ME to play so that the video will start when the application is run. Now if you press F5 to compile and run the application, you will see that it works as expected. That is, in order to start the video, you have to click the play button, and the stop button will stop the video.

Making the video 3D with 3D Tools

OK, before you can move ahead and make the video 3D, you need to know something about DLLs. DLL is short for dynamic link library; I know the name doesn't *really* explain what it is or what it does, so I will. A DLL is the extension for a library of part of an application on Win 32 or .NET platforms. DLLs are similar to executable EXE files but cannot be run directly; instead, functions in your code can make use of methods that are inside of a DLL. This allows you to create projects that are then turned into DLLs, which you can then reference from other projects.

To make sure this is totally clear, let's look at an example. Say somebody has figured out a way to make 2D controls function when painted onto a 3D primitive (which WPF cannot do). And say you have a project where you want to do exactly this. Well, you could sit down and figure it out on your own, but that would take a lot of time and effort. A better solution would be to reference the DLL for a project that can do it in your own project and then make use of the methods that allow you to do it. Then voilà! Your project can now have functional 2D controls on 3D objects. Well, the example I have just provided is a real-world example; 3D Tools does exactly this! With that, go ahead and add the reference to the 3D Tools DLL:

1. In Visual Studio 2008's Solution Explorer, right-click the References folder of the project and click Add Reference.

2. Click the Browse tab.

3. Navigate to where you unzipped the 3D Tools zip file.

4. Double-click 3DTools.dll.

Figure 10-59. Adding a reference to the 3D Tools library to your project

It was just that easy to add a reference to the 3D Tools library. You can see in Figure 10-59 the first reference is to 3DTools.

Now, in Window1.xaml, you need to build a 3D object on which you can place your VideoUserControl. Remember that earlier in this chapter, I said that it is possible to build very simple 3D objects in XAML? Well, to show you I am an honest person, I will walk you through doing that here by building a 3D plane object. A **plane** is just that, a simple, flat object like a piece of paper.

5. Put the following code into a <Window.Resources> node:

```
<MeshGeometry3D x:Key="3DPlane"
    Positions="-1,-1,0 1, -1,0 1,1,0 -1,1,0"
    TextureCoordinates="0,1 1,1 1,0 0,0"
    TriangleIndices="0 1 2 0 2 3"
/>
```

Your Window1.xaml code should now look like this:

```
<Window x:Class="_DMediaElementProject.Window1"
    xmlns="http://schemas.microsoft.com/winfx/2006/xaml/presentation"
    xmlns:x="http://schemas.microsoft.com/winfx/2006/xaml"
    Title="Window1" Height="300" Width="300">
    <Window.Resources>
     <MeshGeometry3D x:Key="3DPlane"
     Positions="-1,-1,0 1, -1,0 1,1,0 -1,1,0"
     TextureCoordinates="0,1 1,1 1,0 0,0"
     TriangleIndices="0 1 2 0 2 3"
   />
    </Window.Resources>


    <Grid>
     <MediaElement Margin="8,8,8,76" Source="MVI_1211.AVI"
x:Name="ME"/>
        <Button HorizontalAlignment="Left" Margin="38,0,0,20"
VerticalAlignment="Bottom" Width="95" Height="22"
Content="Play" x:Name="PlayBtn"/>
        <Button Margin="0,0,31,20" VerticalAlignment="Bottom"
Height="22" Content="Stop" Width="95" HorizontalAlignment="Right"
x:Name="StopBtn"/>

    </Grid>
</Window>
```

What you just did was to create a Window.Resource called 3DPlane. You now can start using your 3D Tools library.

In order to use the classes in the 3D Tools library, you first need to create a namespace that will point to the 3D Tools library:

6. Add the following code to the Window node:

```
xmlns:Interactive3D="clr-namespace:_3DTools;assembly=3DTools"
```

Your Window code should now look like this:

```
<Window x:Class="_DMediaElementProject.Window1"
    xmlns="http://schemas.microsoft.com/winfx/2006/xaml/presentation"
    xmlns:x="http://schemas.microsoft.com/winfx/2006/xaml"
    xmlns:Interactive3D="clr-namespace:_3DTools;assembly=3DTools"
    Title="Window1" Height="300" Width="300">
```

7. Now go into your Grid and make a Viewport3D by adding the following code to your Grid:

```
<Grid>
        <Viewport3D ClipToBounds="False">

        </Viewport3D>
```

8. Add a camera to your Viewport3D.

```
    <Grid>
        <Viewport3D ClipToBounds="False">
            <Viewport3D.Camera>
                <PerspectiveCamera Position="0,0,10"
LookDirection="0,0,-1"/>
            </Viewport3D.Camera>
        </Viewport3D>
```

9. Add an ambient light.

```
    <Grid>
        <Viewport3D ClipToBounds="False">
            <Viewport3D.Camera>
                <PerspectiveCamera Position="0,0,10"
LookDirection="0,0,-1"/>
            </Viewport3D.Camera>
            <ModelVisual3D>
                <ModelVisual3D.Content>
                    <AmbientLight/>
                </ModelVisual3D.Content>
            </ModelVisual3D>
        </Viewport3D>
```

10. Next, you start to use your 3D Tools library with the namespace you created earlier called Interactive3D and bind it to your 3DPlane resource.

```xml
<Grid>
        <Viewport3D ClipToBounds="False">
            <Viewport3D.Camera>
                <PerspectiveCamera Position="0,0,10"
 LookDirection="0,0,-1"/>
            </Viewport3D.Camera>
            <ModelVisual3D>
                <ModelVisual3D.Content>
                    <AmbientLight/>
                </ModelVisual3D.Content>
            </ModelVisual3D>
            <Interactive3D:InteractiveVisual3D Geometry=
"{StaticResource 3DPlane}">
            </Interactive3D:InteractiveVisual3D>
        </Viewport3D>
```

11. You need to add a Grid that will house your MediaElement and Buttons inside of the 3D Tools control called an InteractiveVisual3D (this is a custom UserControl from the 3D Tools DLL) like this:

```xml
<Grid>
        <Viewport3D ClipToBounds="False">
                <Viewport3D.Camera>
                    <PerspectiveCamera Position="0,0,10"
 LookDirection="0,0,-1"/>
                </Viewport3D.Camera>
                <ModelVisual3D>
                    <ModelVisual3D.Content>
                        <AmbientLight/>
                    </ModelVisual3D.Content>
                </ModelVisual3D>
                <Interactive3D:InteractiveVisual3D
 Geometry="{StaticResource 3DPlane}">

                    <Interactive3D:InteractiveVisual3D.Visual>

                        <Grid Margin="8,8,8,20">

                        </Grid>

                    </Interactive3D:InteractiveVisual3D.Visual>
                </Interactive3D:InteractiveVisual3D>
        </Viewport3D>
```

12. Cut and paste the XAML for the MediaElement and Buttons into the Grid inside the Interactive3D.Visual node like this:

```xml
<Grid>
        <Viewport3D ClipToBounds="False">
                <Viewport3D.Camera>
                        <PerspectiveCamera Position="0,0,10"
```

```
LookDirection="0,0,-1"/>
                        </Viewport3D.Camera>
                        <ModelVisual3D>
                            <ModelVisual3D.Content>
                                <AmbientLight/>
                            </ModelVisual3D.Content>
                        </ModelVisual3D>
                        <Interactive3D:InteractiveVisual3D
Geometry="{StaticResource 3DPlane}">

                            <Interactive3D:InteractiveVisual3D.Visual>

                                <Grid Margin="8,8,8,20">
                                    <MediaElement Margin="0,0,0,56"
Source="MVI_1211.AVI" x:Name="ME"/>
                                    <Button HorizontalAlignment="Left"
Margin="30,0,0,0" VerticalAlignment="Bottom" Width="95" Height="22"
Content="Play" x:Name="PlayBtn"/>
                                    <Button Margin="0,0,23,0"
 VerticalAlignment="Bottom" Height="22" Content="Stop
" Width="95" HorizontalAlignment="Right" x:Name="StopBtn"/>

                                </Grid>
                            </Interactive3D:InteractiveVisual3D.Visual>
                        </Interactive3D:InteractiveVisual3D>
                    </Viewport3D>
```

If you were to run the application here, your MediaElement and Buttons would show up but not be interactive yet.

13. Wrap your Viewport3D inside of two other 3D Tools controls like this:

```
<Grid>
        <Interactive3D:TrackballDecorator>
            <Interactive3D:Interactive3DDecorator>



                    <Viewport3D ClipToBounds="False">
                        <Viewport3D.Camera>
                            <PerspectiveCamera Position="0,0,10
" LookDirection="0,0,-1"/>
                        </Viewport3D.Camera>
                        <ModelVisual3D>
                            <ModelVisual3D.Content>
                                <AmbientLight/>
                            </ModelVisual3D.Content>
                        </ModelVisual3D>
                        <Interactive3D:InteractiveVisual3D
 Geometry="{StaticResource 3DPlane}">
```

```
                    <Interactive3D:InteractiveVisual3D.Visual>

                          <Grid Margin="8,8,8,20">
                              <MediaElement Margin="0,0,0,56"
Source="MVI_1211.AVI" x:Name="ME"/>
                                  <Button HorizontalAlignment="Left"
Margin="30,0,0,0" VerticalAlignment="Bottom"
Width="95" Height="22" Content="Play"
 x:Name="PlayBtn"/>

                                  <Button Margin="0,0,23,0"
 VerticalAlignment="Bottom" Height="22"
Content="Stop" Width="95" HorizontalAlignment="Right"
 x:Name="StopBtn"/>

                          </Grid>

                    </Interactive3D:InteractiveVisual3D.Visual>
                  </Interactive3D:InteractiveVisual3D>
              </Viewport3D>
          </Interactive3D:Interactive3DDecorator>
      </Interactive3D:TrackballDecorator>

      </Grid>
</Window>
```

14. Run the application and test it.

When the application runs, it starts to play the video . . . but, wait, it's really small, right? Hold down your mouse button and move your mouse up, and the video will get bigger. Think that's cool? Hold down your mouse button and move your mouse around to rotate the video. Now, *that* is cool. Notice too that the buttons work just as they should (see Figure 10-60).

Figure 10-60. Manipulating the Viewport3D that holds your MediaElement and interactive Buttons

Summary

So what have you learned in this chapter? You learned that WPF has very powerful 3D capabilities that make for pretty visually stunning applications. In this chapter, you learned that WPF itself has a limited capability to create 3D objects such as a 3D image; but you also learned that there is a third-party program called ZAM 3D from Electric Rain that allows you to create cool 3D objects and export them to XAML so you can use them in your projects. Indeed, you did just that and then even made a fun flyby animation with it. You also saw that you can import OBJ files, and that most popular 3D animation programs such as 3ds Max and Maya can export their models into OBJ files. You actually imported a 3D model and then created a button that made it spin. Finally, you learned that WPF out of the box does not allow you to interact with 2D controls when they are painted onto 3D objects. However, you also saw how to download and add a reference to the 3D Tools DLL so that you can interact with 2D controls. Specifically, you created a new project called 3DMediaElementProject for which you created a MediaElement and made a custom VideoUserControl out of it. You then used 3D Tools to paint your new VideoUserControl onto a 3D plane that you created by hand in XAML and were able to manipulate it with your mouse and interact with its buttons as well.

In the next chapter, you will explore DependencyProperties and even learn how to create custom ones that you can make use of.

Chapter 11

DEPENDENCYPROPERTIES

What this chapter covers:

- What are DependencyProperties
- How DependencyProperties are set
- How DependencyProperties can solve a real-world problem
- Creating a custom UserControl with custom DependencyProperties

WPF provides a set of services that are used to extend the functionality of the common language runtime (CLR) property known as the WPF property system. DependencyProperties are properties that are backed by the WPF property system. That, of course, is Microsoft's official definition of DependencyProperties, but it does not tell you the developer much about them or, more importantly, how to use them. Fortunately for you, I have worked with them for quite some time, and I can offer you a much more "human" definition, and also give you hands-on experience in using them and even creating your own custom DependencyProperties. With that, let's get started.

DependencyProperties demystified

Throughout this book, you have worked with many WPF controls such as Buttons, ComboBoxes, Rectangles, Paths, MediaElements, and so on. Because you have worked with these controls and did things such as set the Source property of a MediaElement or the Fill property of a Rectangle, you already have experience in working with DependencyProperties because Fill and Source *are* DependencyProperties. So, in their simplest form, and trust me they *can* get much more complicated, DependencyProperties are properties that allow you to manage in C# or XAML how controls look and behave. Let's take a look at a simple Button with a Background DependencyProperty set to Blue and a Content DependencyProperty set to Dependency Properties Rock!:

```
<Button Background="Blue" Content="Dependency Properties Rock!"/>
```

When you set the Background property to Blue, the XAML loader type converter converts it into a WPF Color using the SolidColorBrush. WPF provides a variety of ways syntactically for setting these properties in both XAML and C#. If you give the Button a Name, like this:

```
<Button x:Name="MyButton" Background="Blue"
Content="Dependency Properties Rock!"/>
```

you can then go into the code-behind file and set the Background property with code like this:

```
// create a variable of the type SolidColorBrush
// and set it to a new Red SolidColorBrush
SolidColorBrush myBrush = new SolidColorBrush(Colors.Red);
// apply the new variable to the Background of MyButton
MyButton.Background = myBrush;
```

There are also different ways available to the developer to set these DependencyProperties in the XAML. Following is an alternative way to set the Background DependencyProperty of a Button in XAML:

```
<Button x:Name="myButton">
<Button.Background>
<SolidColorBrush Color="Green"/>
</Button.Background>
</Button>
```

DependencyProperties can be set through data binding as well. (Remember earlier in the book, in Chapter 9, you used data binding to bind the data from an ObservableCollection to a ComboBox.) The following code creates a SolidColorBrush resource called MyBrush and then binds the Background of a Button to that resource:

```
<Grid>
<Grid.Resources>
<SolidColorBrush x:Key="MyBrush" Color="Aquamarine"/>
</Grid.Resources>
<Button Background="{DynamicResource MyBrush}"
Content="I am Aquamarine"/>
</Grid>
```

DependencyProperties can also be animated. If you recall, you did this way back in Chapter 2 when you created the "Hello World!" application. Remember, if you will, that you created a Storyboard that essentially rotated a TextBlock 360 degrees. In doing that, you changed the DependencyProperty of the TextBlock's Angle property over a period of time.

As you can ascertain, DependencyProperties are a very important part of WPF and Silverlight. But, you may be asking yourself, "What is the big deal, and why are you devoting a chapter to something that seems so relatively straightforward?" Well, the answer is that there is more to DependencyProperties than meets the eye; further, you can do some very cool things with them. In order to demonstrate this, let me present you with a scenario that I have faced in the past:

The design for an application I was working on called for Buttons with images in them. Not a big deal, right? Well, the design mock-up also called for Buttons with images *and text*. Now I had a problem, because although a WPF Button has a Content property, the Content property must be a single item; it cannot be set to an Image *and* a TextBlock. Sure, I could have gone ahead and made a Grid that housed both an image and text, but that would have been cumbersome and take too much time. A better solution was to make a Grid with an image and text and turn it into a custom UserControl. Then in the code-behind, I could set the text of the TextBlock and the source of the Image.

But, what if you as developer, faced with a similar scenario, want to hand off the UserControl to designers to implement? Now you run into another issue, as most designers would have a problem going into the code-behind to set the Text and Source properties for the new custom UserControl. In fact, most designers only use the Expression suite to work on WPF/Silverlight applications. And, as you already know, Blend 2 cannot even open a code-behind file; Blend 2 will automatically open a new instance of Visual Studio if you double-click a code-behind CS file in the Project panel. So then what *is* a viable solution to your dilemma?

What if you could create custom DependencyProperties such as MyIcon and MyText, and then use the values of these properties to set the Text property of the custom UserControl's TextBlock and also use these values to set the Source property of the Image control? The designers could then specify right in the XAML what these values should be and thus never have to open the code-behind files. Well, that is the great thing about DependencyProperties—they allow you to do just that, create something once and hand it off to the designers to use. Do you hear a project coming? You sure do.

A custom UserControl with custom DependencyProperties project

In this section, you'll create a new WPF Application project that features a custom UserControl with custom DependencyProperties that will specify the UserControl's Text and Image Source properties.

Creating the project

You'll start by setting up the project:

1. Fire up Visual Studio 2008 and create a new WPF Application project called DependencyPropertiesProject (see Figure 11-1). Make note of where you save it, as you will be opening this project in Blend 2 as well.

2. Now open Blend 2, navigate to where you saved the project, and open it.

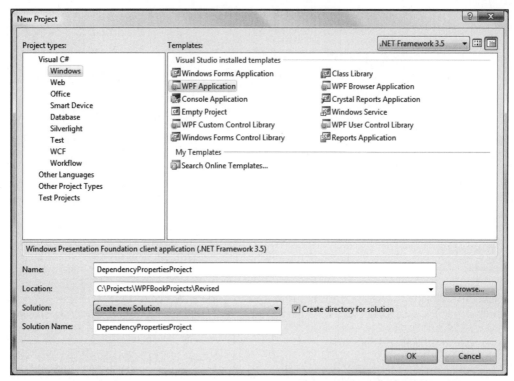

Figure 11-1. Creating a new project in Visual Studio 2008 called DependencyPropertiesProject

Styling the Rectangles and then turning them into a Button control

In Blend 2, the first thing you need to do is create a series of gradient Rectangles that will eventually become your UserControl:

1. Select the Rectangle tool from Blend 2's toolbar.

2. Draw a Rectangle in the Workspace.

3. Select Gradient brush from the Properties panel as shown in Figure 11-2.

4. Select the black color stop and select a color you like (I chose red).

5. Now select the Brush Transform tool like I have done in Figure 11-3.

6. Use the Brush Transform tool to adjust the gradient until you have something like what you see in Figure 11-4.

Figure 11-2. Selecting Gradient brush for the new Rectangle

7. Now press the V key to get your Selection tool back and adjust the radius handles to get rounded edges as shown in Figure 11-5.

Figure 11-3. Selecting the Brush Transform tool

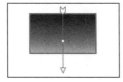

Figure 11-4. Adjusting the gradient

Figure 11-5. Giving your Rectangle rounded edges

8. Next, select the Rectangle if it is not already selected, press Ctrl+C to copy it, and then press Ctrl+V to paste a new copy of it to the Workspace.

9. Select the top Rectangle (lowest in the Objects and Timeline panel) and remove its stroke like I have done in Figure 11-6.

10. Change the fill gradient of the top Rectangle to go from white to white like I have done in Figure 11-7.

I have you do this because the colors of the gradient are irrelevant; what is relevant is the alpha (how much you can see through) one of the gradient colors. Next, you will see how to make one of the gradient's colors completely invisible (alpha of zero).

Figure 11-6. Removing the stroke from the top Rectangle

Figure 11-7. Changing the fill gradient of the top Rectangle to go from white to white

11. Select the right color stop and change its Alpha value to 0% as shown in Figure 11-8.

12. Select the Stroke property and set it to No brush like I have done in Figure 11-9.

Figure 11-8. Selecting the right color stop and dropping its Alpha value down to 0%

Figure 11-9. Setting the Stroke property to No brush

13. With the Selection tool, change the size of the top Rectangle to be smaller than the bottom Rectangle like I have done in Figure 11-10.

14. Use the Brush Transform tool on the top Rectangle until you have something like what you see in Figure 11-11.

15. With the top Rectangle selected, press Ctrl+C to copy and Ctrl+V to paste a copy of it in the Workspace.

16. Press V to select the Selection tool and rotate the new Rectangle (currently on the top in the z order in the Workspace and at the bottom of the Visual Tree in the Objects and Timeline panel) 360 degrees so that you have something like what you see in Figure 11-12.

Figure 11-10.
Resizing the top
Rectangle

Figure 11-11.
Changing the top
Rectangle with the
Brush Transform tool

Figure 11-12.
Rotating the new
Rectangle

Now you have a nice glassy-looking button that you can use for your new custom UserControl. Pretty snazzy, huh?

17. Select everything in the Workspace by pressing Ctrl+A. Right-click the top Rectangle and select Group Into ➤ Grid as shown in Figure 11-13.

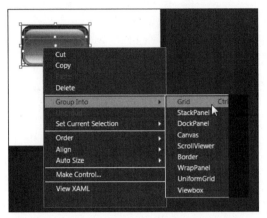

Figure 11-13. Grouping all Rectangles into a Grid

18. Double-click the Grid so that it has a yellow line around it, select the TextBlock tool from the toolbar, and add a TextBlock control like I have done in Figure 11-14.

19. In the Common Properties bucket, set the Text property to read Default Text.

20. In the Text Bucket, click the Paragraph tab and set the text alignment to Center like I have done in Figure 11-15.

Figure 11-14. Adding a TextBlock control into the Grid

Figure 11-15. Specifying Center alignment for the TextBlock

21. In the Brushes bucket, set the Foreground property of the TextBlock to white as shown in Figure 11-16.

Figure 11-16. Changing the Foreground property to white

22. Adjust the positioning and possibly the font of the TextBlock so that it looks like what you see in Figure 11-17.

23. The final thing you need to do to the TextBlock is to give it a unique name so you can code against it. In the Name property of the Properties panel, name the TextBlock MyTextBlock.

Figure 11-17. The final look of the TextBlock

At this point, you need to add a blank Image control to the Grid and give it a unique name as well:

24. Click the Asset Library tool on the toolbar, type Image into the search field, and click Image (see Figure 11-18).

Figure 11-18. Selecting an Image control from the Asset Library

25. Next, draw out an Image control in the Grid (make sure the yellow line is still around the Grid) like I have done in Figure 11-19.

26. In the Name field of the Properties panel, give your Image control a name of MyImage.

27. With the Grid selected, click Tools ➤ Make Control.

28. When the Make Control dialog box pops up, give the control the name of RedButtonUC (UC for UserControl) like I have done in Figure 11-20.

Figure 11-19. Drawing an Image control in the Grid

Figure 11-20. Naming the new UserControl RedButtonUC

Now at this point you have your custom UserControl. You may have noticed that Blend 2 created the control and opened it so that you are now editing RedButtonUC.xaml. Switch back to Window1.xaml, and you may see that your UserControl is showing an error message. If this is the case, press F5 to run the application. You will see RedButtonUC in the running application, and it will refresh; and you will see it also in Blend's Design view. Also, notice that in the Objects and Timeline panel, it shows up as a UserControl of type RedButtonUC.

29. Give the control a name of MyRedButtonUC in the Name section of the Properties panel.

30. Press Ctrl+Shift+B to compile the application, switch back over to Visual Studio 2008, and reload the project when prompted to do so.

Registering the custom DependencyProperties

Now you are going to go ahead and register your custom DependencyProperties in RedButtonUC.xaml.cs.

1. Open RedButtonUC.xaml.cs by double-clicking it in Visual Studio's Solution Explorer.

2. To keep things tidy, place all of your DependencyProperties in C# regions, as shown in the following code. These allow you to collapse chunks of code.

```
using System;
using System.IO;
using System.Net;
using System.Windows;
using System.Windows.Controls;
using System.Windows.Data;
using System.Windows.Media;
```

```
using System.Windows.Media.Animation;
using System.Windows.Navigation;

namespace DependencyPropertiesProject
{
    public partial class RedButtonUC
    {
        public RedButtonUC()
        {
            this.InitializeComponent();

            // Insert code required on
            //object creation below this point.

        }
        #region Dependency Properties

        #endregion
    }
}
```

3. I like to create a region for each DependencyProperty, so I'll have you do that here. As shown in the following code, create a region for your first DependencyProperty called MyTextDP:

```
#region Dependency Properties

#region MyTextDP

#endregion

#endregion
```

4. Now you need to register the MyTextDP property. Here is the code that does this:

```
#region MyTextDP

        public static readonly DependencyProperty MyTextDPProperty =
        DependencyProperty.Register("MyTextDP", typeof(String),
    typeof(RedButtonUC));

        public String MyTextDP
        {
            get { return (String)GetValue(MyTextDPProperty); }
            set { SetValue(MyTextDPProperty, value); }
        }

#endregion
```

5. Switch back to Window1.xaml and add the MyTextDP property into the XAML like this:

```
<DependencyPropertiesProject:RedButtonUC MyTextDP="foo"
 d:LayoutOverrides="HorizontalAlignment, VerticalAlignment"
Margin="61,77,116,125" x:Name="MyRedButtonUC"/>
```

6. Switch back to RedButtonUC.xaml.cs and add a this.Loaded method in the constructor like this:

```
            public RedButtonUC()
        {
        this.InitializeComponent();
this.Loaded += new RoutedEventHandler(RedButtonUC_Loaded);
// Insert code required on
//object creation below this point.

        }

    void RedButtonUC_Loaded(object sender, RoutedEventArgs e)
     {
     throw new NotImplementedException();
     }
```

What this code does is to run RedButtonUC_loaded whenever the RedButtonUC UserControl is loaded. Here you can place a MessageBox to make sure that your MyTextDP is correctly registered and set.

7. Replace the default throw new NotImplementedException(); line with the following line shown in bold:

```
void RedButtonUC_Loaded(object sender, RoutedEventArgs e)
    {
        MessageBox.Show(MyTextDP.ToString());
    }
```

Figure 11-21. A MessageBox with the value of MyTextDP

8. Press F5 to compile and run the application, and if you did everything correctly, you will see something like what I have in Figure 11-21.

Pretty cool, huh? I still get all excited when I see my MessageBox with the correct value of my custom DependencyProperty. Now you need to *do* something with this DependencyProperty.

9. Set the Text property of the TextBlock to the value of MyTextDP as follows:

```
void RedButtonUC_Loaded(object sender, RoutedEventArgs e)
    {
        MyTextBlock.Text = MyTextDP;
    }
```

10. Press F5 again to compile and run the application. Lo and behold, the text for RedButtonUC reads foo (see Figure 11-22). Pretty cool, right?

Figure 11-22. RedButtonUC's text now is equal to the value of the MyTextDP DependencyProperty.

11. Now you need to register the `MyIconDP` DependencyProperty just below the `MyTextDP` region as shown in the following codé:

```
#region MyIconDP

        public static readonly DependencyProperty MyIconDPProperty =
        DependencyProperty.Register("MyIconDP", typeof(String),
typeof(RedButtonUC));

        public String MyIconDP
        {
            get { return (String)GetValue(MyIconDPProperty); }
            set { SetValue(MyIconDPProperty, value); }
        }

    #endregion
```

12. Next, you need to actually add `MyIconDP` into the XAML in `Window1.xaml` as follows:

```
<DependencyPropertiesProject:RedButtonUC MyIconDP="SomeIcon"
MyTextDP="foo" d:LayoutOverrides="HorizontalAlignment,
VerticalAlignment" Margin="61,77,116,125"
x:Name="MyRedButtonUC"/>
```

13. To make certain you registered the `MyIconDP` DependencyProperty correctly, make another `MessageBox` that displays the value of `MyIconDP`. Add this back to `RedButtonUC_Loaded` like this:

```
void RedButtonUC_Loaded(object sender, RoutedEventArgs e)
{
        MyTextBlock.Text = MyTextDP;
        MessageBox.Show(MyIconDP.ToString());
}
```

Figure 11-23. The MessageBox shows the value of `MyIconDP`.

In Figure 11-23, you can see that my `MessageBox` does in fact show the correct value for `MyIconDP`.

Adding an icon image to the project

Now that you know you are registering `MyIconDP` correctly, you need to add an icon image to the project, place the path of that image into the XAML for `MyIconDP`, and then set the `Source` property of RedButtonUC's `MyImage` to the value of `MyIconDP`. Do that now:

1. In Visual Studio 2008, in Solution Explorer right-click the project that reads DependencyPropertyProject (not the solution) and click Add ➤ Existing Item as shown in Figure 11-24.

Figure 11-24. Adding an existing item to the project

2. The Add Existing Item dialog box appears and allows you to browse your hard drive for files. By default, the file type that Visual Studio will be looking for is Visual C# files; you must change the file type to image files as shown in Figure 11-25.

Figure 11-25. Telling Visual Studio to look for image files

3. Navigate to an image on your local hard drive and double-click it.

> Even though an Image *control will resize its source image to fit, it is good practice to take an image into Photoshop and resize it to the size you want it to be in the WPF application. This will also help performance of the application by reducing the size of the image.*

4. Now that you have an image in your project (I named mine icon.png), you can go ahead and code its path into RedButtonUC in Window1.xaml as follows:

```
<DependencyPropertiesProject:RedButtonUC MyIconDP="icon.png"
MyTextDP="foo" d:LayoutOverrides=
"HorizontalAlignment, VerticalAlignment" Margin="61,77,116,125"
x:Name="MyRedButtonUC"/>
```

5. You need to make use of this path by first creating a URI, using that URI to create an ImageSource, and then setting MyImage's Source DependencyProperty to the value of MyIconDP. The following code does this:

```
void RedButtonUC_Loaded(object sender, RoutedEventArgs e)
{
        MyTextBlock.Text = MyTextDP;
        Uri uri = new Uri(MyIconDP.ToString(),
UriKind.RelativeOrAbsolute);
        BitmapImage source = new BitmapImage(uri);
        MyImage.Source = source;
}
```

> The System.Windows.Media.Imaging *namespace is not part of the application by default. You will need to add this namespace to the application by right-clicking* BitmapImage *and choosing* Resolve ➤ using System.Windows.Media.Imaging.

6. Press F5 to compile and run the application, and you will see that the icon shows up just as you would expect (see Figure 11-26).

7. Change MyTextDP in RedButtonUC in Window1.xaml to be something more like a button would normally read, as shown here:

```
<DependencyPropertiesProject:RedButtonUC MyIconDP="icon.png"
MyTextDP="Click Here" d:LayoutOverrides=
"HorizontalAlignment, VerticalAlignment"
Margin="61,77,116,125" x:Name="MyRedButtonUC"/>
```

8. Press F5 to compile and run the application again, and you will see that the text has been updated (see Figure 11-27).

Figure 11-26. Using MyTextDP for the text and MyIconDP for the image

Figure 11-27. Change MyTextDP, and the RedButtonUC text will change.

Making the custom UserControl functional

At this point, the exercise for DependencyProperties is pretty much over. You now know what DependencyProperties are, how to use them, and how to even create custom DependencyProperties of your own. The rest of this chapter is going to show you how to make your sample application a little more useful by having it actually do something. Specifically, I am going to show you how to make another RedButtonUC with different text and a different icon. Then you are going to change the application so that when you click one RedButtonUC, it will become hidden and the other RedButtonUC will become visible, and vice versa. So, if that is something you would be interested in doing, then follow along; if not, feel free to skip ahead to the next chapter.

1. In Window1.xaml, change the Height to 600 and the Width to 800.

2. Copy and paste your XAML for RedButtonUC in Window1.xaml so it looks like this:

```
<DependencyPropertiesProject:RedButtonUC MyIconDP="icon.png"
MyTextDP="Click Here"
d:LayoutOverrides="HorizontalAlignment, VerticalAlignment"
Margin="61,77,116,125" x:Name="MyRedButtonUC"/>

<DependencyPropertiesProject:RedButtonUC MyIconDP="icon.png"
MyTextDP="Click Here"
d:LayoutOverrides="HorizontalAlignment, VerticalAlignment"
Margin="61,77,116,125" x:Name="MyRedButtonUC"/>
```

> *The values for your* RedButtonUC *may vary slightly from mine depending on the icon PNG you use and the margin placement of your* RedButtonUC.

The margin of RedButtonUC determines where in the Workspace it will sit. If both RedButtonUCs have the same margin, one will be directly under the other. Also, the x:Name properties need to be different so you can code against them in the C#.

3. Change both properties right in the XAML, or change the Name property in the Name field of Blend 2's Properties panel. The easiest way to change the margin of a button in Blend 2 is by using the Selection tool and dragging it to where you want it.

4. Change the x:Name property, and change the Margin of the second RedButtonUC so that it now looks something like this:

```
<DependencyPropertiesProject:RedButtonUC MyIconDP="icon.png"
MyTextDP="Click Here" d:LayoutOverrides="HorizontalAlignment,
VerticalAlignment" Margin="61,77,116,125" x:Name="MyRedButtonUC"/>

<DependencyPropertiesProject:RedButtonUC MyIconDP="icon.png"
MyTextDP="Click Here" d:LayoutOverrides="HorizontalAlignment,
VerticalAlignment" Margin="61,250,116,125" x:Name="MyRedButtonUC2"/>
```

5. Press F5 to compile and run the application, and make sure the results are similar to what you see in Figure 11-28.

Figure 11-28. There are now two RedButtonUCs in the application.

6. Put a Cursor property in the XAML for the RedButtonUCs so they look and react more like Buttons.

```
<DependencyPropertiesProject:RedButtonUC MyIconDP="icon.png"
MyTextDP="Click Here" d:LayoutOverrides="HorizontalAlignment,
VerticalAlignment" Margin="61,77,116,125"
x:Name="MyRedButtonUC" Cursor="Hand"/>

<DependencyPropertiesProject:RedButtonUC MyIconDP="icon.png"
MyTextDP="Click Here" d:LayoutOverrides="HorizontalAlignment,
VerticalAlignment" Margin="61,250,116,125"
x:Name="MyRedButtonUC2" Cursor="Hand"/>
```

7. Set the Visibility property of one of the RedButtonUCs to Hidden.

```
<DependencyPropertiesProject:RedButtonUC MyIconDP="icon.png"
MyTextDP="Click Here" d:LayoutOverrides="HorizontalAlignment,
VerticalAlignment" Margin="61,77,116,125" x:Name="MyRedButtonUC"
Cursor="Hand"/>

<DependencyPropertiesProject:RedButtonUC MyIconDP="icon.png"
MyTextDP="Click Here" d:LayoutOverrides="HorizontalAlignment,
VerticalAlignment" Margin="61,250,116,125" x:Name="MyRedButtonUC2"
Cursor="Hand" Visibility="Hidden"/>
```

8. In Window1.xaml.cs, you need to create a Boolean variable to tell whether MyRedButtonUC is visible or hidden. Since by default it *is* visible, you will make this variable true.

```
  public partial class Window1 : Window
  {
        private Boolean _isMyRedButtonUCVisible = true;
```

9. Now you need to listen for the MouseLeftButtonDown event for each RedButtonUC and create methods for each of them in Window1.xaml.cs:

```
public partial class Window1 : Window
{
        public Window1()
```

```
        {
            InitializeComponent();
            MyRedButtonUC.MouseLeftButtonDown +=
new MouseButtonEventHandler(MyRedButtonUC_MouseLeftButtonDown);
            MyRedButtonUC2.MouseLeftButtonDown +=
new MouseButtonEventHandler(MyRedButtonUC2_MouseLeftButtonDown);
        }

            void MyRedButtonUC2_MouseLeftButtonDown
(object sender, MouseButtonEventArgs e)
        {
            throw new NotImplementedException();
        }

        void MyRedButtonUC_MouseLeftButtonDown
(object sender, MouseButtonEventArgs e)
        {
            throw new NotImplementedException();
        }
    }
```

10. Set up conditional statements that check to see whether MyRedButton is visible or not:

```
private Boolean _isMyRedButtonUCVisible = true;
        public Window1()
        {
            InitializeComponent();
            MyRedButtonUC.MouseLeftButtonDown += new
 MouseButtonEventHandler(MyRedButtonUC_MouseLeftButtonDown);
            MyRedButtonUC2.MouseLeftButtonDown +=
new MouseButtonEventHandler(MyRedButtonUC2_MouseLeftButtonDown);
        }

        void MyRedButtonUC2_MouseLeftButtonDown
(object sender, MouseButtonEventArgs e)
        {
            if (_isMyRedButtonUCVisible == false)
            {
                isMyRedButtonUCVisible = true;
                MyRedButtonUC.Visibility = Visibility.Visible;
                MyRedButtonUC2.Visibility = Visibility.Hidden;
            }
        }

        void MyRedButtonUC_MouseLeftButtonDown
(object sender, MouseButtonEventArgs e)
        {
            if (_isMyRedButtonUCVisible == true)
            {
                isMyRedButtonUCVisible = false;
```

```
            MyRedButtonUC.Visibility = Visibility.Hidden;
            MyRedButtonUC2.Visibility = Visibility.Visible;
        }
    }
```

What you have done here is to put a conditional if statement in the EventHandlers for each of the two RedButtonUCs. The statement looks to see whether the variable isMyRedButtonUCVisible is true when MyRedButtonUC is clicked (technically MouseLeftButtonDown). If it is true, the method sets the variable to false and then makes MyRedButtonUC hidden and makes MyRedButtonUC2 visible. Conversely, when MyRedButtonUC2 is clicked, it checks to see whether isMyRedButtonUCVisible is false. If it is, it sets the variable to true and makes itself hidden and MyRedButtonUC visible.

11. Press F5 to compile and run the application. When you click one RedButtonUC, it will disappear and show the other one and vice versa (see Figure 11-29).

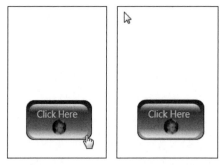

Figure 11-29. Clicking one RedButtonUC will hide it and make the other visible and vice versa.

12. Import a new icon image (I called mine icon2.png) and then set MyRedButtonUC2 to use the new icon and to change the text of MyRedButtonUC2. You can see the code here and the results in Figure 11-30.

```
    <DependencyPropertiesProject:RedButtonUC MyIconDP="icon2.png"
    MyTextDP="No Click Here"
    d:LayoutOverrides="HorizontalAlignment,
VerticalAlignment" Margin="61,250,116,125" x:Name="MyRedButtonUC2"
    Cursor="Hand" Visibility="Hidden"/>
```

Figure 11-30. You can now very easliy change the text and source of your control in the XAML

A compressed file containing a finished version of the application you just created can be found at www.windowspresentationfoundation.com/bookDownloads/ DependencyPropertiesProject.zip.

Summary

In this chapter, you learned that DependencyProperties are properties you can set in XAML or C# that control the way WPF controls look and behave. Some examples of common DependencyProperties are Content for a Button control, Fill for a Rectangle control, Source for a MediaElement control, and Height for an Image control. You learned that you can set the value for DependencyProperties many different ways in XAML and C#, and you can even set them in Storyboards or with data binding. You also saw how you can register your own custom DependencyProperties in C#. You then went on and added additional functionality to the project by making each RedButtonUC have a hand cursor, and to disappear when clicked and show the other RedButtonUC and vice versa. Finally, you changed MyRedButtonUC to have different text and a difference source for its Image control.

In the next chapter, you are really going to start having some fun by taking what you have learned thus far in this book and applying it to creating a real-world application. The project you are going to make is going to showcase some very cool ways that WPF can display an image: specifically, you'll display an image the regular old flat way, then make it a 3D image, and finally visually brush the image onto a spinning 3D box primitive. So, get your thinking cap firmly adjusted, and let's jump right in!

Chapter 12

CASE STUDY A: 3DIMAGEPROJECT

What this chapter covers:

- Creating a new WPF project
- Creating an ObservableCollection of image paths
- Binding the ObservableCollection to a ComboBox
- Creating a DataTemplate to specify how the ComboBox displays the images
- Creating three RadioButtons
- Showing a selected image in three different ways: flat, 3D, and brushed onto a Viewport3D of a 3D box
- Creating a Storyboard named SpinBox that spins the 3D box
- Creating easing behavior for the Storyboard

Now that you are familiar with many basic WPF concepts, it is time to pull them all together and create some cool applications. In this chapter, you are going to create a new application called 3DImageProject. In this project, you will take what you have learned in previous chapters to create an ImageFactory class that will provide you with an ObservableCollection of image paths. You are then going to use that ObservableCollection to create a DataSource. You will bind that DataSource to a drop-down ComboBox. You will then create a DataTemplate to tell the ComboBox how to display its content. Finally, you are going to make three RadioButtons that will determine how the selected image is displayed: flat, 3D, or brushed onto an ever-spinning Viewport3D of a box. With that, let's get started.

Creating the 3DImageProject

First you'll start out by setting up the 3DImage project.

1. Open Visual Studio 2008 and create a new WPF Application project.

2. Name the project 3DImageProject and make sure to make a mental note of where the project is being saved, as you will be opening the project up in Blend 2 as well (see Figure 12-1).

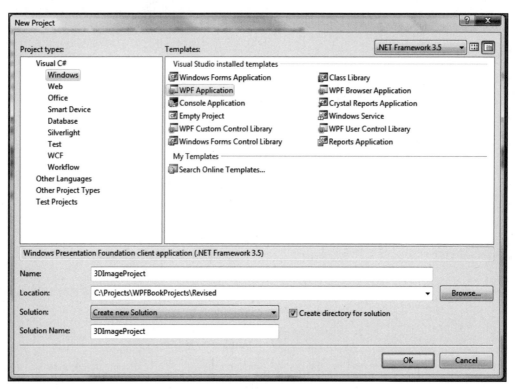

Figure 12-1. Creating a new project named 3DImageProject

Adding images to the project

You will need to import some images into your project.

1. Right-click the project and select Add ➤ New Folder in Solution Explorer like I have done in Figure 12-2.

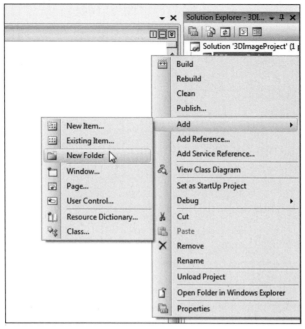

Figure 12-2. Adding a new folder in Solution Explorer

2. Create a new folder called Resources. Then click the Resources folder and add a new folder called Images so that your directory structure looks like mine does in Figure 12-3.

3. Right-click the Images directory and click Add ➤ Existing Item. The Add Existing Item dialog box will appear; make sure that you tell Visual Studio to look for image files as shown in Figure 12-4.

Figure 12-3. Your directory structure should look like this.

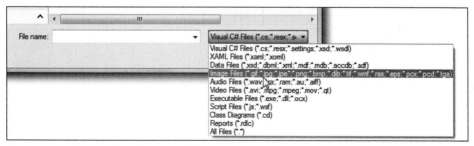

Figure 12-4. Telling Visual Studio to look for image files

4. Navigate to some images on your local hard drive and add them to the Images directory. At this point, your Solution Explorer should resemble what you see in Figure 12-5.

> To make it easier to code later, you can name your images in sequence like this: 1.jpg, 2.jpg, etc.

Creating the ImageFactory

Now you need to create the ImageFactory. You have done this before in Chapter 9, but to reinforce the concepts you learned there, I think it would be good for me to walk you through how to do it again

1. Right-click the project and select Add ➤ New Item. When the Add New Item dialog box appears, select Class and give it a name of ImageFactory like I have done in Figure 12-6.

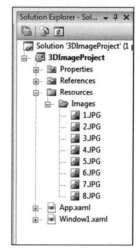

Figure 12-5. Your Solution Explorer should look something like this.

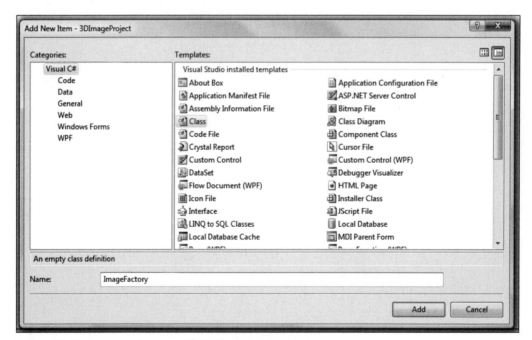

Figure 12-6. Adding a new class named ImageFactory to the project

Visual Studio creates the class for you and opens it so you can start to program in it. You'll do that now:

2. Create a new instance of Images right inside of the ImageFactory class.

```
class ImageFactory
    {
        private static Images _myactauldata = new Images
    }
```

3. Next, specify that this class is public.

```
public class ImageFactory
    {
        private static Images _myactauldata = new Images();
    }
```

4. Create a public variable of the Images type and create a getter that will return _myactualdata.

```
public class ImageFactory
    {
        private static Images _myactauldata = new Images();
        public static Images MyImages
        {
            get
            {
                return _myactauldata;
            }
        }
    }
```

5. Create the Images class within the ImageFactory class.

```
public class ImageFactory
    {
        private static Images _myactauldata = new Images();
        public static Images MyImages
        {
            get
            {
                return _myactauldata;
            }
        }
        public class Images : ObservableCollection<ImageData>
        {

        }
    }
```

6. At this point Visual Studio does not know what an ObservableCollection is, so right-click the word ObservableCollection and select Resolve ➤ using System.Collections.ObjectModel like I have done in Figure 12-7.

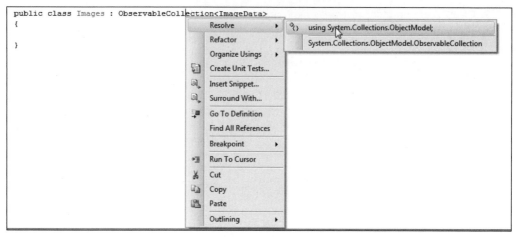

Figure 12-7. Importing the System.Collections.ObjectModel class

7. Create the constructor for your Images class, and in it add the paths of your images.

```
public class Images : ObservableCollection<ImageData>
        {
            public Images()
            {
                this.Add(new ImageData(@"Resources\Images\1.jpg"));
                this.Add(new ImageData(@"Resources\Images\2.jpg"));
                this.Add(new ImageData(@"Resources\Images\3.jpg"));
                this.Add(new ImageData(@"Resources\Images\4.jpg"));
                this.Add(new ImageData(@"Resources\Images\5.jpg"));
                this.Add(new ImageData(@"Resources\Images\6.jpg"));
                this.Add(new ImageData(@"Resources\Images\7.jpg"));
                this.Add(new ImageData(@"Resources\Images\8.jpg"));
            }
        }
```

8. Create the ImageData class directly under the Images class, and make it of the type INotifyPropertyChanged. This class will fire for every Image you add. You will also have to have this class use the System.ComponentModel as shown in Figure 12-8.

9. Create a private string called _sImageName.

```
public class ImageData : INotifyPropertyChanged
        {
            private String _sImageName = "";
        }
```

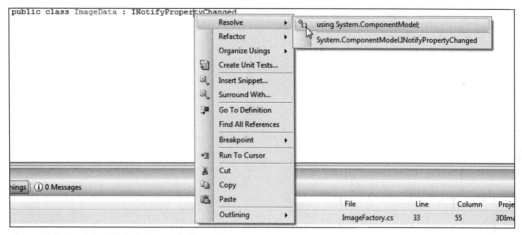

Figure 12-8. Resolving INotifyPropertyChanged

10. Create the constructor for ImageData and pass in sImageName, which is the path that you passed in from the Images class.

```
public class ImageData : INotifyPropertyChanged
        {
            private String _sImageName = "";
            public ImageData(string sImageName)
            {

            }
        }
```

11. Create a variable called ImageName and set it to sImageName.

```
public class ImageData : INotifyPropertyChanged
        {
            private String _sImageName = "";
            public ImageData(string sImageName)
            {
                ImageName = sImageName;
            }
        }
```

12. Create the public String ImageName.

```
public class ImageData : INotifyPropertyChanged
        {
            private String _sImageName = "";
            public ImageData(string sImageName)
            {
                ImageName = sImageName;
            }
```

```
        public String ImageName
        {

        }
    }
```

13. Create getters and setters that will set the `ImageName` string to the image path and also return the `ImageName` string as the image path.

```
public class ImageData : INotifyPropertyChanged
    {
        private String _sImageName = "";
        public ImageData(string sImageName)
        {
            ImageName = sImageName;
        }
        public String ImageName
        {
            get
            {
                return _sImageName;
            }
            set
            {
                _sImageName = value;
                NotifyPropertyChanged(ImageName);
            }
        }
    }
```

14. Add the `PropertyChangedEventHandler` and `NotifyPropertyChanged` method.

```
public class ImageData : INotifyPropertyChanged
    {
        private String _sImageName = "";
        public ImageData(string sImageName)
        {
            ImageName = sImageName;
        }
        public String ImageName
        {
            get
            {
                return _sImageName;
            }
            set
            {
                _sImageName = value;
                NotifyPropertyChanged(ImageName);
            }
        }
```

```
        public event PropertyChangedEventHandler PropertyChanged;
        protected void NotifyPropertyChanged(String sProp)
        {
            if (PropertyChanged != null)
            {
                PropertyChanged(this,
new PropertyChangedEventArgs(sProp));
            }
        }
    }
```

Styling the application and creating the DataSource

At this point, all of the heavy programming is complete. Now you need to open Blend 2 and create a DataSource using the ImageFactory class.

1. Press F6 to compile the application, and switch over to Blend 2 and open the project.

2. In the XAML section of the Split view, change the Height and Width of Window to 600 by 800, respectively.

3. With Grid selected in the Objects and Timeline panel, change the Background property to a gradient in the Brushes bucket of the Properties panel like I have done in Figure 12-9.

Figure 12-9. Changing the background of the Grid to a gradient

275

4. Now change the color of the gradient and use the Brush Transform tool until you have a background that looks something like what you see in Figure 12-10.

Figure 12-10. Your Grid background should look something like this.

5. Click the Project tab, and in the Data bucket click +CLR Object to create a DataSource like I have done in Figure 12-11.

Figure 12-11. Clicking +CLR Object to add a DataSource

6. When the Add CLR Object Data Source dialog box appears, select ImageFactory as shown in Figure 12-12 and click OK.

Just that easily, Blend 2 creates a DataSource for you that you can see in the XAML portion of the Split view:

```
<Window.Resources>
    <ObjectDataProvider x:Key="ImageFactoryDS" d:IsDataSource="True"
ObjectType="{x:Type _DImageProject:ImageFactory}"/>
</Window.Resources>
```

Figure 12-12. Using the `ImageFactory` to create a `DataSource`

Making use of the DataSource

Now you'll put the `DataSource` you just created to use.

1. From the Asset Library, search on ComboBox, and draw a ComboBox control out in the Workspace somewhere in the upper-left corner like I have done in Figure 12-13.

Figure 12-13. Drawing a ComboBox in the Workspace

2. Select the Rectangle tool and draw a Rectangle control in the Workspace as shown in Figure 12-14.

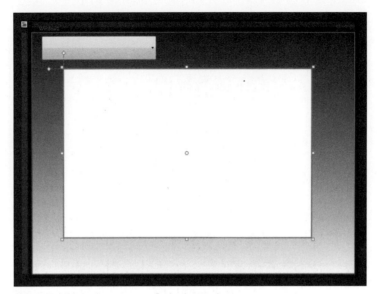

Figure 12-14. Drawing a Rectangle in the Workspace

3. Press F5 to compile and run the application.

I know the application looks very simple at this point, but that is about to change.

4. Switch over to Visual Studio 2008, and reload the project when prompted to do so.

5. Open Window1.xaml, and in the Resources section create a DataTemplate named ImageDT to tell your ComboBox how to display its content, specifically with an Image and a TextBlock.

```
<Window.Resources>
        <DataTemplate x:Key="ImagesDT">
            <StackPanel Orientation="Horizontal">
                <Image Source="{Binding Path=ImageName}"
Height="50" Width="50"/>
                <TextBlock Text="{Binding Path=ImageName}"/>
            </StackPanel>
        </DataTemplate>
        <ObjectDataProvider x:Key="ImageFactoryDS"
d:IsDataSource="True" ObjectType=
"{x:Type _DImageProject:ImageFactory}"/>
        </Window.Resources>
```

6. Locate the XAML for the ComboBox; it will look something like this:

```
<ComboBox IsSynchronizedWithCurrentItem="True"
HorizontalAlignment="Left" Margin="23.5,8,0,0"
 VerticalAlignment="Top" Width="282" Height="55"/>
```

7. Add an ItemsSource property, and tell it to use MyImages from the ImageFactoryDS that you created earlier, and also tell it to use the ImagesDT DataTemplate that you just created.

```
<ComboBox ItemsSource="{Binding Path=MyImages,
Source={StaticResource ImageFactoryDS}}"
ItemTemplate="{StaticResource ImagesDT}"
 IsSynchronizedWithCurrentItem="True"
 HorizontalAlignment="Left" Margin="23.5,8,0,0"
VerticalAlignment="Top" Width="282" Height="55"/>
```

8. Press F5 to compile and run the application, and you should see that the ComboBox is now populated with the images that you added to the ImageFactory (see Figure 12-15).

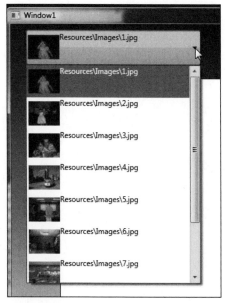

Figure 12-15. The ComboBox is now populated with your image data.

Now you'll brush the selected item of the ComboBox onto the Rectangle in the Workspace.

9. Locate the Rectangle in the XAML; it should look something like this:

```
<Rectangle Margin="78,84,104,84" Fill="#FFFFFFFF" Stroke="#FF000000"/>
```

10. Modify it so that it has a fill not of #FFFFFFFF (be sure and remove the old Fill property) but of an ImageBrush like this:

```
<Rectangle Margin="78,84,104,84" Stroke="#FF000000">
            <Rectangle.Fill>
               <ImageBrush
ImageSource="{Binding Path=SelectedItem.ImageName,
 ElementName=MyCB}"/>
            </Rectangle.Fill>
    </Rectangle>
```

11. Notice that the preceding code says to bind to the selected item of the element named MyCB? Well, you have not yet named the ComboBox, so do that now.

```
<ComboBox x:Name="MyCB" ItemsSource="{Binding Path=MyImages,
Source={StaticResource ImageFactoryDS}}"
ItemTemplate="{StaticResource ImagesDT}"
IsSynchronizedWithCurrentItem="True"
 HorizontalAlignment="Left" Margin="23.5,8,0,0"
 VerticalAlignment="Top" Width="282" Height="55"/>
```

12. Press F5 to compile and run the application.

Lo and behold, whatever item is selected in the ComboBox is now brushed onto the Rectangle (see Figure 12-16). Cool, huh? Now, let's go ahead and really make this application cool by giving the option of viewing a selected image three different ways: flat (as it is currently), in 3D, and brushed onto all visible sides of a 3D spinning box. I'm sure you can hardly wait, so let's get to it!

Figure 12-16. The selected item of the ComboBox is now brushed onto the Rectangle.

Creating viewing choices

To create different viewing choices for your images, follow these steps:

1. Decrease the width of the Rectangle to give you some room on the left for the RadioButton controls. Switch back to Blend 2 and do that visually with the Selection tool as shown in Figure 12-17.

Figure 12-17. Decreasing the width of the Rectangle in Blend 2

2. Now add a Grid and in it place three RadioButtons like this:

```
<Grid Margin="8,109.25,0,0" VerticalAlignment="Top" Height="84"
 HorizontalAlignment="Left" Width="210">

     <RadioButton Margin="0,0,0,30" Content="Flat View"
IsChecked="True" x:Name="FlatRB"/>

     RadioButton Margin="0,30,0,0" Content="Image 3D"
IsChecked="False" x:Name="Image3DRB"/>

     <RadioButton Margin="0,0,8,-8" Content=
"Visual Brush onto 3D Primitive"
IsChecked="False" x:Name="Animated3DRB"
VerticalAlignment="Bottom" Height="31"/>

</Grid>
```

You can see the results in Figure 12-18.

Figure 12-18. A Grid with RadioButtons

3. Select the Rectangle and in the Appearance bucket change the Visibility drop-down menu option to Collapsed as shown in Figure 12-19.

Figure 12-19. Changing the Rectangle to have a Visibility value of Collapsed

4. Click Blend 2's Project tab, locate the folder named Resources/Images, and drag an image into the Workspace.

5. With the Image control selected, click Tools ➤ Make Image 3D as shown in Figure 12-20.

6. Notice that the Image turns into a Viewport3D in the Objects and Timeline panel. With the Viewport3D selected, uncheck ClipToBounds in the Appearance bucket of the Properties panel like I have done in Figure 12-21.

Figure 12-20. Changing the Image control in the Workspace into an Image3D control

Figure 12-21. Unchecking ClipToBounds

7. Double-click the Viewport3D and use the gimbal tool to skew the image like I have done in Figure 12-22.

Figure 12-22. Using the gimbal tool to skew the Viewport3D

8. Now you need to find the `DiffuseMaterial.Brush` node of the Viewport3D and bind it to the `SelectedItem` of the ComboBox. So, in the XAML, locate `DiffuseMaterial.Brush` and change it to what you see here:

```
<DiffuseMaterial.Brush>
    <ImageBrush ImageSource="{Binding Path=SelectedItem.ImageName,
ElementName=MyCB}" Stretch="Fill"/>
</DiffuseMaterial.Brush>
```

9. Once you are happy with your Image3D, go ahead and set its Visibility property to Collapsed in the Appearance bucket of the Properties panel.

10. Now it is time for the BIG GUN . . . the box Viewport3D. I have taken the liberty of creating a nice 3D box for you in 3ds Max. If you paste the link http://windowspresentationfoundation. com/bookDownloads/3DBox.txt into your browser, you should be able to copy it right into the browser window; if not, download it, open it, and then copy its contents.

11. Once you have the Viewport3D named box in your clipboard, paste it just above the last `</Grid>` in the project:

```
<!--paste here-->
</Grid>
</Window>
```

I have already taken the liberty of binding the ImageBrush in the Viewport3D for you so, if you named everything exactly as I have, as soon as you paste it in, you should see that the selected item of the ComboBox already shows up like it does in Figure 12-23.

Figure 12-23. The Viewport3D named box

12. With the box Viewport3D selected, set its Visibility property to Collapsed in the Appearance section of the Properties panel.

13. In the Objects and Timeline panel, select the Rectangle, give it a name of Flat, and set its Visibility property back to Visible, because you want it to be visible when the application starts.

14. In the Objects and Timeline panel, select [Viewport3D] and give it a name of Image3D. The Viewport3D already has the name of box, so there is no need to do anything with it.

15. Press F5 to compile and run the application.

You'll see that your RadioButtons don't work yet. Close the application and switch back over to Visual Studio 2008 so you can wire them up.

Wiring up the RadioButton controls

To wire up your RadioButton controls, follow these steps:

1. Open Window1.xaml.cs so you can listen for Click events for the three RadioButtons as follows:

```
public partial class Window1 : Window
    {
        public Window1()
```

```
        {
            InitializeComponent();
            FlatRB.Click += new RoutedEventHandler(FlatRB_Click);
            Image3DRB.Click += new RoutedEventHandler(Image3DRB_Click);
            Animated3DRB.Click +=
    new RoutedEventHandler(Animated3DRB_Click);
        }

        void Animated3DRB_Click(object sender, RoutedEventArgs e)
        {
            throw new NotImplementedException();
        }

        void Image3DRB_Click(object sender, RoutedEventArgs e)
        {
            throw new NotImplementedException();
        }

        void FlatRB_Click(object sender, RoutedEventArgs e)
        {
            throw new NotImplementedException();
        }
    }
```

2. When a RadioButton is clicked, all you have to do is make the corresponding control Visible and make the others Collapsed.

```
    void Animated3DRB_Click(object sender, RoutedEventArgs e)
    {
        Flat.Visibility = Visibility.Collapsed;
        Image3D.Visibility = Visibility.Collapsed;
        box.Visibility = Visibility.Visible;
    }

    void Image3DRB_Click(object sender, RoutedEventArgs e)
    {
        Flat.Visibility = Visibility.Collapsed;
        Image3D.Visibility = Visibility.Visible;
        box.Visibility = Visibility.Collapsed;
    }

    void FlatRB_Click(object sender, RoutedEventArgs e)
    {
        Flat.Visibility = Visibility.Visible;
        Image3D.Visibility = Visibility.Collapsed;
        box.Visibility = Visibility.Collapsed;
    }
```

3. Press F5 to compile and run the application, click the different RadioButtons, and you should see they work just as planned (see Figure 12-24).

Figure 12-24. The different views can be seen by clicking the RadioButtons.

Spinning the box

But wait, I bet right now you are saying, "Hey, you said that the 3D box would be spinning." Well, you'll make it do that next:

1. Switch back over to Blend 2 and reload the project when prompted.

2. Click the box Viewport3D and set its Visibility property to Visible so you can see it.

3. Press F7 to switch to Blend 2's Animation Workspace.

4. Click the + Event button to add a new event as shown in Figure 12-25.

5. Click the New Storyboard button to add a new Storyboard as shown in Figure 12-26.

Figure 12-25. Clicking the + Event button

Figure 12-26. Clicking the New Storyboard button

6. When the Create Storyboard Resource dialog box appears, type SpinBox in the text field and click OK (see Figure 12-27).

Figure 12-27. Entering the name SpinBox in the Create Storyboard Resource dialog box

7. Move your playhead out to 2 seconds like I have done in Figure 12-28.

Figure 12-28. Moving the playhead to 2 seconds

8. Turn down all the arrows in the box Viewport3D until you come to Box01, and then turn down the arrow beside that to display geometryModel3D as shown in Figure 12-29.

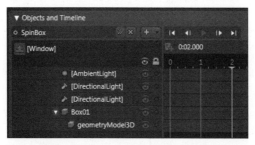

Figure 12-29. Drilling down in the box Viewport3D

9. In the Transform bucket of the Properties panel, select the Rotation tab and set the Z angle to 90 like I have done in Figure 12-30.

10. Move the playhead out to 4 seconds and set the Z angle to 180 like I have done in Figure 12-31.

Figure 12-30. Setting the Z angle to 90

Figure 12-31. Setting the Z angle to 180 at 4 seconds

11. Move the playhead out to 6 seconds and set the Z angle to -90 like I have done in Figure 12-32.

12. Move the playhead out to 8 seconds and set the Z angle to 0 like I have done in Figure 12-33.

Figure 12-32. Setting the Z angle to -90 at 6 seconds

Figure 12-33. Setting the Z angle to 0 at 8 seconds

13. Now click the play button as shown in Figure 12-34, and you will see your box spin 360 degrees.

Figure 12-34. Clicking the play button

If you press F5 to compile and run the application now, you would see that the 3D box does in fact spin, but wouldn't it be nice if the 3D box slowed for just a split second so you could get a good look at each side? To accomplish this, you could add easing to the animation. You'll do that now:

14. In the timeline, click the first keyframe like I have done in Figure 12-35.

Figure 12-35. Clicking the first keyframe

15. Notice in the Properties panel an Easing panel shows up (see Figure 12-36). Click and drag the yellow dots so they look like what you see in Figure 12-37. This will cause the spinning animation to start slowly, move quickly through the middle, and end slowly.

Figure 12-36. The Easing panel

Figure 12-37. The Easing panel with adjusted easing

16. Adjust the easing for all four keyframes.

17. You need to add a RepeatBehavior property to the SpinBox Storyboard so that it will continuously loop. Find it in the XAML and change it to read like this:

```
<Storyboard x:Key="SpinBox" RepeatBehavior="Forever">
```

18. Press F5 to compile and run the application.

Ahh, now that is much better. There's only one thing left to do:

19. Close the Storyboard by clicking the Close Storyboard button as shown in Figure 12-38 and then click the box Viewport3D and set its Visibility property back to Collapsed in the Appearance bucket of the Properties panel.

Figure 12-38. Closing the Storyboard

Now when you run the application by clicking F5 and click the Visual Brush onto 3D Primitive radio button, you see a nice spinning 3D box complete with easing to give you time to admire the image painted on the box (see Figure 12-39).

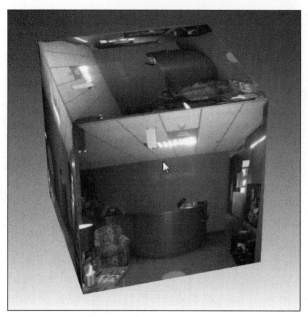

Figure 12-39. The spinning 3D box

You can download the source application at www.windowspresentationfoundation.com/ bookDownloads/3DImageProject.zip.

Summary

In this chapter, you pulled together all of the concepts that you have learned previously to create a class called ImageFactory that created an ObservableCollection of image paths. You then used Blend 2 to create a DataSource using the ImageFactory class. You constructed a ComboBox and a DataTemplate to tell the ComboBox how to display its content and a Rectangle with a visual brush that was bound to the selected item of the ComboBox. You then generated RadioButtons that would eventually show the selected image in three different views: flat, 3D, and finally brushed onto a Viewport3D of a 3D box. You created the Image3D in Blend 2 and then pasted in the Viewport3D named box that I had you download. In C#, you then wired up the RadioButtons to control the visibility of the different views. Finally, you made Storyboards to spin the 3D box complete with easing.

In the next chapter, you are going to take the things you have learned and build an application that will spin around a model of a *Star Wars* Tie Fighter to show off its key features.

Chapter 13

CASE STUDY B: 3DTIEFIGHTERPROJECT

What this chapter covers:

- Importing the free Tie Fighter model that ships with ZAM 3D
- Adding a lighting scheme to the model in ZAM 3D
- Exporting the model to XAML
- Creating a new WPF project
- Importing the XAML of the model
- Cleaning the XAML
- Creating buttons that are placed next to the model (windshield, left wing, right wing, etc.)
- Spinning the model to show a particular model part better, while repositioning the buttons next to their respective model parts
- In C#, creating a TextBlock placed outside the visual Workspace that describes the selected model part
- Brushing the content of the description onto a Viewport3D of a 3D plane primitive

Now that you know how to use ZAM 3D, you are going to import a 3ds model into ZAM 3D and export it as XAML. You will then create a new WPF Application project in Visual Studio 2008 called 3DTieFighterProject and pull the XAML model into the project. You will create buttons all around the model (windshield, left wing, right wing, etc.) and then use your knowledge of Triggers and Storyboards so that when a button is clicked, the model will rotate to show the corresponding part better. Further, you are going to add dummy text to a TextBlock off the Workspace and then use a VisualBrush to brush that text onto a 3D plane you are going to create. With that, let's get cracking!

Importing a model from ZAM 3D

First, you'll need to import the free Tie Fighter model from ZAM 3D as XAML. Start by doing the following:

1. Open ZAM 3D and select File ➤ New From 3DS to open the Import 3DS File dialog box.

2. By default, ZAM 3D will give you options to import 3ds files that ship with the product. Select E-tie-dv.3ds by double-clicking it. You will then see the model shown in Figure 13-1.

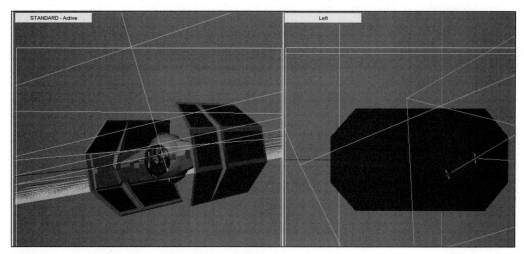

Figure 13-1. The 3ds Tie Fighter model imported into ZAM 3D

The lighting scheme that is included with this project is very dark, so you need to add a new one.

3. In the lower-right portion of the ZAM 3D IDE, click Lighting Schemes as shown in Figure 13-2.

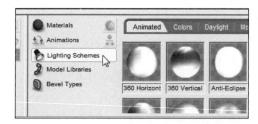

Figure 13-2. Clicking the Lighting Schemes button

4. Click and hold the tab that reads Daytime (it is the third one in the top row of schemes).

5. Drag it onto the view that reads STANDARD – Active until your cursor has a + (plus) icon on it like mine does in Figure 13-3.

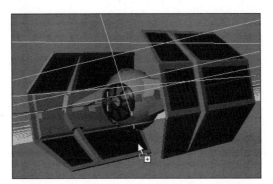

Figure 13-3. Dragging the Daytime lighting schema onto the model

6. Let go of your mouse, and the lighting schema will be applied to the model.

7. Click Edit ➤ Copy XAML. ZAM 3D copies the XAML to your clipboard, and now you are ready to create the project.

Creating the 3DTieFighterProject

Next, you'll set up your 3DTieFighterProject.

1. Open Visual Studio 2008 and create a new WPF Application project called 3DTieFighterProject (see Figure 13-4). Make a mental note of where the project is being saved, as you will be opening the project up in Blend 2 as well.

2. Once the project is created, make the Height and Width properties for the main window 600 by 800, respectively.

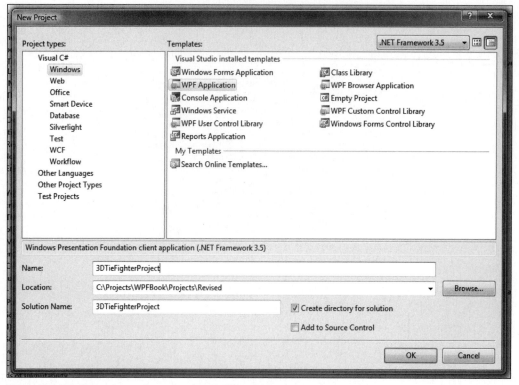

Figure 13-4. Creating a new project named 3DTieFighterProject

Cleaning the XAML

While creating this exercise, when I pasted the XAML the ZAM3D copied to the clipboard into my application, it failed to render. I worked through what the issues were, and here I am going to walk you through the steps I followed to get the Tie Fighter model to render correctly.

1. Go into Blend 2 and open the 3DTieFighterProject project.

2. In the XAML portion of the Split view, place your cursor between the `<Grid>` and `</Grid>` tags, and press Ctrl+V to paste in the Viewport3D code.

When you do this, you will get an error in your Results panel in the Errors tab that reads "Cannot convert '1.#IND'." To fix this, continue with these steps:

3. Double-click the error message in the Errors tab, and Blend 2 will take you to where the problem is. The following code is what Blend has trouble with:

```
<TranslateTransform3D OffsetX="-1.#IND"
OffsetY="-1.#IND" OffsetZ="-1.#IND"/>
```

4. Change this code to read

```
<TranslateTransform3D OffsetX="-1 " OffsetY="-1 " OffsetZ="-1 "/>
```

Once you do this, the Tie Fighter model will show up in the Design portion of the Split view. But if you were to press F5 to compile and run the application at this point, you would get another error that reads "'Blast_.copy01OR47' Name property value is not valid. Name must start with a letter or an underscore and can contain only letters, digits, and underscores." Because Visual Studio is better suited for editing XAML, what with its robust search feature and the ability to collapse blocks of code, you'll switch over to Visual Studio to take care of this problem.

5. Save the project by pressing Ctrl+S or by selecting File ➤ Save in the top menu. Switch back over to Visual Studio and reload the project.

6. Press Ctrl+F (or click Edit ➤ Find and Replace ➤ Quick Find) to bring up the search dialog box. In the Search field, type blast.

7. Locate the following code block and delete it:

```
<Model3DGroup x:Name="Blast_.copy01OR47"
Transform="{DynamicResource Blast_.copy01OR47TR46}">
 <!-- Blast .copy01 (XAML Path = (Viewport3D.Children)
[0].(ModelVisual3D.Content).(Model3DGroup.Children)[15]) -->
    <GeometryModel3D x:Name="Blast_.copy01OR47GR48"
     Geometry="{DynamicResource Blast_.copy01OR47GR48}"
     Material="{DynamicResource BLAST_REDMR7}"
     BackMaterial="{DynamicResource BLAST_REDMR7}"/>
</Model3DGroup>
```

Note also that ZAM 3D exported the model with animations and Triggers. I am going to show you how to strip these out of the XAML, because you are going to add your own animations.

8. In Visual Studio, find Viewbox.Resources and click the – (minus) icon to collapse the entire node. Do this also for Viewbox.Triggers. Figure 13-5 shows you what the code blocks look like when collapsed.

Figure 13-5. Collapsed code blocks in Visual Studio

9. Select these two collapsed code blocks and delete them.

Your Tie Fighter model will now compile and run. Try it out if you like by pressing F5.

In the next section, you are going to add the buttons for parts of the Tie Fighter.

Creating the buttons

You are now going to create buttons that are just simple Ellipses and place them next to key parts of the model. To do that, follow these steps:

1. Select the Ellipse tool and draw an Ellipse in the Workspace like I have done in Figure 13-6.

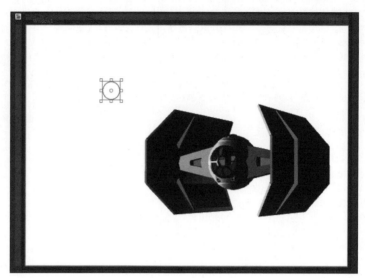

Figure 13-6. Drawing an Ellipse in the Workspace

2. Give the Ellipse a radial gradient fill with no stroke, and then use the Brush Transform tool to move the gradient like I have done in Figure 13-7.

3. Copy the Ellipse and paste one by the left wing, one by what I suppose is a laser cannon, one by the cockpit, one near the back engine, and one near the right wing, or what I will call the deflector shield, as shown in Figure 13-8.

Figure 13-7. Giving the Ellipse a radial gradient fill with the colors of your choice and no stroke (my gradient is blue with a white highlight)

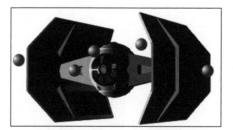

Figure 13-8. From left to right, the Ellipses represent the left wing, a laser cannon, the cockpit, the rear engine, and a deflector shield.

4. Name the buttons from left to right as follows: LeftWing, LaserCannon, Cockpit, Engine, and Deflector.

Creating the Storyboard animations

Now that you have your model and your buttons in place, you can go ahead and start creating the animations.

1. Press F6 to show Blend 2's Animation Workspace.

2. Click the New Storyboard button as shown in Figure 13-9.

3. When the Create new Storyboard dialog box appears, name the Storyboard ShowLeftWing and click OK.

Figure 13-9. Clicking the New Storyboard **button**

4. Move the playhead out to 1 second in the timeline like I have done in Figure 13-10.

Figure 13-10. Moving the playhead out to 1 second in the timeline

5. Double-click the model two times to bring up the gimbal control as shown in Figure 13-11.

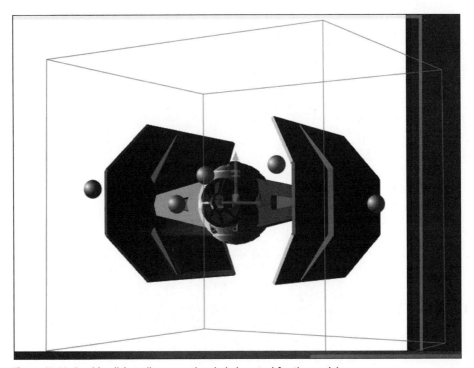

Figure 13-11. Double-click until you see the gimbal control for the model.

6. Use the handles until the left wing is shown clearly like I have done in Figure 13-12.

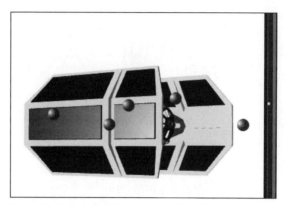

Figure 13-12. Rotating the model to show the left wing

7. Now move the LeftWing Ellipse to the top-left corner of the Workspace.

8. Reposition the other Ellipses so they are once again next to their respective model parts (e.g., the Cockpit Ellipse needs to be moved to the cockpit again) as shown in Figure 13-13.

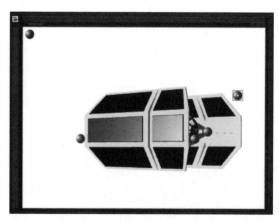

Figure 13-13. Repositioning the Ellipses

9. Close the Storyboard by clicking the Close Storyboard button shown in Figure 13-14.

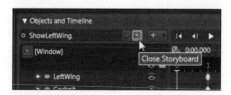

Figure 13-14. Closing the Storyboard

10. With the LeftWing Ellipse selected, go to the Triggers section of the Interaction panel and, using the various drop-down menus, change the event from When [Window].Loaded is raised to When LeftWing.MouseDown is raised ShowLeftWing.Begin like I have done in Figure 13-15.

Figure 13-15. Changing the event so that ShowLeftWing begins when LeftWing raises a MouseDown event

11. Press F5 to compile and run the application, and click the LeftWing Ellipse to make certain that it runs as you expect it to.

12. Close the running application.

Next, you'll create the Storyboard for the LaserCannon.

13. Click the New Storyboard button and give the new Storyboard the name of ShowLaserCannon.

14. Move the playhead out to 1 second in the timeline.

15. Double-click the model twice until you see the gimbal control.

16. Rotate the model so that you can clearly see the laser cannon like I have done in Figure 13-16.

Figure 13-16. Rotating the model to show the laser cannon

17. Move the LaserCannon Ellipse to the top left of the Workspace.

18. Move the other Ellipses so that they are next to their respective parts.

Now that I have run you through this procedure twice, you should be able to make adjustments for the remaining Ellipses on your own. Once you have done so, run the application, make sure that all of the buttons work properly, and then move on to the next sections so you can style up the background and then add some text about the parts of the Tie Fighter.

Styling the background

At this point, your model doesn't much look like it's in space. That is about to change as you follow the next set of steps:

1. Click F6 to get back to the Design view.

2. Find an image of space. If you cannot find one, you can use the one I created here: www.windowspresentationfoundation.com/bookDownloads/spaceBg.jpg. Or you can download high-resolution images from NASA's web site, located here: www.nasa.gov/multimedia/imagegallery/iotd.html.

3. To get the image, open the URL in an IE browser, right-click the space image, and then click Save Picture As.

4. Save the image to your local hard drive and then drag it into the 3DTieFighterProject folder in the Blend 2 Project panel.

5. Double-click the image, and it will appear in the Workspace.

6. Move the image up to the top of the Visual Tree in the Objects and Timeline panel so it appears behind the model and the Ellipses (see Figure 13-17).

Figure 13-17. Moving the background image up so that it is above the model and Ellipses in the Visual Tree

That looks a little better. It does now in fact appear that your model is in space (see Figure 13-18). Cool!

Figure 13-18. The space background is now behind the model and Ellipses.

Adding descriptive text to a 3D plane

Now you need to start adding some descriptive text that you can then brush onto a 3D plane. With that, let's get started.

1. Add a Grid with a TextBlock in it that is not in the visual area of the application like I have done in Figure 13-19.

2. Name the Grid TextGrid.

3. Name the TextBlock inside TextGrid TieText.

4. Next you need a Viewport3D of a plane. You can download the XAML for this here: www.windowspresentationfoundation. com/bookDownloads/3DPlane.txt.

5. Paste the XAML for this in right under the TextGrid. Because I have already bound the visual brush of the _3DPlane Viewport3D, you should immediately see that it will show whatever text you have in your TextGrid. Mine currently says TextBlock (see Figure 13-20).

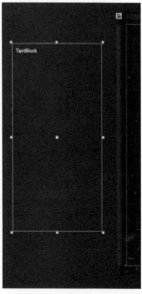

Figure 13-19. Creating a Grid with a TextBlock in it placed off the visual space of the application

Figure 13-20. When you paste the Viewport3D named _3DPlane under TextGrid, it will immediately bind to the TextBlock in TextGrid.

Coding the text in Visual Studio

Now you'll wire up the functionality that changes the text in TextGrid when an Ellipse is clicked.

1. Press Ctrl+S or select File ➤ Save in Blend 2, switch back over to Visual Studio, and reload the project.

2. Open Window1.xaml.cs and in the constructor, create events and method stubs for each of the Ellipses as shown here:

```
namespace _DTieFighterProject
{
    /// <summary>
    /// Interaction logic for Window1.xaml
    /// </summary>
    public partial class Window1 : Window
    {
        public Window1()
        {
            InitializeComponent();
            LeftWing.MouseDown +=
new MouseButtonEventHandler(LeftWing_MouseDown);
            LaserCannon.MouseDown +=
new MouseButtonEventHandler(LaserCannon_MouseDown);
            Cockpit.MouseDown +=
new MouseButtonEventHandler(Cockpit_MouseDown);
            Engine.MouseDown +=
new MouseButtonEventHandler(Engine_MouseDown);
```

```
        Deflector.MouseDown +=
new MouseButtonEventHandler(Deflector_MouseDown);
        }

        void Deflector_MouseDown(object sender, MouseButtonEventArgs e)
        {
            throw new NotImplementedException();
        }

        void Engine_MouseDown(object sender, MouseButtonEventArgs e)
        {
            throw new NotImplementedException();
        }

        void Cockpit_MouseDown(object sender, MouseButtonEventArgs e)
        {
            throw new NotImplementedException();
        }

        void LaserCannon_MouseDown
(object sender, MouseButtonEventArgs e)
        {
            throw new NotImplementedException();
        }

        void LeftWing_MouseDown(object sender, MouseButtonEventArgs e)
        {
            throw new NotImplementedException();
        }
    }
```

3. Now all that you need to do is set the Text property of TieText to dummy text in each of the method stubs.

```
void Deflector_MouseDown(object sender, MouseButtonEventArgs e)
{
TieText.Text = "The Deflector can stand blasts from
10 X-Wing Fighters simultanously and still have enough
left to take on a Y-Wing or two";
}

void Engine_MouseDown(object sender, MouseButtonEventArgs e)
{
TieText.Text = "The newly deisgned Tie Fighter Engine is the only one
of its kind and can even boast hyperdrive functionality.
Need to get out of a battle fast? This is the Tie Fighter for you";
}

void Cockpit_MouseDown(object sender, MouseButtonEventArgs e)
{
```

```
TieText.Text = "The newly designed Tie Fighter cockpit has plush
 racing seats, a wood trimmed dash, and even dual cup holders";
}

void LaserCannon_MouseDown(object sender, MouseButtonEventArgs e)
{
TieText.Text = "The most powerful destructive Laser Cannon of its kind.
This new cannon can even take down a Star Destroyer";
}

void LeftWing_MouseDown(object sender, MouseButtonEventArgs e)
{
TieText.Text = "The new aerodynamic sleek wing structure makes the
new Tie Fighter more maneuverable than any X-Wing in production today";
}
```

OK, so my descriptions may have you cracking up. I don't know if any of what I have there is true, but it sounds pretty good to me. Now if you were to run the application at this point, you would notice that you can't click any Ellipse that is behind the Viewport3D named _3DPlane.

4. To solve this problem, move the _3DPlane above the Ellipses in the Objects and Timeline panel as shown in Figure 13-21.

Figure 13-21. Moving the Viewport3D named _3DPlane above the Ellipses

You are getting close to finishing! Just one more step:

5. Change the TieText in the constructor of Window1.xaml.cs so that it doesn't say TextBlock when the application starts:

```
public Window1()
    {
        InitializeComponent();
        LeftWing.MouseDown += new
MouseButtonEventHandler(LeftWing_MouseDown);
```

```
        LaserCannon.MouseDown +=
new MouseButtonEventHandler(LaserCannon_MouseDown);
        Cockpit.MouseDown +=
new MouseButtonEventHandler(Cockpit_MouseDown);
        Engine.MouseDown +=
 new MouseButtonEventHandler(Engine_MouseDown);
        Deflector.MouseDown +=
 new MouseButtonEventHandler(Deflector_MouseDown);
        TieText.Text = "Tie Fighter";
    }
```

Now you have completed the case study application for this chapter. However, if you want to challenge yourself, try the following improvements:

1. Create a reflection for the Tie Fighter model.

2. Add more Ellipses.

3. Add a MediaElement with Tie Fighter sounds (you can easily find *Star Wars* WAVs on the Internet for free).

> You can download the source application at www.windowspresentationfoundation.com/bookDownloads/3DTieFighterProject.zip.

Summary

In this chapter, you have taken what you learned about events, Triggers, Storyboards, ZAM 3D, and Viewport3Ds and created the cool 3DTieFighterProject. The project has buttons that, when clicked, will rotate the Tie Fighter model to give the user a better view of a particular part. The button that was clicked will move to the top-left corner of the application, while the other buttons will reposition themselves to once again be next to their respective Tie Fighter parts. Also, descriptive text is set off the visible Workspace to describe the selected Tie Fighter part. That text is then brushed onto a 3D plane primitive Viewport3D.

In the next chapter, you are going to create a Silverlight paging system that can be used as a web site template.

Chapter 14

CASE STUDY C:
SILVERLIGHTPAGINGSYSTEMPROJECT

What this chapter covers:

- Creating a Silverlight 1.1 project
- Creating styled Rectangles and placing them in a Grid to act as navigation buttons
- Creating XAML UserControls that will be sections that are loaded when a navigation button is clicked
- Creating variables in C# that instantiate the XAML sections
- Loading in the section that corresponds to the navigation button that was clicked and unloading any previously loaded sections

> *This being the first of two Silverlight-specific chapters, in order to work through this case study and the one in the next chapter, you will need to download and install the Silverlight 1.1 Alpha Refresh developer plug-in from* www.microsoft.
> com/silverlight/installation-win-dev.aspx. *I instructed you to do this in Chapter 1, but I want to mention it here again in case you didn't install it then, as you will need this plug-in to work through this chapter.*

While WPF can make web applications, known as XAML browser applications or XBAPs for short, the applications can only be viewed on a PC. Further, the PC has to be running Vista or Windows XP Service Pack 2 with the .NET Framework 3.0 or later installed. This being the case, WPF is probably not the best choice for developing web sites.

Silverlight 1.1, however, can be viewed on both Macs and PCs and does not need the .NET Framework installed. This makes Silverlight a much better choice for creating Rich Internet Web Applications. Although you have only created WPF applications up to this point in the book, if you can develop in WPF, you can also develop in Silverlight, because as you already know Silverlight is a stripped-down version of WPF. And, because Silverlight *is* in fact the best choice for web sites, I thought it would be good to show you how to create a Silverlight 1.1 web site template with navigation buttons that, when clicked, load XAML pages that represent the content associated with those buttons. The XAML pages you are going to create are very simple, but this template can be used to create much more complex web sites. With that, let's get started creating your first Silverlight 1.1 application.

Creating the SilverlightPagingSystemProject

You'll start by setting up your Silverlight project in Visual Studio 2008.

1. Open Visual Studio 2008.
2. Create a new project, but this time, instead of creating a WPF Application project, select Silverlight as the project type and Silverlight Project for the template, and name the project SilverlightPagingSystemProject as shown in Figure 14-1. Make certain to make a mental note of where your project is being saved, as you will be opening this project in Blend 2.

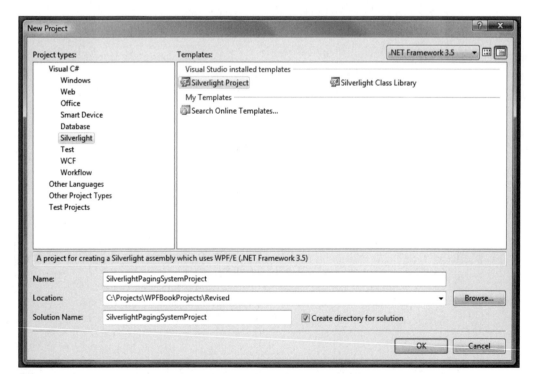

Figure 14-1. Creating a Silverlight project called SiverlightPagingSystemProject

Visual Studio 2008 creates a new Silverlight 1.1 project for you. Notice that instead of Window1.xaml, you get a file called Page.xaml. This is the first page that is loaded into the TestPage.html (the default page that will be loaded into the browser when the application is run).

Setting up various page properties

The first thing you are going to do is change some of the page properties.

1. Open Page.xaml, and in the main Canvas, change the Background property from White to Blue as in the following bold code line:

```
<Canvas x:Name="parentCanvas"
        xmlns="http://schemas.microsoft.com/client/2007"
        xmlns:x="http://schemas.microsoft.com/winfx/2006/xaml"
        Loaded="Page_Loaded"
        x:Class="SilverlightPagingSystemProject.
Page;assembly=ClientBin/SilverlightPagingSystemProject.dll"
        Width="640"
        Height="480"
        Background="Blue"
        >
```

2. Press F5 to compile and run the application, and a browser will open showing your project with a blue background. Close the browser.

3. In Page.xaml, change the main Canvas to have a Height of 600 and a Width of 800 as shown in the following code:

```
<Canvas x:Name="parentCanvas"
        xmlns="http://schemas.microsoft.com/client/2007"
        xmlns:x="http://schemas.microsoft.com/winfx/2006/xaml"
        Loaded="Page_Loaded"
        x:Class="SilverlightPagingSystemProject.
Page;assembly=ClientBin/SilverlightPagingSystemProject.dll"
        Width="800"
        Height="600"
        Background="Blue"
        >
```

If you were to run the application again, you would see that it looks the same. This is because you need to change the Height and Width in the JavaScript of TestPage.html as well; the JavaScript creates the Silverlight window (called a SilverlightHost), and it must be the same size as the XAML.

4. Open `TestPage.html` and make the changes shown here in bold:

```
<head>
    <title>Silverlight Project Test Page </title>

    <script type="text/javascript" src="Silverlight.js"></script>
    <script type="text/javascript" src="TestPage.html.js"></script>
    <style type="text/css">
        .silverlightHost { width: 800px; height: 600px; }
    </style>
</head>
```

5. Now run the application, and you will see that it is in fact 800 by 600.

But wait, the white margin in the browser window looks strange. You can fix this in the `Style` section of `TestPage.html`.

6. Add the body style shown in the following code in bold into your `TestPage.html`:

```
<head>
    <title>Silverlight Project Test Page </title>

    <script type="text/javascript" src="Silverlight.js"></script>
    <script type="text/javascript" src="TestPage.html.js"></script>
    <style type="text/css">
        .silverlightHost { width: 800px; height: 600px; }
        body {  padding: 0;  margin-left: 0;  margin-top: 0;
width: 100%;  }

    </style>
</head>
```

Now if you were to run the application, you would see that the blue background is 800 by 600 and has no top or left margin. Great! Now you'll move forward and add some navigation buttons.

7. Open Blend 2 and then open your Silverlight project.

Right away you will see the bold blue background; you'll change that now:

8. In the Objects and Timeline panel, select `parentCanvas`.

9. In the Properties panel in the Brushes bucket, choose Background and change it to a gradient.

10. Change the default black color to a color of your liking (I chose a dark purple).

11. Use the Brush Transform tool to change the gradient to go from top to bottom like I have done in Figure 14-2.

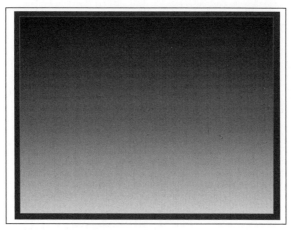

Figure 14-2. Changing the background to be a top-to-bottom gradient

Creating the navigation buttons

Next, you will next create a series of Rectangles in a Canvas that you will then use as your navigation buttons. Before you do that, however, it would be good for you to understand the differences between WPF and Silverlight. As you know, WPF has many built-in controls such as the Button control. Silverlight, however, does not have very many built-in controls at all, for example, it does not even include a Button control. In fact, if you look in the Asset Library and select Show All, you will see that Silverlight 1.1 only has ten controls. So basically, if you want something that acts like a WPF control, such as a Button, RadioButton, etc., you are going to have to build it yourself.

I come from a background in Flash, and up until Flash CS3, this is exactly what Flash developers had to do, because the Flash components were not very good and made the application quite large. So, with that, let's go ahead and build a control that acts just like a WPF Button control.

1. Select the Rectangle tool from the toolbar and draw a Rectangle in the Workspace.

2. Use the radius handles to give the Rectangle rounded edges.

3. Give the Rectangle a solid fill of red (see Figure 14-3).

Figure 14-3. A solid Rectangle with rounded edges

4. Copy the Rectangle and paste another one on top of the first.

5. Change the fill to a gradient with the left color being white and the right color being white with an Alpha property of 0% (Figure 14-4 shows the settings for the fill).

Figure 14-4. The fill settings for the second Rectangle

6. Use the Brush Transform tool to make the gradient go from top to bottom.

7. Use the Selection tool to make the second Rectangle a little smaller than the red Rectangle. Figure 14-5 presents my two Rectangles zoomed in to show detail.

Figure 14-5. My two Rectangles

8. Copy the top Rectangle and paste in another instance of it.

9. Use the Selection tool to rotate the Rectangle 180 degrees.

10. Change the fill to a radial fill and adjust it so that it looks like what I have in Figure 14-6.

Figure 14-6. The three Rectangles that will represent your navigation buttons

Not a bad-looking button. Now you need to wrap this button into a layout control:

11. Select all three Rectangles by pressing Ctrl+A.

12. Right-click the grouped Rectangles to bring up the context menu and select Group Into ➤ Canvas (this is an easy choice because Canvas is the only layout control that Silverlight 1.1 currently has).

13. In the Properties panel, name the Canvas Section1Btn.

14. In the Common Properties bucket in the Properties panel, change the Cursor value to Hand.

If you were to run the application now, you would see that your navigation button looks like a Button control and even has a hand-shaped cursor when you mouse over it. But wait, you need to add some text, so do that now:

15. In the Objects and Timeline panel, double-click the Section1Btn Canvas so it has a yellow line around it.

16. Select the TextBlock tool and draw a TextBlock in the Section1Btn Canvas.

17. Leave the TextBlock with the default black foreground, and in the Properties panel in the Common Properties bucket, make the Text property read Section 1.

18. Copy the TextBlock and paste in another TextBlock on top of the first.

19. Make the foreground for this TextBlock white.

20. Use your Selection tool to move the top TextBlock a little left and up so it looks like the bottom TextBlock is a shadow of the top one as shown in Figure 14-7.

Figure 14-7. The navigation button with two TextBlocks

Now that looks like a custom WPF button control.

21. Copy the Section1Btn and paste it three times so that you have four navigation buttons.

22. Change the names of the buttons so that they are Section1Btn, Section2Btn, Section3Btn, and Section4Btn. Make sure and also change their respective TextBlocks like I have done in Figure 14-8.

Figure 14-8. All of my navigation buttons

Next, you'll group all of the navigation buttons into a Canvas just to be neat.

23. Click the first button, hold down the Shift key, and click each of the remaining buttons so they are all selected.

24. Right-click the buttons and select Group Into ➤ Canvas.

25. Name the Canvas NavigationCanvas.

Creating the content Canvas container and the content pages

Now that you have your navigation buttons, you need a Canvas that will house the content that will be loaded when a navigation button is clicked. Add that now:

1. Select the Canvas tool from the toolbar and draw a Canvas in the Workspace. It should take up the entire Workspace minus the navigation buttons as shown in Figure 14-9.

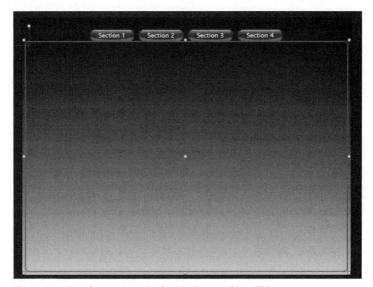

Figure 14-9. Drawing a Canvas in the Workspace that will house your content

2. Name the Canvas ContentCanvas so that you can code against it in C#.

You need to create your sections as separate XAML files, but first you'll import four images that you can use as content for each section.

3. Open the folder containing the images that you'd like to use.

4. In Blend, select the Project tab.

5. Right-click the project and select New Folder.

6. Right-click the new folder and select Rename.

7. Name the folder Images.

8. Drag the images from your local folder into the Images folder.

Now you can go ahead and create your XAML sections:

9. In Blend, right-click the project and select Add New Item.

10. When the Add New Item dialog box appears, name the UserControl Section1 and make sure Include code file is checked.

11. Click OK, and the Section1.xaml file will be created.

12. Repeat this process for Section2.xaml, Section3.xaml, and Section4.xaml.

Your Project tab should look something like what I have in Figure 14-10, except for the image names.

13. Open Section1.xaml and drag an image into the Workspace.

14. Resize the image so it is about 200 pixels wide and looks like what I have in Figure 14-11.

Figure 14-10. The Project tab

Figure 14-11. Section1.xaml has an image and a TextBlock that reads Section 1.

15. Select the TextBlock tool from the toolbar and drag out a TextBlock under the image.

16. Give the TextBlock a red foreground.

17. Give the TextBlock a Text property that reads Section 1.

18. Open Section2.xaml.

19. Drag an image into the Workspace and resize it to have a width of about 200 pixels so that it looks something like what you see in Figure 14-12.

317

Figure 14-12. Section2.xaml has an image and a TextBlock that reads Section 2.

20. Add a TextBlock with a red foreground that reads Section 2.

21. Open Section3.xaml.

22. Drag an image into the Workspace and resize it so that it looks like what I have in Figure 14-13.

Figure 14-13. Section3.xaml has an image and a TextBlock that reads Section 3.

23. Add a TextBlock with a red foreground that reads Section 3.

24. Finally, open `Section4.xaml` and repeat the preceding steps so that it looks like what you see in Figure 14-14.

Figure 14-14. `Section4.xaml` has an image and a `TextBlock` that reads Section 4.

Creating the functionality in Visual Studio

Now that you have all of your sections built, you can switch to Visual Studio 2008 and wire up the functionality.

1. Press Ctrl+Shift+B to compile the application, switch over to Visual Studio, and reload the project.

2. Create variables `s1` through `s4` and instantiate them as `Section1` through `Section4` using the following code:

```
public partial class Page : Canvas
    {
        Section1 s1 = new Section1();
        Section2 s2 = new Section2();
        Section3 s3 = new Section3();
        Section4 s4 = new Section4();
```

3. Now that you have your sections instantiated, you need to create events for each navigation button. Do so by adding the following code in bold:

```
public partial class Page : Canvas
    {
        Section1 s1 = new Section1();
        Section2 s2 = new Section2();
        Section3 s3 = new Section3();
        Section4 s4 = new Section4();
```

319

```csharp
        public void Page_Loaded(object o, EventArgs e)
        {
            // Required to initialize variables
            InitializeComponent();
            Section1Btn.MouseLeftButtonDown += new
    MouseEventHandler(Section1Btn_MouseLeftButtonDown);
            Section2Btn.MouseLeftButtonDown += new
    MouseEventHandler(Section2Btn_MouseLeftButtonDown);
            Section3Btn.MouseLeftButtonDown += new
    MouseEventHandler(Section3Btn_MouseLeftButtonDown);
            Section4Btn.MouseLeftButtonDown += new
    MouseEventHandler(Section4Btn_MouseLeftButtonDown);
        }

        void Section4Btn_MouseLeftButtonDown
    (object sender, MouseEventArgs e)
        {
            throw new NotImplementedException();
        }

        void Section3Btn_MouseLeftButtonDown
    (object sender, MouseEventArgs e)
        {
            throw new NotImplementedException();
        }

        void Section2Btn_MouseLeftButtonDown
    (object sender, MouseEventArgs e)
        {
            throw new NotImplementedException();
        }

        void Section1Btn_MouseLeftButtonDown
    (object sender, MouseEventArgs e)
        {
            throw new NotImplementedException();
        }
    }
```

4. In each method, add the section for that method and remove any others, just in case they exist.

```csharp
    public partial class Page : Canvas
    {
        Section1 s1 = new Section1();
        Section2 s2 = new Section2();
        Section3 s3 = new Section3();
        Section4 s4 = new Section4();
```

```
public void Page_Loaded(object o, EventArgs e)
{
    // Required to initialize variables
    InitializeComponent();
    Section1Btn.MouseLeftButtonDown += new
MouseEventHandler(Section1Btn_MouseLeftButtonDown);
    Section2Btn.MouseLeftButtonDown += new
MouseEventHandler(Section2Btn_MouseLeftButtonDown);
    Section3Btn.MouseLeftButtonDown += new
MouseEventHandler(Section3Btn_MouseLeftButtonDown);
    Section4Btn.MouseLeftButtonDown += new
MouseEventHandler(Section4Btn_MouseLeftButtonDown);

}



void Section4Btn_MouseLeftButtonDown(object sender,
MouseEventArgs e)
{
    ContentCanvas.Children.Remove(s1);
    ContentCanvas.Children.Remove(s2);
    ContentCanvas.Children.Remove(s3);
    ContentCanvas.Children.Add(s4);
}

void Section3Btn_MouseLeftButtonDown(object sender,
MouseEventArgs e)
{
    ContentCanvas.Children.Remove(s1);
    ContentCanvas.Children.Remove(s2);
    ContentCanvas.Children.Add(s3);
    ContentCanvas.Children.Remove(s4);
}

void Section2Btn_MouseLeftButtonDown(object sender,
MouseEventArgs e)
{
    ContentCanvas.Children.Remove(s1);
    ContentCanvas.Children.Add(s2);
    ContentCanvas.Children.Remove(s3);
    ContentCanvas.Children.Remove(s4);
}

void Section1Btn_MouseLeftButtonDown(object sender,
MouseEventArgs e)
{
    ContentCanvas.Children.Add(s1);
    ContentCanvas.Children.Remove(s2);
```

321

```
                ContentCanvas.Children.Remove(s3);
                ContentCanvas.Children.Remove(s4);
            }
        }
```

5. Press F5 to run the application, and you will see that it works just as you hoped it would.

Congratulations! You have just created a very simple Silverlight 1.1 web site paging system. As a challenge to you, I would like you to try the following exercises on your own:

1. Create a new XAML section called WelcomeScreen.xaml.

2. Place a styled TextBlock in WelcomeScreen.xaml that says, of course, "Welcome."

3. In C#, change the code so this new welcome section is loaded when the project is loaded.

4. Make all navigation buttons unload this section when clicked.

If you have any trouble with these exercises, take a look at my downloadable project, in which I've added the functionality. The URL follows. Good luck!

> *You can download the source application at* www.windowspresentationfoundation.
> com/bookDownloads/SilverlightPagingSystemProject.zip.

Summary

In this chapter, you have taken what you learned and created a Silverlight 1.1 application complete with styled navigation buttons and XAML sections that you then load into the main page when a navigation button is clicked.

In the next chapter, I am going to show you how to build a Silverlight 1.1 media player because media, video especially, is a very big part of Silverlight.

Chapter 15

CASE STUDY D:
SILVERLIGHTVIDEOPLAYERPROJECT

What this chapter covers:

- Creating a Silverlight 1.1 MediaElement project

In this chapter, I am going to show you how to build a Silverlight 1.1 video player with custom stop, play, and pause buttons.

Creating the SilverlightVideoPlayerProject

As with the case study in the last chapter, you'll start by setting up a new Silverlight project.

1. Open Visual Studio 2008 to create a new project. Select Silverlight as the project type, choose Silverlight Project for the template, and name the project SilverlightVideoPlayerProject as shown in Figure 15-1. Make certain to make a mental note of where your project is being saved, as you will be opening this project in Blend 2.

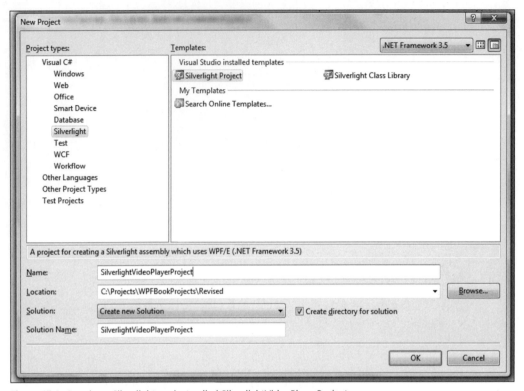

Figure 15-1. Creating a Silverlight project called SilverlightVideoPlayerProject

The first thing you need to do is to open the project in Blend 2 and add a MediaElement. Here is how to do that:

2. Click the Asset Library in the toolbar and select MediaElement.

3. Draw a MediaElement control in the Workspace like I have done in Figure 15-2.

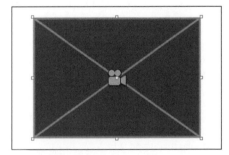

Figure 15-2. Drawing a MediaElement in the Workspace

4. Name the MediaElement me.

5. In the Properties panel in the Media bucket, click the button with the ellipsis to browse for a video source as shown in Figure 15-3.

Figure 15-3. Browsing for a video to be the source of the MediaElement

6. Choose a source video in WMV or AVI format on your local hard drive (my video is in WMV format and has a width of 320 and a height of 420).

> Your video can have different dimensions and can be scaled in Blend 2; however, a very large video will have an impact on performance.

Now that you have done that, it's time to create the buttons:

7. Draw a Rectangle with a height and width of about 30 pixels in the Workspace. Give it rounded edges and a black background like I have done in Figure 15-4. This will eventually become the play button.

Figure 15-4. Drawing a Rectangle in the Workspace

8. Next, copy the Rectangle and paste another one atop the first in the Workspace.

9. Make the top Rectangle a little smaller than the bottom Rectangle using the Selection tool.

10. Make sure the top Rectangle has no stroke and add a gradient fill that goes from top to bottom.

11. Make the gradient fill go from white to white, and set the bottom white color's Alpha property to 0% so that you have something like what you see in Figure 15-5.

Figure 15-5. The two Rectangles zoomed in to show detail

12. Select both Rectangles and group them into a Canvas.

13. Copy and paste the Canvas so that you have three buttons like I have in Figure 15-6.

Figure 15-6. Copy and paste the Canvas so that you have three buttons.

Now that you have done this, you can go ahead and double-click the first button and create the play symbol:

14. To make the play button triangle, turn on Blend 2's snap grid by clicking the grid icon located in the toolbar directly under the Workspace and then use the Path tool to draw the triangle. Do that so that you have something like what you see in Figure 15-7.

Figure 15-7. Using the Path tool to create the play button triangle

15. Name the Canvas PlayBtn.

16. Double-click the next button along so that it has a yellow line around it, and draw a square rectangle in it for the stop button icon like I have done in Figure 15-8.

Figure 15-8. Using the Rectangle tool to create the stop button icon

17. Name this Canvas StopBtn.

18. Double-click the last button and draw two rectangles to represent the pause icon like I have done in Figure 15-9.

Figure 15-9. Using the Rectangle tool to create the pause button icon

Creating the functionality in Visual Studio 2008

Now you are ready to start adding the functionality to your SilverlightVideoPlayerProject.

1. Press Ctrl+Shift+B to compile the application and switch over to Visual Studio 2008 to wire up the functionality. When prompted by Visual Studio, reload the project.

2. The first thing you need to do is to create a Boolean variable called _isPlaying and set it to true, because you want your MediaElement, named me, to play when the application starts.

```
private Boolean _isPlaying = true;
public void Page_Loaded(object o, EventArgs e)
{
    // Required to initialize variables
    InitializeComponent();

}
}
```

3. Now you need to create events and EventHandlers for each of the three buttons.

```
public partial class Page : Canvas
{
    private Boolean _isPlaying = true;
    public void Page_Loaded(object o, EventArgs e)
    {
        // Required to initialize variables
        InitializeComponent();
        PlayBtn.MouseLeftButtonDown +=
new MouseEventHandler(PlayBtn_MouseLeftButtonDown);
        PauseBtn.MouseLeftButtonDown += new
 MouseEventHandler(PauseBtn_MouseLeftButtonDown);
        StopBtn.MouseLeftButtonDown += new
MouseEventHandler(StopBtn_MouseLeftButtonDown);
    }

    void StopBtn_MouseLeftButtonDown
(object sender, MouseEventArgs e)
    {
        throw new NotImplementedException();
    }
```

```
        void PauseBtn_MouseLeftButtonDown
(object sender, MouseEventArgs e)
        {
            throw new NotImplementedException();
        }

        void PlayBtn_MouseLeftButtonDown
(object sender, MouseEventArgs e)
        {
            throw new NotImplementedException();
        }
    }
```

4. Code the play button, which will check to see whether _isPlaying is false. If it is, it will play the MediaElement named me.

```
        void PlayBtn_MouseLeftButtonDown
(object sender, MouseEventArgs e)
        {
            if (_isPlaying == false)
            {
                _isPlaying = true;
                me.Play();
            }

        }
```

5. Code the stop button. The stop button does not care whether _isPlaying is true or false because you want to stop the video even if it is paused.

```
        void StopBtn_MouseLeftButtonDown
(object sender, MouseEventArgs e)
        {
         _isPlaying = false;
          me.Stop();
        }
```

6. Lastly, code the pause button that will pause the video if it is playing and play it if it is paused.

```
        void PauseBtn_MouseLeftButtonDown
(object sender, MouseEventArgs e)
        {
            if (_isPlaying == true)
            {
                _isPlaying = false;
                 me.Pause();
            }
            else
            {
                _isPlaying = true;
                 me.Play();
            }
        }
```

7. Now press F5 to compile and run the application. You will see that your video buttons are functional and work the way you had hoped (see Figure 15-10).

That is all there is to it. You now have a Silverlight video player that can be viewed on a Mac or a PC. If you have a web site and want to add your Silverlight video player to it, all you have to do is go to where you saved the project. You will then see the SLN file and a directory with the same name as your project, namely SilverlightVideoPlayerProject. Go into that directory and upload the following files to your web site:

Figure 15-10. The functional Silverlight 1.1 video player

- Your video file
- Page.xaml
- Page.xaml.cs
- Silverlight.js
- TestPage.html
- TestPage.html.js

Now that you've finished this chapter's case study, I challenge you to extend it to do the following:

1. Create a rewind button that stops the video and restarts it from the beginning.
2. Create a next button that loads a new video the first time it is clicked, and then when it is clicked again, it reloads the original video (hint: you are going to need a variable that knows which movie is currently playing).
3. When the video ends, set _isPlaying to false so all the user has to do is click the play button again for the video to play.

Good luck! If you would like to see this project as an actual web site, you can do so here: www.windowspresentationfoundation.com/bookDownloads/SilverlightVideoPlayerProject/TestPage.html.

> *You can download the source application (with the video removed to reduce download time) at* www.windowspresentationfoundation.com/bookDownloads/SilverlightVideoPlayerProject.zip.

Summary

In this chapter, you created a Silverlight 1.1 project and put a MediaElement with a source video into the Workspace. You then created styled buttons to play, stop, and pause the video. Finally, you went into Visual Studio 2008 and coded up the functionality in C#.

Now you've just about come to the end of this book. In the Appendix that follows, I give you some good resources to help you continue to learn about WPF and Silverlight.

Appendix

WPF AND SILVERLIGHT RESOURCES

If you like what you have learned thus far and want to keep on developing in WPF and/or Silverlight, I suggest you keep this list of resources handy. You never know when you will need to take a look at the documentation to learn about a certain class. Or you may just want to keep up on the latest and greatest with some great blogs. Or possibly you just want to take more tutorials. Finally, maybe you are in the middle of a WPF/Silverlight application and you are stuck on a problem; the forums are a great place to turn for help. As this information may change over time, you can view the same information updated on my book's web site, www. windowspresentationfoundation.com.

References

- **MSDN Windows Presentation Foundation**: This is the place to find the documentation for all of WPF.

  http://msdn2.microsoft.com/en-us/library/ms754130.aspx

- **Silverlight homepage**: This site is a great place to find everything Silverlight.

  http://silverlight.net/

- **WPF FAQ Index**: Here, you'll get answers to frequently asked questions about WPF.

  http://wpfwiki.com/WPF%20FAQ%20Index.ashx

- **MSDN Windows Presentation Foundation (Avalon) FAQ**: This is another good site for getting answers to frequently asked questions about WPF.

  http://msdn2.microsoft.com/en-us/windowsvista/aa905016.aspx

Blogs

- **Beatriz Costa**: If you are looking for great WPF insight, sample code, and sample projects, this site is for you.

  www.beacosta.com/blog/

- **IRhetoric**: This is the blog of Karsten Januszewski, a Technical Evangelist for Microsoft, and it's a great site for all things WPF and Silverlight.

  http://rhizohm.net/irhetoric/

- **Tim Sneath**: Tim is a Group Manager for Microsoft. His blog also has great WPF and Silverlight resources.

  http://blogs.msdn.com/tims/

- **The WPF Blog**: This is the blog of Lee Brimelow. Although Lee has recently moved away from WPF development and back to Flash, his blog has an archive of wonderful articles and tutorials.

  www.thewpfblog.com/

Tutorials

- **ContentPresenter**: Here you'll find some really great WPF tutorials from Lee Brimelow.

  www.contentpresenter.com/

- **Lynda**: This is a pay site, but it has some very good Expression Blend and Silverlight tutorials. You can start to take the first few lessons for free. If you like the tutorials, you can subscribe.

  http://lynda.com/

- **Silverlight homepage**: There are some very cool video tutorials here for Silverlight 2.0 and 1.0 if you are interested.

  http://silverlight.net/Learn/videocat.aspx?cat=2

Tools

- **Blendables—Tools and Components for Designers and Developers**: If you plan on doing WPF development professionally, save yourself a lot of time and headaches by checking out this set of tools.

  http://blendables.com/

Community sites

- **The MSDN Silverlight Community**: If you get stuck with Silverlight, this site is the place to go to ask questions and get answers, oftentimes from Microsoft developers themselves!

  http://msdn2.microsoft.com/en-us/silverlight/bb187454.aspx

- **The Silverlight Forums**: Here you'll find more Silverlight forums to help you solve your Silverlight issues.

  http://silverlight.net/forums/

- **The MSDN WPF Forums**: These forums are dedicated to everything WPF.

  http://forums.microsoft.com/MSDN/ShowForum.aspx?ForumID=119&SiteID=1

- **ExpressionBlend.com**: You'll find Blend forums at this site.

  http://expressionblend.com/forums/default.aspx

- **MSDN Visual Studio Setup and Installation**: If you are having trouble installing Visual Studio, check this site out.

  http://forums.microsoft.com/MSDN/ShowForum.aspx?ForumID=26&SiteID=1

Professional WPF/Silverlight development resources

- **IdentityMine**: This is the site for the leading development house for WPF and Silverlight and a Gold Vendor for Microsoft. If you need professional WPF Silverlight development, they are the ones to contact.

  www.identitymine.com/

INDEX

QR

 **XML for Flash**
1-59059-543-2 $39.99 [US]

 **Actionscript Animation**
1-59059-518-1 $39.99 [US]

 **Flash 8**
1-59059-542-4 $36.99 [US]

 **ASP.NET 2.0 for Flash**
1-59059-517-3 $39.99 [US]

 **Flash 8 Video**
1-59059-651-X $44.99 [US]

EXPERIENCE THE DESIGNER TO DESIGNER™ DIFFERENCE

 **Flash Applications for Mobile Devices**
1-59059-558-0 $49.99 [US]

 **New Masters of Flash**
1-59059-314-6 $59.99 [US]

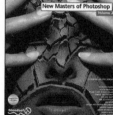 **New Masters of Photoshop**
1-59059-315-4 $59.99 [US]

 **Object-Oriented ActionScript for Flash 8**
1-59059-619-6 $44.99 [US]

 **Extending Flash MX 2004**
1-59059-304-9 $49.99 [US]

 **Apache Essentials**
1-59059-355-3 $24.99 [US]

 **Dreamweaver MX 2004 Design, Projects**
1-59059-409-6 $39.99 [US]

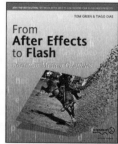 **From After Effects to Flash**
1-59059-748-6 $49.99 [US]

 **ActionScript Components**
1-59059-593-9 $49.99 [US]

 **Flash Interface Design**
1-59059-555-6 $44.99 [US]

 **DOM Scripting**
1-59059-533-5 $34.99 [US]

 **Web Accessibility**
1-59059-638-2 $49.99 [US]

 **HTML Mastery**
1-59059-765-6 $34.99 [US]

 **Blog Design Solutions**
1-59059-581-5 $39.99 [US]

 **CSS Mastery**
1-59059-614-5 $34.99 [US]

 **Flash Application Design Solutions**
1-59059-594-7 $39.99 [US]

 **WEB STANDARDS SOLUTIONS**
1-59059-381-2 $34.99 [US]

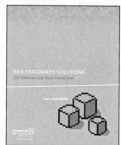 **PODCAST SOLUTIONS**
1-59059-554-8 $24.99 [US]